Becoming Parents

Exploring the Bonds between Mothers, Fathers, and Their Infants

Becoming Parents presents a landmark study of the transition to parenthood and its effects on individual well-being and couple relationships. It tracks the experiences of couples becoming parents for the first time, from the second trimester of pregnancy to six months after birth. The book addresses such key issues as the division of domestic labor, the changing nature of couples' marital relationships, changes in new parents' attachment networks, postnatal depression, and factors predicting the ease of transition. The research was based on adult attachment theory, an exciting new approach to couple relationships. The insights gleaned from interviews, questionnaires, and diaries reveal a unique, intriguing picture of parenthood.

Judith Feeney is Senior Lecturer in Psychology at the University of Queensland in Brisbane. She has published a number of widely cited articles and books in the areas of marital and family relationships, interpersonal communication, and the link between personal relationships and health.

Lydia Hohaus is Lecturer in Lifespan Development at Griffith University and has conducted research in the areas of caregiving, memory, and aging.

Patricia Noller is Professor of Psychology at the University of Queensland. She has published extensively in the area of marital and family relationships, including attachment relationships. She received an Early Career Award from the Australian Psychological Society and is a Fellow of the Academy of the Social Sciences in Australia. She is foundation editor of *Personal Relationships: Journal of the International Society for the Study of Personal Relationships.*

Richard P. Alexander holds an MA in psychology and has extensive experience working as a practitioner in child and family welfare.

Becoming Parents

Exploring the Bonds between Mothers, Fathers, and Their Infants

Judith A. Feeney

University of Queensland

Lydia Hohaus

Griffith University

Patricia Noller

University of Queensland

Richard P. Alexander

University of Queensland

CAMBRIDGE
UNIVERSITY PRESS

PUBLISHED BY THE PRESS SYNDICATE OF THE UNIVERSITY OF CAMBRIDGE
The Pitt Building, Trumpington Street, Cambridge, United Kingdom

CAMBRIDGE UNIVERSITY PRESS
The Edinburgh Building, Cambridge CB2 2RU, UK
40 West 20th Street, New York, NY 10011–4211, USA
10 Stamford Road, Oakleigh, VIC 3166, Australia
Ruiz de Alarcón 13, 28014 Madrid, Spain
Dock House, The Waterfront, Cape Town 8001, South Africa

http://www.cambridge.org

© Judith A. Feeney Lydia Hohaus Patricia Noller Richard P. Alexander 2001

First published 2001

Printed in the United States of America

Typeface Utopia 9.75/14   *System* Quark XPress™   [HT]

A catalog record for this book is available from the British Library

Library of Congress Cataloging-in-Publication Data

The transition to parenthood : an attachment perspective /
Judith A. Feeney ... [et al].
p. cm.
Includes bibliographical references and index.
ISBN 0-521-77250-8 – ISBN 0-521-77591-4 (pb.)
1. Parenthood. 2. Attachment behavior. I. Feeney, Judith.

HQ755.8 .T729 2001
306.874 – dc21   00-065172

ISBN 0 521 77250 8 hardback
ISBN 0 521 77591 4 paperback

Contents

Preface

Our aim in writing this book was to draw together two important concepts in the area of couple and family relationships. The first concept concerns the importance of the transition to parenthood: Parenting is one of the most crucial tasks that human beings engage in, and first-time parenthood brings significant changes to the parents as individuals and to their ongoing relationships. The second concept is that of attachment, or bonding, between adult partners. Recent years have seen great advances in the study of adults' attachment relationships; that is, relationships such as marriage that play a special role in meeting our innate needs for comfort and emotional security. As a result, attachment is now recognized as central to personal well-being and effective functioning across the life span. To date, much has been written about the transition to parenthood and about couple relationships as attachments, but these concepts have rarely been drawn together. We see the transition to parenthood as a time when attachment issues are extremely important, as partners must reshape their couple relationship to accommodate a new and highly dependent individual. In fact, a key challenge of new parenthood involves parents tending to the emotional needs of their infant and of each other, while managing the many practical tasks of the household.

For these reasons, we decided to conduct a study that would explore, in detail, the effects of first-time parenthood on individuals and their attachment relationships. Using interviews, questionnaires, and diaries, we were interested in assessing parents' perceptions of stress, coping and well-being, their developing relationships with their infants, and their ways of relating to close friends, family members, and each other. More specifically, we addressed questions such as these:

- How do different couples react to finding out about their first pregnancy?
- What do couples see as the best and worst features of becoming parents?
- How do couples cope with the stress of having a new baby in the home?
- What factors are linked to postnatal depression, and what are its effects on partners?
- How involved are new fathers in helping out with household and baby-care tasks?
- Does parenthood change the attachment network of men and women?
- Why do some couples emerge relatively unscathed from this transition, whereas others struggle to adjust?

Despite the amount of planning that went into this study, we were somewhat surprised by the wealth of information and insights that the couples provided, and by the diversity of their experience. We soon realized that a book was needed to summarize this information, and make the findings available to those who would benefit from them. The book is designed for two main groups of readers. First, it is intended to help prospective parents, and those people (close friends and family members) who wish to support them during this challenging time. Second, the book provides information relevant to students and professionals in a number of areas, including psychology, counseling, social work and social welfare, nursing, and relevant branches of medical practice (general practice, obstetrics, and pediatrics).

In presenting the results of this study, we would like to acknowledge several sources of assistance. First, we wish to thank the Australian Research Council, which provided funding for the research project.

Second, we would like to thank those individuals and groups who assisted with the recruitment of couples. In particular, we are grateful to Carla Ward, Sue-Ann Ward, and Ailie Perich, who worked as research assistants on the project, and to the staff of the Royal Women's Hospital in Brisbane, who allowed us to make regular visits to their antenatal clinic. Finally, and most important, we owe a debt of gratitude to the couples who took part in the study – we made considerable demands on their time and energy during the challenging time of new parenthood, and this book was made possible by their willingness to share their experiences.

ONE

The Transition to Parenthood

The transition to parenthood is not a new topic for research and discussion. In fact, this topic has been studied at some depth for more than half a century, by researchers interested in life-span development and in the structure and functions of the family. Moreover, it has undoubtedly been discussed informally throughout most of the history of the human race, as young people have wondered about the impact of this event and their elders have tried to share their own experience and advice. In this chapter, we trace the development of studies in this area, and present the main findings that these research projects have generated.

WHY STUDY THE TRANSITION TO PARENTHOOD?

Perhaps the first question that we should consider is *why* the transition to parenthood arouses so much interest. At least two broad reasons can be suggested. First, parenthood is a topic that is of direct interest to most people. As children, we experience parental relationships on a personal and ongoing basis, and as adults, we may recognize that this experience plays a formative role in the way we develop and function. Further, the majority of people have at least one child during their life span, and almost everyone has seen close friends or family members dealing with pregnancy and new parenthood. This almost universal experience of parenthood applies across cultures and across eras, despite the fact that more adults in western societies are now remaining single, choosing not to become parents, or having only one or two children, than in the past.

Survey studies show that most young people still envisage their future as including the traditional aspects of family life, including a wedding, honeymoon, and children (e.g., Kilmartin, 2000), and still see marriage as playing an important role in fulfilling personal needs for companionship and emotional security (Barich & Bielby, 1996). Similarly, recent British survey data show that when people are asked about the "important events" that have happened to them during the last year, almost half of the events mentioned involve the family unit; in addition, of these family-related events, pregnancy and birth are mentioned more often than any other type of event (Newman & Smith, 1997).

In fact, the tendency for adults to show an interest in babies and young children may be "hardwired," as part of our evolutionary heritage. After all, our survival as a species depends, at one level, on our urge to reproduce; further, both couple relationships and parent-child relationships are crucial for our reproductive success (Buss, 1994). According to many researchers, the relevance of evolutionary principles to parenthood is not confined to the acts of conceiving, bearing, and giving birth to children. Rather, because humans take many years to reach maturity, it is important that parents be willing to nurture and care for their offspring during these formative years. Parents' involvement in protecting and teaching their children helps to ensure the safety of the offspring, and the passing on of their genetic heritage (Bell & Richard, 2000). In other words, from an evolutionary perspective, it is important that adults produce children, and that they are prepared to invest time, energy, and material resources to foster their development.

The second reason for the interest in the transition to parenthood is slightly more academic, although the relevance to individuals and families is very clear. This reason centers on the remarkable changes that are implicit in the arrival of a new infant. Prior to first-time parenthood, the "family" (or at least the "nuclear family") simply consists of the couple. With the arrival of the first baby, the family becomes much more complex: There are now three dyadic relationships, instead of one. Further, as we have already mentioned, the new arrival is relatively helpless, and dependent on the parents for care and protection. Hence, new parents have to respond to their infants' needs and signals, and the responses are quite far-reaching. For instance, new mothers and fathers generally experience strong emotional responses to their babies (although these responses vary from one parent to another, and from one point in time to another). In addition, these emotional responses of love and concern (and, at times, frustration), are interwoven with the practical aspects of parenting: Many new tasks have to be tackled in households with young babies.

In short, the role of parent is a demanding one; moreover, because it is acquired fairly abruptly, there is often a sense of anxiety and inadequate preparation (Miller & Sollie, 1980). Given the pressures and demands that come with parenthood, it seems only natural that the relationship between the mother and the father will undergo some changes. In fact, these changes are likely to be quite diverse, and to involve both rewards and stresses. Hence, these shifts are of interest to researchers and practitioners who are interested in couple and family relationships, as well as to prospective parents.

PLANNING FOR PARENTHOOD

As we will see shortly, researchers who want to document the experience of new parenthood generally study individuals or couples who have recently become parents, or those who are expecting their first child when they are recruited for the study. However, in a very real sense, the transition to parenthood begins for many couples long before these events. That is, the transition may begin with a prior period of planning and decision making.

To Have or Not to Have?

Of course, pregnancy is not always the result of planning, and it may seldom occur at the exact time that the parents might hope. When children are born into a stable relationship, however, the partners are likely to have put a considerable amount of time and effort into planning for parenthood. Many couples recognize the importance of joint decision making in this area, and opt for direct discussion and negotiation of their plans; that is, should they have children at all and, if so, when would be the "right" time?

At the start of this chapter, we noted that most young people see having children as part of their future, but that more are deciding to remain childless than in the past. Together, these two facts highlight the importance of how people see both the rewards and the costs associated with parenting.

Researchers interested in these issues have developed questionnaires designed to measure various aspects of attitudes to parenting: how strongly individuals desire offspring, how well they think they can relate to young children, how much satisfaction they think they would derive from caring for infants, and how much aggravation they might experience in relation to child-rearing (e.g., Rholes, Simpson, Blakely, Lanigan, & Allen, 1997). These studies confirm the idea that people differ quite widely in their desire for children, and in their expectations of the rewards and costs of having children.

Costs of Parenting. The perceived costs (or "barriers") of parenting can be categorized into a number of broad areas.

■ Ability to relate: Some people report concerns about how well they would relate to offspring. For example, they may feel "uncomfortable" in the presence of young children, or worry that they could not become emotionally attached to them.

- Responsibility: Other people express concerns about the amount of work and responsibility involved in child-rearing, and the emotional strain associated with ensuring the child's health, safety, and general well-being.
- Lifestyle: The restrictions that parenting places on social activities and shared couple activities are salient to many people. Similarly, some individuals fear that parenthood will interfere with their pursuit of important individual achievements, such as meeting educational, financial, and career goals.
- Effects on marriage: Another concern expressed by some people is that children will put a lot of strain on their marriage, by placing extra demands on partners' time, attention, and energy.

Rewards of Parenting. On the other hand, people also perceive many rewards associated with parenting, and give many reasons for wanting to have children. In fact, according to Clements and Markman (1996, p. 292), there are "almost as many reasons for having children as there are couples who have them". Individuals may not always be clearly aware of these reasons. It has been argued, for example, that "unplanned" pregnancy, stemming from a careless use of contraception, sometimes reflects an unconscious desire to have children (Harris & Campbell, 1999). Although some individuals may not be clearly aware of their motivations for having children, others are able to provide one or more reasons for their decision. Again, these reasons can be classified into several broad areas.

- Biological need: Having children can be seen as the fulfillment of strong biological needs to procreate. As mentioned earlier, the urge to reproduce is crucial to the survival of the species; infants are cute and cuddly, and tend to trigger responses of love and care in prospective parents.
- Emotional rewards: Some individuals claim that they want to have children because of the affection and companionship they will provide. In addition, they may anticipate parenthood as involving both fun and challenge, or as giving them a sense of personal achievement.
- A symbol of love: Others see parenthood as a way of partners' expressing their love and affection for each other, or as a symbol of

that love. They may also believe that having children will keep them close, and promote cohesion and stability in the relationship.

■ A sense of continuity: Some people see having children as a way of extending their sphere of influence; that is, they express a desire to "live on" through their children and grandchildren. Similarly, they may report a desire to carry on the "family name," or perpetuate the "family line."

■ Improving on experience: Another reason some individuals give for having children is that they want to "do things better" than their own parents did; put another way, they want to show that they will not make the same mistakes.

■ Social pressure: For some people, parenthood may be a response, in part, to the expectations of others. These expectations may come from society at large, from friends, or from family members who exert pressure on couples to produce grandchildren.

■ Overcoming problems: Finally, some people may see pregnancy as a way of cementing a troubled relationship, or of overcoming feelings of loneliness or being unloved. It is important to note that these expectations are likely to be unrealistic, however; in fact, the demands of new parenthood are likely to *increase* the problems of those who are already struggling in their relationships or their personal lives.

In short, despite the costs associated with child-rearing, people offer many reasons for wanting to have children. In cases where parenthood is jointly planned, questions also arise about how long couples should wait before they embark on their first pregnancy.

When Is the Right Time?

First-time parenthood occurs at very different ages and stages of the life cycle. Nevertheless, there is a clear demographic trend in western societies whereby age at first birth is increasing, with many couples choosing to postpone having children until they are in their 30s and beyond. This is an interesting trend, because it means that many couples are tending to ignore their "biological clocks", and trying to conceive beyond their most fertile age.

How couples decide when to have their first child is not well understood. Demographers have put a lot of effort into studying how the timing of the first birth relates to the social characteristics of one partner. In most cases, the focus of these studies has been on the characteristics of the woman; for instance, researchers might ask how the timing of parenthood is related to the wife's work patterns or level of education. The focus on areas such as education and occupation seems well justified: Women who emphasize achievement in these areas are likely to delay their first pregnancy, and conversely, pregnancy and parenthood tend to interrupt activity in these areas. However, a limitation of many of these studies is that they have ignored the joint decision-making processes that take place in couple relationships. It is only fairly recently that these processes have been examined.

The results emerging from these studies of couple relationships are quite complex, and suggest that the decision-making process may work differently in different cultures. For example, in cultures with a fairly traditional family orientation, characteristics of the woman seem to be the most important factors influencing the timing of the first pregnancy. This is not surprising, because in these cultures, parenting tends to be seen as primarily the province of women. In contrast, in cultures that tend to emphasize the equal roles of men and women, the characteristics of *both* partners seem to be important to the timing of parenthood, presumably because both partners have substantial input into family-related decisions (Corijn, Liefbroer, & de Jong Gierveld, 1996).

EARLY STUDIES OF THE TRANSITION TO PARENTHOOD: A TIME OF CRISIS

In contrast to the relatively limited research on how couples plan parenthood, many studies have attempted to show how the birth of the first child affects new parents. In trying to make sense of this large body of work, it becomes clear that the research methods used and the conclusions reached have tended to shift over time. We will start by describing the early studies conducted in this area, and go on to explain why certain limitations of these studies prompted calls for more sophisticated kinds of research.

For roughly 50 years, researchers have been investigating the effects of new parenthood. In an influential book published in 1949, Hill developed a model of family stress and crisis. In this book, he suggested that in some cases, parenthood was so stressful and required such a drastic reorganization of roles and interaction patterns that it could precipitate a crisis for spouses. The idea that parenthood represents a crisis point in individuals' and couples' lives persisted over the next couple of decades, as reflected in the classic studies of that era. These studies were of two main types: clinical studies and retrospective interviews.

Clinical Studies

The early clinical studies of parenthood came primarily from within the psychoanalytic tradition (e.g., Benedek, 1959; Bibring, Dwyer, Huntington, & Valentine, 1961; Caplan, 1957). These studies were based on clinicians' evaluations of expectant women or new mothers, and their husbands, and tended to focus on the internal conflicts facing these individuals.

Although this approach can provide some insights into the issues that trouble new or prospective parents, the samples studied were often quite small. More important, the samples were certainly not typical of new parents. Rather, they consisted of women and men who had been in therapy for some time, or who presented with significant emotional problems that had begun during pregnancy or shortly after the birth of the baby. Because the samples were so atypical, the findings are unlikely to apply outside of the clinical setting.

Interviews "Looking Back"

The second type of study within the "crisis" viewpoint used somewhat larger samples, and involved interviewing parents about their recollections of the arrival of their first child. For example, LeMasters (1957) interviewed 48 couples, and concluded that the transition to parenthood had been a crisis for the vast majority of them. A few years later, Dyer (1963) conducted a similar study and reached similar conclusions, although he advanced previous findings by noting a link between the state of the marriage *before* the birth and the amount of crisis experienced.

Again, however, studies of this type suffered from severe limitations. Not only were the interviews retrospective (i.e., looking back on events that had occurred earlier), in many cases, they took place several years after the birth. Retrospective reports of events are always potentially flawed, because they rely on people having accurate and complete memories of the events in question. As Grossman (1988, p. 89) has noted, however, retrospective reports are likely to be *especially* problematic in the case of new parenthood, given that the experience that people are asked to recall is "complicated, intense, and fatiguing."

LATER STUDIES: IMPROVING RESEARCH METHODS

In another series of studies of the transition to parenthood, Hobbs (e.g., 1965, 1968) assessed parents when their babies were relatively young (between about one and eight months of age). He also used a more structured approach to assessment; namely, a checklist of specific problems or stresses that might be associated with new parenthood (e.g., interruption of routine habits, tiredness, and fatigue, etc.). Hobbs's studies consistently suggested that although new parenthood is stressful, it does *not* involve high levels of crisis.

Why was Hobbs's conclusion so different from that of the earlier researchers? The most likely explanation lies in the different methods used. It is almost inevitable that clinical studies will portray new parenthood as fraught with danger, because only those who experience it as traumatic will find their way into the samples. In terms of the interview studies, we have already suggested that people are unlikely to have complete and accurate memories of their past experiences of parenting. Rather, the things that come to mind some years later may be the most striking (and possibly the most stressful) aspects.

Research Design and the Effects of Parenthood

The methods that are used to study the transition to parenthood are likely to affect the outcomes. The early methods suggested that new parenthood results in major adjustment problems, but this conclusion may not be warranted. This point was clearly made by Cook and Campbell (1979), who identified three kinds of evidence that are essential if researchers are to be confident that parenthood *causes* any problems that might be reported by individuals or couples. That is, if researchers wish to claim that parenthood causes a drop in marital quality (to take a specific example), they need to be able to show that parenthood

- is associated with lower marital quality (cause and effect go together)
- comes before a lowering in marital quality (cause precedes effect)
- is the best explanation of the lower marital quality (other explanations ruled out).

Coming up with these kinds of evidence requires two main "design features." First, researchers need to use longitudinal designs, in which they follow a group of couples from pregnancy until after the births of the babies. Second, they need to include a group of "comparison" couples who are *not* going through the transition to parenthood, and to follow them over the same period of time. In this way, it is possible to monitor changes in couples' relationships as they occur. It is also possible to see whether any changes in marital quality are similar for the two groups (a finding that would suggest an effect due simply to the amount of time spent in the relationship), or greater for the transition group (suggesting an effect due specifically to parenthood).

Other Developments in Studying New Parenthood

There are two other important respects in which studies of the transition to parenthood have become more sophisticated. The first of these concerns the *methods* used to assess people's experiences of parenthood. We have seen that the early studies relied either on clinical assessments, or on retrospective reports obtained by interviews. Although it is easy to be critical of these methods, in fact there is no perfect way of documenting parents' experiences.

For example, interviews can be a rich and detailed source of information, as long as they do not involve retrospective reports. However, precisely because they provide so much information, limits have to be placed on the number of questions asked and the number of people interviewed. By comparison, structured questionnaires or checklists are much easier to administer and score, but do not give respondents the opportunity to raise issues that are important to them or to express their reactions in their own words. Moreover, because each questionnaire item usually asks about people's "typical" or "general" experiences, it can be difficult for respondents to remember the various situations that might be relevant, and come up with a single answer that best sums up their experiences. An approach that overcomes this problem is the diary record, which requires people to record specified events either as they occur, or at least once each day. This method can be rather onerous for those who are asked to complete the records, but is likely to provide more reliable information about the frequency and nature of the specified events.

Because each of these methods has particular strengths and weaknesses, researchers have increasingly tended to use a combination of methods within the same study. In this way, the strengths of one method tend to compensate for the limitations of another, and a more complete picture of people's experiences can be obtained.

The second respect in which studies of parenthood have become more sophisticated concerns the recognition of the important role of *fathers*. In the past, some studies tended to focus on parenthood as "women's experience." Other studies gathered information from fathers, but only in a fairly superficial way (e.g., comparing the overall levels of stress reported by mothers and fathers). Presumably this relative neglect of fathers' role reflected the fact that mothers were usually seen as the primary caregivers of their young children.

Although it is still true that more mothers than fathers take on this primary caregiving role, fathers clearly play an extremely important part in the transition from couple to fully-fledged family. Most fathers are actively involved in tending to and playing with their babies. In fact, babies form strong bonds, or "attachments," both to mothers and to fathers (as we discuss further in Chapter 2). These facts attest to the vital ways in which fathers contribute to the development of their children. Their contribution to the running of the household during this time of transition is also very important. In fact, as we will see shortly, men's involvement in household tasks is a key predictor of husbands' and wives' adjustment to parenthood. For these reasons, a comprehensive study of new parenthood requires assessment of both women's and men's views of the experience.

HOW DOES PARENTHOOD CHANGE COUPLE RELATIONSHIPS?

Having pointed out the advances made in studying this period of transition, we turn now to the major findings from more recent research, focusing in particular on changes to couples' relationships. The findings described below are drawn from a number of important studies in the area, including those of Belsky and colleagues (Belsky & Kelly, 1994; Belsky & Pensky, 1988; Belsky & Rovine, 1990), Philip and Carolyn Cowan and colleagues (Cowan & Cowan, 1988; Cowan, Cowan, Heming, & Miller, 1991), Crohan (1996), Huston and colleagues (Huston & Vangelisti, 1995; Huston, McHale, & Crouter, 1986; Johnson & Huston, 1998), Levy-Shiff (1994), and Osofsky and Culp (1993).

Earlier in this chapter, we commented on the remarkable changes that take place in the family with the arrival of the first child: The structure of the family becomes more complex, and the new infant is totally dependent on the parents. Given these changes in the structure and functioning of the family unit, it is not surprising that researchers have looked for changes in couples' relationships throughout this transition. The changes studied can be grouped into four broad aspects of couple relationships: division of household work; leisure, companionship, and intimacy; emotional tone of couple interactions (positivity and negativity); and relationship satisfaction.

Division of Household Work

In describing the changes that occur in couples' relationships, the performance of household duties is a fitting place to start. After all, it is fairly obvious that parenthood brings many new tasks and responsibilities. Moreover, this is the area in which couples most consistently report changes in their relationships.

Regardless of whether researchers have studied small samples of couples or conducted large-scale surveys, they have usually found parenthood to be associated with a more traditional division of labor. In other words, the arrival of the baby seems to crystallize a gender-based division of labor, with men focusing on paid work outside the home (the "breadwinner" role), and women focusing on infant care and other responsibilities around the home (the "homemaker" role).

How does this change come about? As we said earlier, a new baby clearly means "extra work." Some studies indicate that men's patterns of paid and unpaid work show little change at this point in the life cycle, but others suggest that men actually *increase* their hours of paid work when they become fathers (Bittman, 1991). The latter suggestion fits with anecdotal and interview data, which point to new fathers' awareness of their additional responsibilities, including the responsibility to "provide" for the family.

At the same time, women's work routines change very markedly with pregnancy and parenthood. Generally, this change involves women leaving paid employment, or at least cutting back their hours, and becoming much more heavily involved with chores around the house. Not only do most wives take on the lion's share of the tasks related to infant care, they also increase their hours of general household work. It is also important to note that most new mothers report doing much more of the housework and infant care than they had expected. Not surprisingly, this discrepancy between expectation and experience tends to create disappointment and dissatisfaction for some wives.

As this point suggests, the tendency for parenthood to bring more traditional division of labor is often neither planned nor expected. A major factor behind this development seems to be the sheer number of demands that new parents face: Their resources of time and energy are limited, and a traditional form of task allocation may seem to be the most efficient way of doing things (especially if the wife stays at home). A second factor involves issues of earning power and job stability: In many couples, the man still enjoys greater earning power than the woman, but also has less freedom to adapt work schedules to fit with the demands of family life. For these couples, financial considerations can limit men's active involvement in fatherhood (Schwartz, 1994). Yet another relevant factor is that wives tend to "go along" with husbands' preferences for how tasks are allocated. Although this finding might seem to point to men's greater power and dominance in decision making, it is not as simple as this. Wives' tendency to accept husbands' preferences is more marked if their feelings of love for their partners are very strong, suggesting that this compliance represents a deliberate focus on minimizing conflict and maximizing family harmony.

Of course, not all new parents adopt highly traditional approaches to task allocation. Several studies of new parenthood have focused specifically on patterns of household work (e.g., Deutsch, Lussier, & Servis, 1993; Sanchez & Thomson, 1997); these studies show that husbands' involvement in baby care and other household tasks varies greatly from couple to couple, and that the reasons for this variation are complex. The extent of husbands' involvement in chores has been linked to broader work patterns, including both parents' work hours, income, and occupational status. It has also been linked to partners' attitudes towards gender roles and feminism, and to complex dynamics within the marriage, involving partners' perceptions of satisfaction, togetherness, and conflict.

Interestingly, although housework and child care have often been considered collectively (as "domestic labor"), the factors affecting partners' involvement in these two types of tasks seem to be quite different. For example, fathers' involvement in housework is predicted by dynamics within the marriage, whereas their involvement in child care is predicted by their nontraditional gender role attitudes and by mothers' hours of paid work. For these reasons, housework and child care are best considered as two separate issues that couples need to confront.

Leisure, Companionship, and Intimacy

How does new parenthood affect the extent to which couples share leisure time, general companionship, and intimacy? As we might expect, the conclusion drawn from most studies is that these aspects of the relationship tend to decline after the birth of the baby. That is, most new parents report a lessening of shared leisure activities, joint decision making, and general companionship. They also report that they have less opportunity to converse with each other, particularly in terms of sharing small talk.

According to most studies, parenthood does not produce much change in the *absolute* amount of time that husbands and wives spend together. What changes is the way that time is spent. New parents have less leisure time, and their choice of leisure activities tends to be restricted: They spend less time going out to dinner or to the movies than before the baby was born, and often look for joint activities that allow them to watch over the baby. New parents (especially new fathers) are also less likely to engage in independent leisure pursuits, that is, activities that they may enjoy, but their partner does not. In short, when partners spend time together, they are likely to be looking after their baby, or to be doing other instrumental tasks. Despite the lack of change in the absolute amount of time spent together, this *relative* lack of couple intimacy is a common source of complaint among new parents. Clearly, not all "time together" is equal!

A recent review of studies of new parenthood suggests that it is also common for couples to report changes in their sexual relationship (von Sydow, 1999). These changes include reductions in sexual interest, responsiveness, activity (both coital activity and other forms of stimulation), and enjoyment. There can be many reasons for the changes. In late pregnancy, there may be fears that sexual activity will harm the baby (although these fears are generally unfounded). For some women, intercourse can become painful; for others, enjoyment is inhibited because they feel less attractive or are concerned about their partner's sexual satisfaction.

After the baby is born, lack of sleep and general fatigue can dampen sexual desire. New parents may also find that the presence of the new baby inhibits their spontaneity, or interrupts their attempts at physical intimacy. For many couples, the first intercourse after the birth of the baby can pose particular problems: These problems can be physical (e.g., milk leakage, or pain), or emotional (again, being worried about physical attractiveness or about the sexual satisfaction of the partner). New parents' reports of their sexual relationships vary widely, however; some report few changes, and where changes do occur, they can be either short-lived or quite lasting.

Emotional Tone of Interactions: Positivity and Negativity

Emotional climate is another crucial aspect of couple relationships. People experience their most intense emotions in the context of their close relationships, and the emotions experienced by one partner are usually communicated to the other, either directly or indirectly. Given

their increased task load and reduced opportunities for companionship and intimacy, we might expect new parents to report a change in
the emotional climate of their relationship. That is, we might expect
them to report fewer positive interactions than beforehand, and more
negative interactions. Some studies of new parenthood suggest that
this is the case.

For instance, both questionnaire responses and direct observation of
couples have suggested that parenthood brings a decline in expressions
of affection and other positive interactions (e.g., spouses paying attention
to one another). In addition, new parents often report wishing that positive interactions occurred more frequently than they actually do.

In terms of negativity, some researchers have found that new parents report more frequent arguments and conflict, and increases in
general feelings of marital tension. There is also some evidence that
parenthood is associated with a tendency for one or both partners to
engage in conflict avoidance. In other words, new parents may tend to
respond to marital conflict by becoming quiet and pulling away from
the spouse, perhaps because disagreements make them feel more vulnerable after the arrival of the baby.

Although these findings suggest that the emotional climate of marriage is less positive for new parents than for other couples, it is important to note that this suggestion has not gone unchallenged. For
example, Huston and Vangelisti (1995) compared the interactions of
childless couples and new parents, using telephone interviews to sample specific behaviors across several days. This fairly objective method
of assessment revealed no difference between the two groups of couples in the frequency of positive behaviors (e.g., saying "I love you"), or
negative behaviors (e.g., registering complaints or criticisms).

Relationship Satisfaction

Although it is important to look at the kinds of interactions that new
parents engage in, it is equally important to know how they *feel* about
their relationship. The changes that we have described so far (e.g., division of labor, less companionship) might seem to imply that couples
should be less satisfied with their relationships than they were before
the birth. However, common sense suggests that this is not necessarily

the case. If couples *expect* the birth of their baby to bring these sorts of changes, they may accept them fairly readily.

Studies of new parenthood shed some light on this issue, but also highlight its complexity. One point to note is that the research findings have been inconsistent. Many studies have associated parenthood with declines in relationship satisfaction, but almost as many have shown that any decline is roughly similar in size to that shown by childless couples (and hence cannot be attributed to parenthood). The difference in findings across studies suggests that any reports of "average amounts of change" are likely to mask important differences between different couples. In fact, some researchers now focus on trying to identify different *trajectories of satisfaction*. For example, Belsky and Rovine (1990) identified four groups of new parents, defined by patterns of relationship satisfaction from pregnancy to parenthood: Two groups showed declines in satisfaction (one more marked than the other), one showed fairly stable levels, and one actually showed a slight increase in satisfaction.

Another source of debate concerns possible gender differences in the course of relationship satisfaction. In particular, some studies have shown that declines in satisfaction are more marked for mothers than for fathers. However, it seems that this apparent gender difference may depend on the timing of the assessments. If relationship satisfaction is measured when the babies are only a few months old, women are more likely than men to show a drop in satisfaction. On the other hand, after a year or so of parenthood, fathers often show a similar drop. In short, men may be slower to experience the impact of parenthood, perhaps because their day-to-day involvement in tending to the baby is usually not as great. Of course, for some couples, this difference in spouses' feelings over the first few months may, in itself, create distance or conflict.

Summing Up the Changes

To summarize what we have discussed so far, parenthood is most likely to bring changes in the areas of task allocation and performance, and leisure, companionship, and intimacy. These findings are not surprising, because these areas are most directly affected by the presence of the baby. In contrast, changes in the emotional climate of marriage and in overall levels of satisfaction are less clear-cut. When differences are found in these areas, they are usually small in size, and there is a great deal of similarity in the reports of childless couples and new parents. In other words, some couples report significant problems in their relationships around the birth of the first baby, but others fare quite well. In the next section, we explore possible reasons for these different experiences of the transition to parenthood.

WHY DO SOME COUPLES FARE BETTER THAN OTHERS?

As we have suggested, the effects of new parenthood on couples vary enormously, and it is important to understand the factors that are linked most closely to adjustment to the transition. According to Belsky and Pensky (1988), four sets of factors are important: factors associated with the infant, with the parents as individuals, with the couple relationship, and with the broader social network.

Infant Characteristics

It is not surprising that infant characteristics play an important part in the adjustment process. Specific characteristics that are very relevant to parents' adjustment include temperament and physical health. In terms of temperament, for example, it is clear that not all babies are alike: Some are generally placid and easy to soothe, whereas others are irritable, "fussy" or "difficult." Irritable babies place greater demands on parents, making the adjustment more difficult.

More severe conditions of the infant, such as prematurity, illness, and physical handicap, are associated with higher levels of parental stress. These conditions usually involve additional tasks and demands of infant care. Parents also have to cope with violated expectations of a "normal" birth, and with a situation that is largely beyond their control (Parke & Beitel, 1988).

The Parents as Individuals

Individual characteristics of the parents are also associated with the ease or difficulty of adjustment following the first birth. For example, parents who are prone to depression or low self-esteem are more likely to struggle with new parenthood. Other aspects of personality and behavioral style are also relevant. For instance, Levy-Shiff (1994) found that the transition to parenthood was easier for women who were low in autonomy and high in the ability to organize, and for men who saw themselves as caring and nurturing. Presumably these characteristics make it easier for new parents to accept the demands of parenthood, and work together to respond to the baby's needs.

Traditional gender role attitudes also seem to promote a relatively easy adjustment, particularly for women. We have already seen that new parenthood usually brings a more traditional division of labor. Spouses who hold traditional gender role attitudes seem to accept this change more readily. Wives with traditional attitudes tend to be comfortable with their role of nurturing and caring for the infant, and often see child care as their own domain. This arrangement can suit husbands with traditional attitudes, who may prefer to focus most of their energy on providing for the family and doing other "masculine" tasks.

Similarly, expectations of parenthood are very important to the transition. Many parents report a marked discrepancy between their expectations and their actual experiences. In particular, they may find that they spend more time tending to the baby than they had expected, and less time engaged in leisure and social activities. Discrepancies of this sort have been associated with a more difficult adjustment to parenthood.

The Couple Relationship

There is no doubt that the couple relationship plays a central role in the adjustment to parenthood. Where levels of relationship satisfaction and cohesion are high before the birth, parents tend to cope better. This finding has emerged quite consistently from studies over a 40-year period. In fact, longitudinal studies comparing transition and childless couples show that initial levels of relationship satisfaction explain later satisfaction better than whether the couple had a child or not. The crucial role of relationship satisfaction seems to apply to both women and men. According to Grossman (1988), having a satisfying couple relationship increases women's sense of comfort and confidence during this time of transition. In addition, relationship satisfaction and support from partner predict fathers' level of involvement with the baby, as well as their parenting competence.

Although overall relationship satisfaction is clearly important to new parenthood, satisfaction with the allocation and performance of tasks is particularly important. For instance, Levy-Shiff (1994) found that low involvement on the part of fathers (especially in regard to infant care), was the major factor predicting declines in satisfaction for both fathers and mothers. What seems to matter most is not the sheer amount of fathers' involvement, but whether partners see that involvement as fair or unfair. Terry, McHugh, and Noller (1991) found that women who saw their husbands as making a fair contribution actually *increased* in satisfaction across the transition to parenthood. Again, the match between expectations and reality is crucial: When women find themselves doing more of the child care and housekeeping than they expected (and, as already noted, this is a common occurrence), they experience more dissatisfaction. Further, it seems that adjustment to new fatherhood is affected by satisfaction with the process of decision-making about allocation of tasks, rather than by "who does what."

The Social Network

According to several researchers, the adjustment to parenthood is easier when couples can draw on the help and support of others. This finding is easy to understand, given the many changes and demands that come with parenthood. Relationships both inside and outside the family can be important in this regard.

More specifically, Belsky (1984) has pointed out that other people can help new parents in any of three different ways. First, they can provide emotional support and acceptance, by being available to talk about issues and by showing an understanding of the joys and challenges that the new parent is experiencing. Second, they can provide practical, or instrumental, assistance. For instance, they can help with meal preparation and other household tasks, enabling the mother to concentrate on caring for the baby. Finally, friends and family members who have experienced parenthood can be a source of appropriate expectations, and help new parents to deal with their anxieties and fears. Of course, the advice and comments of others can sometimes be a source of strain, rather than a source of support, particularly if they are seen as intrusive, irrelevant, or outdated.

Links Between Factors that Predict Adjustment

Although it is convenient to talk about *sets* of factors that explain differences in adjustment (factors of the infant, the parents as individuals, the couple relationship, and the social network), these factors do not work in isolation. Rather, characteristics of the infant (including temperament) can affect the individual adjustment of the parents, and the patterns of interaction between them. For example, having an "easy" baby tends to foster a sense of competence and general well-being in the parents, which is likely to make their couple interactions more agreeable. In addition, the combination of low self-esteem and lack of social support seems to place new mothers at particular risk of adjustment problems. In other words, the transition to parenthood is best seen as "part of an interrelated system of factors and events" (Osofsky & Culp, 1993, p. 79).

SUMMARY

Parenting is a topic of almost universal interest: Most people have strong ideas about the parenting they experienced as children, and about the costs and benefits of becoming parents themselves. Although parenthood is no longer widely regarded as a time of crisis, it is a transition that can have marked effects on individuals and their relationships. These effects are particularly evident in the areas of household duties and couple intimacy. Some people handle the transition to parenthood more easily than others, and the couple relationship is a key factor in promoting adjustment. In the next chapter, we introduce the concept of attachment, which provides a relatively new way of thinking about couple relationships. The attachment perspective helps to explain why couple bonds are so important to our sense of comfort and security, and why some couples find it easier than others to cope with challenge and change.

TWO

Attachment in Childhood and Beyond

The concept of attachment has had a central place in the literature on parent–child relationships for several decades. Most experts in this area would agree that a secure attachment bond with at least one nurturing adult is a key factor in producing happy and well-adjusted children. It seems that these bonds help children develop feelings of trust and confidence, enabling them to move out into the world and acquire the skills they need to deal with new situations. Similarly, recent research suggests that attachment is a useful concept for understanding the bonds that adults form with intimate partners, and the way that couples respond to stress and change. But how can attachment be defined?

DEFINING ATTACHMENT

In everyday language, it is common for people to talk about being "attached" to someone or something. According to the *Concise Oxford Dictionary,* this everyday use of the term *attachment* refers to feelings of affection and devotion. In writings on religious and philosophical topics, however, the term *attachment* often implies something more than this: a very strong desire to have or to keep the object of affection, and conversely, an extreme reluctance to give up the object, or do without it.

In all these respects, researchers' use of the term *attachment* is similar to the use in everyday language. The best-known figure in this area of research has been John Bowlby, an English scholar who studied and wrote about childhood attachment from the 1940s through to the 1980s. In particular, he is renowned for his trilogy of books on attachment and loss (Bowlby, 1969, 1973, 1980).

Bowlby defined attachment behavior as "any form of behavior that results in a person attaining or retaining proximity to some other differentiated and preferred individual, usually conceived as stronger and/or wiser" (Bowlby, 1973, p. 292). Although this definition is very broad in scope, Bowlby was especially interested in the attachment behaviors that infants and young children direct toward their mothers. He argued that these behaviors, such as crying, smiling, clinging, babbling, and following, were instinctive in nature. That is, these behaviors serve to keep young children close to the "attachment figure" (often the mother), and also act as a kind of "social releaser" that cues the attachment figure to respond with love and care. In this way, young children's relationship-seeking behaviors help to ensure their safety.

Bowlby's definition of attachment behavior focused on the idea of "proximity seeking." In other words, broadly speaking, the goal of attachment behavior is to ensure that young children remain close to their caregivers. However, he also identified other important functions of attachment that are related to this broad goal. In general, the attachment figure provides a "secure base" from which the child can feel safe to explore the environment and master new skills. In fact, in familiar situations, children are more likely to engage in exploratory activity than in attachment behavior, although they tend to check on the caregiver's availability from time to time. By contrast, in unfamiliar or threatening situations, attachment behavior predominates; hence, in times of stress, the attachment figure acts as a "safe haven" to which the child can retreat for comfort and reassurance. According to Bowlby, proximity seeking (including distress at separation), secure base, and safe haven are the defining features, and the functions, of attachment relationships.

ATTACHMENT: BACKGROUND TO THE THEORY

Although attachment theory is most often associated with the name of Bowlby, he was influenced, of course, by the findings of earlier researchers. In fact, Bowlby was very widely read, and the theory he formulated was a brilliant integration of ideas drawn from several disciplines, including psychoanalysis, developmental psychology, and ethology (the study of social behavior in animals and humans).

Bowlby was trained in psychoanalytic theory and practice, but became troubled by what he saw as psychoanalysts' overemphasis on unconscious motives or drives, and underemphasis on people's actual relationship experiences. In the 1940s, he carried out a number of studies that looked at the effects of disruptions to the bond between children and their mothers. In the report of one of these studies (Forty-four Juvenile Thieves), he documented the high proportion of delinquent boys who had experienced separations from their mothers early in life. Some years later, he wrote a report for the World Health Organization, describing the mental health problems faced by children who had been separated from their mothers. In this report (Maternal Care and Mental Health), he argued that maternal separations were a clear risk factor for mental illness, and that institutional care was very damaging to children unless it provided them with a true "mother substitute."

In the 1950s, Bowlby became familiar with the work of ethologists, including Konrad Lorenz, who were studying the bonding behavior of birds and mammals. One of the intriguing findings of these researchers concerned a phenomenon known as "imprinting". This term refers to the fact that when creatures such as ducks and geese are born, they attach themselves to the first moving object they see. Of course, this object is usually the mother, but if a human researcher happens to be the first in view, the baby bird will become imprinted on the researcher, and follow him or her everywhere. Bowlby was struck by this finding, because it fitted with his own ideas about human development: that infants come into the world predisposed to relate to others, and that nature's plan for the bonding between parent and offspring can go wrong if the parent is not available to meet the child's needs.

At about the same time, Bowlby was impressed by work carried out by James Robertson, a member of his own research unit. Robertson was a social worker who had been carefully observing young children during their stays in hospital. At that time, visiting hours in hospitals were very restricted, even for the parents of young children. Robertson observed the extreme distress that children suffered as a result of being separated from their parents, and was furious when psychiatric experts of the day refused to concede that these separations could be traumatic. To convince them otherwise, he bought a simple hand-held camera, selected one hospitalized child at random, and recorded her behavior at selected points throughout her eight-day stay in hospital. The resulting film, *A Two Year Old Goes to Hospital,* provided a graphic picture of the child's suffering. The film was highly controversial at the time, but was instrumental in bringing about more flexible arrangements for hospital visits.

Another study that had an impact on Bowlby was reported in 1958 by Harry Harlow. Harlow, in turn, had been influenced by reports of infants who had been orphaned or abandoned, and who were raised in foundling homes: These infants received very little in the way of affection, physical comfort, and touch, and often died at a young age. Harlow was interested in animal behavior, and decided to investigate the importance of contact and warmth to the development of young rhesus monkeys. He separated monkeys from their mothers soon after birth, and assigned them to one of two surrogate mothers: One was made of wire mesh, and the other was made of soft terry-cloth, but both could be fitted with a feeding nipple. Harlow showed that the infant monkeys became more attached to the cloth "mother" than to the wire "mother", even when the wire mother was the only one providing food. This attachment was reflected in the young monkeys' tendency to cuddle the cloth mother, use it as a base for their explorations, and cling to it when unfamiliar objects were brought into the environment (see Figure 2.1). In short, warm contact was clearly important to

Figure 2.1. Young monkey and surrogate mothers used in Harlow's research.

the infant monkeys, and promoted attachment behaviors (proximity seeking, secure base, and safe haven).

FUNDAMENTALS OF THE THEORY

Based on his own observations and those of researchers such as Lorenz and Harlow, Bowlby became convinced that a secure attachment bond was crucial to children's social and emotional development. He also concluded that attachment behavior forms an organized behavioral system. In other words, many different behaviors (including crying, smiling, and clinging) serve the single function of maintaining closeness to caregivers. Because observational studies had shown strong similarities in bonding between humans and other animal species, Bowlby argued that attachment behavior was universal in nature, and had evolved through a process of natural selection. Put another way, attachment behavior is adaptive, and protects infants from danger by keeping them close to a caring adult.

In his writing, Bowlby tended to emphasize the bond between infant and *mother,* an emphasis that reflected the traditional view of gender roles prevailing at the time. However, he recognized that human infants usually become attached to more than one person, even within the first year of life. The person who provides most of the care usually becomes the primary attachment figure, and is preferred as a safe haven when the infant is distressed. Although there have been recent trends in western countries towards more varied and complex patterns of child care, mothers are still likely to occupy the role of primary attachment figure.

Fathers and older siblings are likely to become secondary attachment figures. In other words, these family members occupy an important place in the infant's social world, although they may not be able to soothe the distressed child as easily as the mother can. In recent years, attachment scholars have looked more closely at the bond between infants and fathers, a point we return to later in this chapter.

As we have seen, Bowlby's discussions of attachment focused mainly on the bonds between infants and their caregivers. This focus was a deliberate one, and based on the recognition that early social experiences are very important: They occur when the individual is highly dependent and vulnerable, and tend to shape the developing personality. This does not mean, however, that attachment is restricted to the young or the "immature." In fact, Bowlby argued that the attachment system plays a crucial role across the life span, and that human beings engage in attachment behavior "from the cradle to the grave" (Bowlby, 1979, p. 129).

DESCRIBING DIFFERENCES IN ATTACHMENT BONDS

In 1950, a young scholar named Mary Ainsworth joined Bowlby's research unit. For the next four years, she was responsible for analyzing and interpreting data collected by members of the research team, and planning new research projects. She was particularly impressed by Robertson's work on hospitalized children, which showed how much researchers could learn by observing parents and offspring in their natural settings. As a result, she decided to use similar methods in her own research.

This decision was put into place four years later, when Ainsworth and her husband moved to Uganda. She located 28 young babies, and began a longitudinal study in which she observed the babies and their mothers in their own homes. She documented the growing sophistication of the babies' attachment behavior, from crying, to smiling, to vocalizations. She also noted that some babies seemed more secure in their maternal bond than others, and began to develop measures of mothers' sensitivity and responsiveness to their babies' needs and signals.

This work was extended when she moved to Baltimore, Maryland. With the aid of a research grant, she and a team of observers studied 26 babies and their mothers, collecting a massive amount of data during the course of 18, four-hour home visits to each family. The attachment behaviors that the team observed were similar to those seen in the Ugandan families, supporting Bowlby's claim that attachment behaviors are universal. The research conducted in Baltimore went a step further, however, and included a laboratory technique designed to assess how babies responded to separations from their mothers. This technique allowed researchers to measure both attachment behavior and exploratory behavior (attractive toys were placed in the room to encourage exploration), and came to be known as the Strange Situation.

Based mainly on the babies' reactions to the comings and goings of their mothers, Ainsworth identified three main "attachment styles": secure, ambivalent, and avoidant (Ainsworth, Blehar, Waters, & Wall, 1978). Secure babies were quite comfortable exploring their surroundings when the mother was present. They usually cried when the mother left the room, but were obviously happy to greet her when she came back, often stretching out their arms to reach her. Ambivalent babies tended to be "clingy" even when the mother was present, and seemed afraid to explore their surroundings. They became extremely upset when the mother left the room, and were difficult to soothe when she came back, often appearing to want contact, but at the same time arching away from her angrily. Finally, avoidant babies seemed unusually independent in the Strange Situation. They tended to explore the room without checking on the mother's availability, showed little distress when she left, and often avoided or "snubbed" her when she came back. (Findings from later studies suggest that avoidant babies *do* become upset when their mothers leave them, and that their apparent indifference is a defensive reaction.)

Ainsworth's findings (from the Strange Situation and the home visits) were immensely important, for two related reasons. First, they showed that attachment needs, although universal, can be expressed in quite different ways. Second, these differences in attachment patterns seemed to be explained, to a considerable degree, by mothers' caregiving behavior. Mothers of babies who were classified as secure in the Strange Situation were generally quite responsive to their babies' signals, trying to soothe them when they were upset and returning their smiles when they were happy. On the other hand, mothers of ambivalent babies were more inconsistent, sometimes responding appropriately to their babies' signals, but at other times being insensitive or intrusive; and mothers of avoidant babies were often unresponsive or rejecting of their babies' needs and demands (see Figures 2.2, 2.3, and 2.4).

Since Ainsworth's early work, hundreds of studies have explored similar questions about caregiving and babies' development as social beings. Overall, this research has supported her major findings. Babies clearly show varying reactions to separations and reunions with their caregivers. Moreover, these reactions can be explained, in part, by the style of caregiving that the babies have experienced.

Equally important, a large number of follow-up studies have pointed to longer-term implications of secure and insecure attachment: On average, children who have been classified as secure in infancy seem to show more curiosity, more self-reliance, and better relationships with their peers than those classified as insecure. Interestingly, the link between mothers' responsiveness and children's adjustment supports what is, for most parents, a matter of intuition: to pick up and soothe a distressed baby. Certainly, they run counter to the opposing view (which held sway for some time), that picking up a crying baby reinforces the crying, and "spoils" the child.

Although most studies of infant attachment have focused on mothers as attachment figures, a smaller number have looked at the role of fathers (e.g., Grossmann, Grossmann, & Zimmermann, 1999; Kerns & Barth, 1995;

Exploration from a Secure Base

© Candida Peterson

Figure 2.2. Secure attachment in infancy.

van IJzendoorn & De Wolff, 1997). This work suggests that interactions with fathers also shape children's attachment security, though possibly to a lesser degree than those with mothers. In addition, fathers contribute to their children's development in other vital ways. For example, many fathers engage in physical play with their offspring, issuing directives and responding to children's needs and suggestions; in this way, they foster the capacity for cooperative play with family members and peers. Fathers

Remains Upset and Resists Caregiver
on Reunion

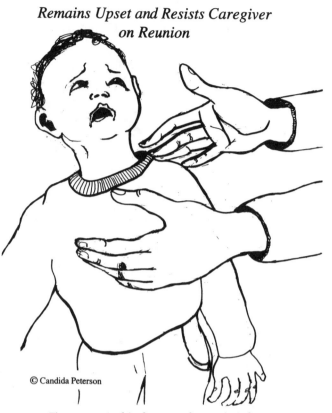

© Candida Peterson

Figure 2.3. Ambivalent attachment in infancy.

can also influence children's adjustment indirectly, by impacting on the mother's sensitivity to her offspring.

As with many research findings, the results of studies of infant attachment have not gone without criticism. Some critics have questioned the usefulness of the Strange Situation technique, seeing it as rather artificial and limited in scope. Others have queried the meaning of differences in attachment patterns, arguing that insecure attachment can be explained by innate differences in infant temperament, rather than by differences in mothers' behavior. In other words, some children may simply be genetically predisposed to feel insecure or rejected. As we noted in Chapter 1, it is certainly true that some babies are more difficult to handle than others. Nevertheless, how parents

Avoids Caregiver on Reunion

Figure 2.4. Avoidant attachment in infancy.

respond to the particular needs of their baby is important, and it would be surprising if this were not the case! Babies and young children experience countless interactions with their caregivers, and these interactions convey, at least implicitly, important messages about love, trust, and self-worth.

In this way, according to Bowlby and Ainsworth, children and adolescents gradually internalize their relationship experiences. In other words, over time, repeated interactions with caregivers give rise to a set of expectations about what will happen in close relationships. These expectations, usually referred to as "mental models of attachment," reflect the individual's ideas about his or her self-worth and about the dependability of others. Because these expectations are based on actual interactions, they can be revised in the light of new experiences. If caregiving circumstances are fairly stable, however, the expectations tend to become stronger over time, and more resistant to change.

DO ADULTS FORM ATTACHMENT BONDS?

Can adults' close relationships be regarded as attachments? According to Ainsworth (1989), attachment relationships must meet several criteria: They must be relatively long-lasting bonds involving a desire to be close to the relationship partner; moreover, the partner must play a unique role in providing feelings of comfort and security. Similarly, Weiss (1982, 1986) has argued that the defining features of attachment bonds, as outlined by Bowlby, suggest several criteria of attachment:

- the person wants to be with the partner, especially in times of stress
- s/he derives comfort and security from the partner
- s/he protests when the partner becomes, or threatens to become, unavailable.

These criteria are certainly consistent with the idea of couple relationships as attachments – most adults are familiar with the special feelings of intimacy enjoyed with romantic partners, the sense of confidence and security derived from them, and the extreme distress that occurs when relationships are lost or threatened. In later work, Weiss (1991) identified other striking parallels between infant and couple relationships. For instance, in both kinds of relationships, the individual's sense of attachment to the partner does not habituate (or fade) over time; if anything, it becomes stronger. In addition, feelings of attachment usually continue, even in the face of physical separation, and loss of the attachment figure results in a predictable sequence of reactions, known as grief.

Despite the various logical arguments for the concept of adult attachment, it took an innovative research project to test these ideas. In

1987, Hazan and Shaver reported the results of this project, which was based on a simple proposition: If people's experiences throughout childhood and adolescence produce relatively lasting expectations about relationships, and if those expectations guide behavior, different attachment styles should be evident amongst adults, just as they are amongst young children.

To test this proposition, Hazan and Shaver developed a simple questionnaire measure of adult attachment style. They derived the measure by considering the characteristics of the three infant styles, and asking how these basic styles might be played out in couple relationships. For example, individuals whose primary relationships have been emotionally distant are likely to expect others to reject them or ignore their needs; because of this, they may be uncomfortable and defensive in close interactions (a style that only serves to heighten the chance that the negative expectations will be confirmed). In this way, Hazan and Shaver developed one-paragraph descriptions for each of the three styles, with respondents being asked to indicate which paragraph best described their feelings in close relationships.

- **Secure:** I find it relatively easy to get close to others and am comfortable depending on them and having them depend on me. I don't often worry about being abandoned or about someone getting too close to me.
- **Avoidant:** I am somewhat uncomfortable being close to others; I find it difficult to trust them completely, difficult to allow myself to depend on them. I am nervous when anyone gets too close, and love partners often want me to be more intimate than I feel comfortable being.
- **Ambivalent:** I find that others are reluctant to get as close as I would like. I often worry that my partner doesn't really love me or won't want to stay with me. I want to merge completely with another person, and this desire sometimes scares people away.

Using this measure in studies with two different samples of adults, Hazan and Shaver found considerable support for the concept of adult attachment styles. Most adults were able to select a description that "best" fitted them, and the relative frequencies of the three styles were very similar to those typically observed among infants: Just over half of the respondents chose the secure description, and of the remainder, slightly more described themselves as avoidant than as ambivalent.

Equally important, the three groups of adults differed in predictable ways. Secure respondents recalled their early family relationships as generally warm and caring; they saw themselves as easy to get to know and others as well-intentioned, and described their most important love relationships as friendly, happy, and trusting. In contrast, avoidant respondents perceived their mothers as rather cold and rejecting. They tended to question the existence of romantic love, and their most important relationships were marked by fear of intimacy and difficulty in accepting their love partners. Respondents who chose the ambivalent description saw their fathers as having been unfair towards them. They also felt misunderstood, and reported that it was hard to find love and commitment. Their most important relationships were marked by strong feelings of attraction, but also by jealousy and concerns about whether partners reciprocated their feelings.

These findings generated an enormous amount of interest amongst relationship researchers. A major reason for this interest was that the research seemed to herald a more scientific approach to the study of love. Although many previous writers and researchers had tried to describe or define love, much of their work focused on the more extreme or maladaptive forms of love. (Tennov's [1979] work on "limerence" is a good example of this more restricted approach, portraying the anxiety and obsession that some people experience as "love.") Descriptions of anxiety and obsession make interesting reading, but they shed little light on *why* some people experience love in this way. In contrast, attachment theory makes sense of different experiences of love, by linking them to earlier relationship experiences and the expectations they create.

UNDERSTANDING ADULT ATTACHMENT

Although there are striking parallels between infant and adult attachments, there are also some major differences. In fact, both the similarities and the differences help us to understand the important features of adult attachment relationships.

Attachment, Caregiving, and Sexuality

If we stop to think about how adults relate to their intimate partners and how they relate to their offspring, two obvious differences soon come to mind. First, the relationship between intimate partners is essentially one between peers: Although there are some couples in which one partner tends to dominate the other, most aspire to relationships marked by equality and mutual support. In other words, caregiving within couple relationships is usually reciprocal, with each partner being called on at times to help and support the other. In contrast, caregiving of infants tends to be a "one-way street" (as the very term *caregiver* implies); infants are helpless, and depend on their parents for support and protection.

The other obvious difference between couple and parent–child relationships lies in the role of sexuality. Sexual attraction and sexual behavior play an important part in couple relationships, contributing to partner's sense of intimacy and passion. Infants, on the other hand, have a very limited capacity for sexual response, and the parent–child bond is usually seen as an inappropriate context for the expression of sexuality. In fact, almost all cultures have a taboo against incestuous relationships between parents and offspring.

In light of these differences between infant and adult attachments, Shaver and Hazan (1988; Hazan & Shaver, 1994) suggested that couple relationships could be understood in terms of the interplay among three behavioral systems: attachment, caregiving, and sexuality. According to this view, the three systems of behavior are interrelated, and are all integral to the experience of romantic love. (Similarly, Bowlby had argued that several interlocking systems of behavior, including attachment, caregiving, and sexual mating, worked together to ensure the survival of the species.) The three systems vary in importance from one relationship to another, and from one point in time to another; for example, sexual attraction is especially important in the early stages of couple relationships. However, the attachment system is seen as fundamental: Our first attachment experiences occur very early in life, and the mental models that emerge from these experiences are likely to shape our approach to caregiving and to sexual relating.

Individual Differences: Types or Dimensions?

Earlier in this chapter, we noted that the first studies of adult attachment set out to describe three attachment styles (secure, ambivalent, and avoidant), analogous to those observed among infants. Although those studies were largely successful (the three groups showed predictable differences in their reports of early parenting, social attitudes, and love experiences), the search for ways to measure different attachment orientations in adults had just begun.

Even in the area of infant attachment, measuring attachment styles is not a simple or straightforward matter. Ainsworth had carefully observed both infants and their mothers. Her work involved not only classifying the infants into groups, but also measuring aspects of parenting that could be linked to their attachment style; in addition, she focused on identifying subgroups of infants within the three main groups. Other researchers had argued the need for a fourth attachment group that would accommodate infants not readily classifiable as secure, ambivalent, or avoidant.

If the emerging picture of infant attachment styles was quite complex, surely adult relationship behavior would be even more complex. As several researchers were quick to point out, most adults have a wealth of relationship experience, involving innumerable interactions with many different kinds of people. Based on that broad experience, they are likely to have developed rather complex views about themselves, human nature, and the costs and rewards of intimate relationships. Can these different views actually be summed up in just three styles?

One reaction to this type of concern was to propose a four-group model of adult attachment. Based on Bowlby's work, Bartholomew (1990; Bartholomew & Horowitz, 1991) argued that we develop mental models both of ourselves (are we worthy of love and attention?) and of other people (are others generally reliable and trustworthy?). Assuming a simple yes/no answer to each of these questions, four styles can be defined (see Figure 2.5).

The main features of the four adult attachment styles can be summed up as follows:

■ *Secure:* confidence in dealing with close relationships; sense of comfort with both intimacy and autonomy

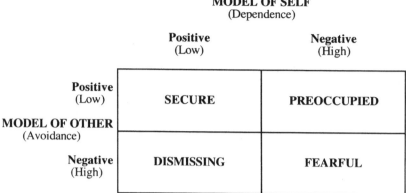

Figure 2.5. Four-group model of adult attachment.

- *Preoccupied* (similar to the ambivalent style): extreme dependence on others; preoccupation with concerns about partners' love and commitment
- *Dismissing-avoidant:* denial of need for close relationships; emphasis on self-reliance and achievement, rather than intimacy
- *Fearful-avoidant:* desire for intimacy, but distrust of others; avoidance of situations that might entail a risk of rejection

In recent years, this typology has been used more widely than the three-group model. However, even the four-group model has been subject to criticism. In essence, critics suggest that it is a waste of time to argue about whether there are three attachment groups, or four, or even more: People simply do not fit neatly into discrete groups. According to this view, it is more useful to think about the *dimensions* along which people differ. (This suggestion has parallels with discussions about personality; attempts to "type" people have generally been less fruitful than attempts to measure important dimensions of difference, such as extraversion and agreeableness.)

There is now a fair degree of consensus about the dimensions that underlie adults' sense of attachment security. Although different researchers have used slightly different labels, the two main dimensions can be described as *discomfort with closeness* and *anxiety over relationships* (Brennan, Clark, & Shaver, 1998).

Discomfort with closeness is a bipolar dimension, that is, one that contrasts two opposing tendencies. Essentially, it contrasts avoidant and secure approaches to close relationships. People who score high on this dimension find it difficult to get close to others; they feel nervous when other people get too close, and prefer to keep to themselves rather than depend on other people. In contrast, those who score low on this dimension find it easy to get close to others, and feel comfortable depending on others and having others depend on them.

The other dimension, anxiety over relationships, is similar to the ambivalent (or preoccupied) style of relating. This dimension deals with the desire for extreme closeness and union with the partner. It also taps fears about lack of love, and about possible rejection and abandonment by relationship partners.

Together, these two dimensions seem to provide a good assessment of adults' attachment concerns. They can also be linked to the typologies mentioned earlier; for example, avoidant groups (dismissing and fearful) report more discomfort with closeness than other groups, and preoccupied and fearful groups report more relationship anxiety than other groups. Compared with simple categorical measures, however, the dimensions allow finer distinctions to be made between individuals.

Attachment Style and Attachment Strength

A final difference between infant and adult attachment concerns the nature of the attachment network. As we mentioned earlier, infants usually form attachments to more than one person. However, they have limited control over the course of their interactions, and generally have to rely on whoever is available to meet their needs. In contrast, adults are mostly free to decide how they will have their needs met. For instance, if a young woman has an upsetting confrontation with someone at work, she may want to turn to someone for comfort (the "safe haven" function of attachment). In this event, she can decide whether to confide in a romantic partner (if she has one), her mother, her best friend, or some other close confidant.

Because adults are usually free to choose their interaction partners, it is interesting to see who they rely on to meet their attachment needs; that is, how important are the different members of the attachment network?

Whereas the dimensions we described in the previous section (discomfort with closeness, anxiety over relationships) ask about an individual's sense of *security* in intimate relationships, measures of the attachment network ask about the *importance* of various attachment figures.

Both these issues are important to understanding attachment, especially at transition points. For example, Hazan and Zeifman (1994) reported a study of attachment relationships in childhood, adolescence, and early adulthood. These researchers used a simple interview technique, which involved asking young people to name their preferred attachment figures (e.g., "Who do you like to spend time with?"; "Who do you miss most during separations?"; "Who do you turn to for comfort when you're feeling down?"). Their results showed a gradual shift in reliance on different attachment figures: All age groups preferred to spend time in the company of their peers (proximity seeking), but it was only in late adolescence that peers came to replace parents as the preferred secure base and source of greatest separation distress. More generally, the findings suggest the importance of applying this kind of assessment technique in longitudinal research. As we saw in Chapter 1, adjustment to change is best studied by tracking people over time, and shifts in the attachment network are likely to be an important aspect of that adjustment.

IMPLICATIONS OF ATTACHMENT SECURITY

Earlier in this chapter, we noted the implications of attachment security for children's development: Those classified as securely attached in infancy tend to be more sociable and well-adjusted as young children. The major focus of this book, however, is the link between attachment security and relationship functioning in *adults*. This issue has been explored with regard to a number of aspects of couple interaction (see Feeney, 1999, for a review):

- relationship satisfaction
- caregiving
- sexuality
- communication and conflict patterns
- stress and coping.

Relationship Satisfaction

Perhaps the most important question about attachment style and couple interaction is whether secure adults are happier with their relationships than insecure adults. This question is fundamental, because relationships that are satisfying are more stable, and contribute strongly to people's overall sense of well-being.

A large number of studies have looked at this issue, and the findings suggest that the link between security of attachment and relationship satisfaction is quite robust. That is, on average, secure adults report their couple relationships as more happy and satisfying than do insecure adults.

In terms of the attachment dimensions discussed earlier, it seems that men's discomfort with closeness and women's anxiety over relationships have the clearest links with relationship dissatisfaction. This pattern seems to reflect well-established gender role stereotypes about relationship behavior, with women expected to be more "clingy" and dependent, and men expected to be more distant and self-reliant. Extreme adherence to these stereotypical behaviors is likely to have a negative impact on couple relationships: It tends to pit men and women against each other in a kind of tug-of-war, rather than allowing them to work together as a team.

Caregiving

As we mentioned earlier, one of the important features of couple relationships is the provision of mutual care and support. From time to time, each partner will be called on to help the other deal with their problems and concerns. Although most adults regard this caregiving role as an implicit part of the marital contract, some fulfill the role more easily and successfully than others. Ideally, when one partner needs care, the other should be sensitive to his or her needs, and willing to show affection and support. At the same time, the caregiver should not become over-involved in the partner's problems, or take on their issues to the point where they lose sight of their own needs: An over-involved or "compulsive" style of caregiving can affect relationships adversely, by creating dependence in the person needing care and a sense of burden in the person providing it.

As would be expected from attachment theory, a number of studies suggest that secure adults respond more constructively than insecure adults to their partners' needs for care. In other words, secure adults are more responsive and less compulsive when it comes to providing their partners with emotional care and support.

Of course, caregiving is not always emotional in nature. Spouses often perform practical tasks to help each other, and this kind of tangible support is likely to be especially important when there is a new baby in the home. At this stage, little is known about whether attachment security affects spouses' willingness to help each other in these more practical ways.

Sexuality

Sexuality is another feature that distinguishes between parent–child bonds and couple bonds. According to attachment theory, basic expectations about the rewards and costs of close relationships affect our approach to sexuality. For instance, people who see others as trustworthy and well-intentioned will generally approach relationships optimistically, and expect intimacy and mutual satisfaction in their sexual relationships. On the other hand, those who have problems with close relationships may prefer a rather distant and uncommitted approach to sexual interactions, or may focus on sex as a way of trying to establish intimacy.

According to a study by Hazan, Zeifman, and Middleton (1994), there are consistent links between adult attachment styles and styles of sexual relating. Secure persons report more enjoyment of physical contact, more mutually initiated sex, and less sex outside of their primary relationships. Avoidant persons, on the other hand, are less likely to regard casual sex as inappropriate or unacceptable and, consistent with these attitudes, are more likely to have sex with people they do not feel particularly close to. Ambivalent individuals often report enjoying hugs and cuddles more than explicitly sexual acts, although ambivalent females seem to be more sexually adventurous than their male counterparts. These findings have emerged fairly consistently, but it is important to note that most of the research has looked at the sexual attitudes and behaviors of young single people. In contrast, relatively little is known about the links between attachment security and sexual expression in stable long-term relationships.

Communication and Conflict Patterns

Communication is at the very heart of close relationships – communication is the vehicle by which partners share their thoughts and feelings, make decisions, and deal with differences and disagreements. In fact, some researchers have argued that "good communication" and "good relationships" are one and the same thing. Because responsive caregivers generally encourage their offspring to be quite open in expressing their thoughts and feelings, securely attached children are thought to develop more effective patterns of communication.

Similarly, attachment security has been linked to key aspects of couple communication, including self-disclosure and conflict resolution. For example, secure adults engage in more self-disclosure, overall; their approach to disclosure is flexible, however, varying widely according to the demands of the particular situation. In contrast, those who are uncomfortable with intimacy are reluctant to disclose personal information, and those who are anxious about their relationships (i.e., concerned about issues of love and commitment) engage in self-disclosure fairly readily, but with little regard for the constraints of the situation.

Secure adults also adopt more constructive approaches to conflict resolution; that is, they tend to express their own point of view, listen to that of their partner, and try to work together to find solutions and compromises. On the other hand, those who are uncomfortable with intimacy tend to show low levels of acceptance and support of partners in the face of relationship conflict. Individuals who are anxious about their relationships often adopt a coercive and dominating stance when relationship conflict arises. Ironically, this coercive style of response only tends to fuel conflict, and may bring about the very outcome that these individuals fear most: alienation from their partners.

The link between attachment security and responses to conflict is very important, because failure to deal effectively with differences and disagreements can put relationships in jeopardy. The different conflict styles adopted by secure and insecure individuals are particularly evident when relationship conflict is intense, or involves issues that are central to the relationship (Feeney, 1998; Rholes, Simpson, & Stevens, 1998). This finding is not surprising: When people feel threatened, they tend to react in ways that are relatively automatic, "overlearned," and often immature (e.g., aggressively or defensively).

This type of response to threat is particularly problematic for insecure individuals, who are likely to "expect the worst" from their partners, and hence to interpret many events in a negative or threatening light. After all, almost any relationship event can be interpreted in a variety of ways. (For example, why is my partner home so late from work? Is it because that important work meeting took longer than expected? Or is it because he prefers to spend his free time with someone else?)

Stress and Coping

As we have just seen, adults who are insecure in their relationships often respond negatively to conflict. More generally, they may find it very difficult to cope with stressful situations. According to attachment theory, the different attachment styles observed in infancy reflect different rules and strategies for dealing with distress (Kobak & Sceery, 1988; Sroufe & Waters, 1977). Secure infants, for instance, generally have caregivers who are quite responsive to their needs; hence, the message they learn from them is that it is okay to express distress, and to turn to others for help. Insecure infants, on the other hand, have caregivers who are less consistently responsive. As a result, they learn either to suppress their negative feelings, so as to avoid irritating their caregivers, or to be particularly vocal about them, in order to force their caregivers to attend to their needs.

Similar styles of coping can be found amongst adults in their dealings with stressful relationship events, such as periods of physical separation from partners. Secure individuals, for example, are usually less worried than others about risks to the relationship, and more likely to focus on keeping in touch with the partner and making joint plans for the future. Insecure individuals are generally more distressed by separations (although dismissing-avoidants often report a lack of emotion, or even a sense of enjoyment of their newfound freedom). This distress can be associated with destructive coping responses, such as "picking fights" with the partner, abusing alcohol or drugs, and "catastrophizing" (e.g., imagining the partner being unfaithful).

"Partner" Effects

In our discussion of attachment so far, we have focused on the effects of the individual's own insecurities. Because adult attachments involve two relatively equal partners, however, the interaction patterns that develop should be influenced by the attachment concerns of *both* partners.

Available research supports this claim. For example, some researchers have compared three types of couples: secure (both partners secure), insecure (both partners insecure), and mixed (one partner secure and the other insecure). Although these studies ignore potentially important differences between different *types* of insecurity, they provide a simple way of looking at different combinations of attachment styles. Secure couples consistently show better relationship functioning than insecure couples. Mixed couples generally fall somewhere in between, but there seem to be some situations where the secure individual buffers the effect of the partner's insecurity, and others where insecure behavior predominates.

Similarly, other research shows that couple relationships are influenced by the attachment dimensions of both partners. For example, when the couple includes a man who is uncomfortable with closeness or a woman who is anxious about relationship issues, *both* partners tend to feel dissatisfied with the relationship. In short, a given individual may think and act quite differently in relationships, depending on whether the partner encourages or rebuffs attempts at intimacy, and whether the partner is confident or anxious about the state of the relationship.

ATTACHMENT AND THE TRANSITION TO PARENTHOOD

Why choose the attachment perspective as a way of understanding the transition to parenthood? Although basic insecurities about love and intimacy seem to have fairly pervasive effects on couple relationships, pregnancy and parenthood are likely to bring these issues to the fore.

As we saw in Chapter 1, new parenthood is an important developmental phase for most couples. The role of new parent is a demanding one, which involves substantial changes both at the personal level and in terms of the couple relationship. Couples often report a more traditional division of labor, and a decrease in intimacy and shared leisure activities. For some couples, new parenthood also seems to be accompanied by an increase in conflict and a decrease in satisfaction with the relationship.

Because the new member of the family is highly dependent on the parents for all its needs, the adjustments that are required at this time have implications for the three systems of behavior discussed earlier in this chapter: attachment, caregiving, and sexuality. First, the couple's attachment bond needs to expand to include the new member. That is, each parent needs to form a bond with the baby, without losing the security and comfort derived from the bond previously established with their partner. Second, patterns of caregiving in the marriage may change; the baby will demand a great deal of care and attention, but it is important that partners not lose sight of their spouse's emotional needs. Third, the sexual relationship is likely to be affected by the demands of new parenthood, including factors such as fatigue, sudden interruptions, limited time for intimacy, and various kinds of physical changes.

Where partners are secure in their relationship, they should find it somewhat easier to deal with these issues and changes. They are less likely to see the changes as threatening the bond with the partner, and more likely to negotiate new ways of relating that satisfy the needs of the partner, while accommodating those of the infant. In short, secure partners should find their relationships changed, but still satisfying.

SUMMARY

The bond between infant and parent is crucial to the social development of the child, and is also marked by strong emotions for both parties. A similar bonding process seems to link intimate partners in adulthood, although their relationships are also enriched by sexual passion and by mutual support and caregiving. The concept of attachment helps explain these universal processes, but also highlights the differences between secure and insecure bonds, especially when individuals face stressful situations. In this book, we focus on the attachment bonds between intimate partners as they make the transition to first-time parenthood. Attachment issues are central to this transition, which requires each parent to bond with their infant, while maintaining the unique support features of their couple relationship. Throughout the following chapters, we describe couples' varying responses to the demands of parenthood and to the reshaping of their relationships.

THREE

The Study

The study we report in this book was designed to provide a comprehensive picture of couples' responses to the transition to parenthood. Based on attachment principles and on previous research into first-time parenthood, the areas we selected for study included relationship satisfaction, attachment, caregiving, sexuality, general psychological adjustment, coping resources and coping styles, and division of household labor. As described in more detail in the next chapter, we recruited two groups of couples: one group who were experiencing their first pregnancy (called the transition group), and another group who reported that they were not planning to have children in the near future (called the comparison group).

OVERVIEW OF THE DESIGN

In Chapter 1, we pointed out the importance of longitudinal studies, which allow researchers to observe couples as they experience pregnancy and new parenthood. The study we designed involved couples providing major sets of data at three points in time: during the second trimester of pregnancy, about six weeks after the baby was born, and when the baby was six months old (couples in the comparison group were assessed at similar time intervals). Between the second and third assessment points, spouses also completed structured diaries detailing their involvement in household and baby-related tasks over a four-day period. By following the couples throughout pregnancy and the first six months of parenthood, we were able to chart the course of their relationships and identify changes linked to this major event in the life cycle.

One of the important features of this study was the variety of methods that we used to assess partners' adjustment as individuals and as couples. We used interviews, questionnaires, and structured diary records, as different ways that couples could tell us about their experiences of the transition. The chronology of the testing sessions is shown in Figure 3.1.

ASSESSING THE IMPACT OF NEW PARENTHOOD

In the rest of this chapter, we describe the various methods that we used to assess couples' responses to new parenthood. Further details of these methods can be found in the remaining chapters, as we present our findings for the different measures.

Interviews

At the first and second assessment times, we interviewed the couples in the transition group about their recent experiences of pregnancy and parenthood. These interviews helped us to get to know the couples, and to tell them about the purpose and progress of the study; they also gave couples the opportunity to talk at some length about their reactions to the pregnancy, their thoughts and feelings about the birth, and their experiences of becoming parents. By allowing couples to express

Chronology and events

	3-4 months	6 weeks		6 weeks	3 months	
Second trimester assessment	--->	Birth of child	--->	First post- birth interview (6 weeks post-partum)	--->	Diary data	--->	Second post- birth interview (6 months post-partum)

Measures

Interview	Interview	Household tasks	Core questionnaires
Core questionnaires	Core questionnaires	Baby-care tasks*	
Coping resources	Coping strategies		
	Parenting stress*		

Core questionnaires: marital satisfaction, attachment, caregiving, sexuality, individual adjustment.
* Completed by transition group only.

Figure 3.1. Chronology of the testing sessions.

their reactions in their own words, we were able to obtain quite detailed and vivid descriptions of their varying experiences. In contrast to the questionnaire and diary methods, these interviews also enabled the spouses to interact as a couple, and to express areas of agreement and disagreement. The content of the interviews conducted at the first and second assessments is detailed in Chapters 5 and 6, respectively.

To ensure that the two groups of couples had similar amounts of contact with the members of the research team, we also conducted interviews with the comparison couples. These interviews covered issues such as important events in their relationships, and spouses' thoughts and feelings about the possibility of having children in the future. Because these issues are not central to the research project, we will not present any findings from the interviews with comparison couples.

Questionnaires

As another means of collecting data, we asked spouses to complete a set of standardized questionnaires at each of the three major assessment times. These questionnaires covered a range of aspects of individual and couple adjustment. (The core questionnaires, which were completed at all three times, can be found in Appendix A, and sample items from all the questionnaires are presented in tables throughout this chapter. An additional measure, requiring spouses to list the various people they relied on to meet their attachment needs, is detailed in Chapter 10.)

On each occasion, we asked members of the couple to complete the questionnaire measures without any joint discussion of either the questions or their answers. This procedure allowed spouses to retain their privacy and to be more open and honest in their responses; it also enabled us to obtain independent evaluations from husbands and wives.

The questionnaires were designed to provide information about eight different aspects of couple and individual adjustment. Couples' marital relationships were assessed in terms of relationship satisfaction, and the three systems of behavior that we discussed in Chapter 2 (attachment, caregiving, and sexuality). The four remaining sets of measures were concerned with general psychological adjustment, coping resources, coping strategies, and appraisals of stress. We included these measures because the transition to parenthood, like any major transition, tends to be stressful; for this reason, it is important to consider aspects of stress and coping, together with possible changes in individual adjustment.

Relationship Satisfaction. In Chapter 2, we noted why relationship satisfaction is regarded as such an important issue: Relationships that are satisfying are more likely to last, and they also foster a general sense of well-being. Satisfaction with the marital relationship was assessed using four scales drawn from a measure developed by Snyder (1979): global distress (an individual spouse's general feelings of unhappiness and disappointment in the relationship), affective communication (satisfaction with the amount of affection and understanding expressed by the spouse), problem-solving communication (satisfaction with spouses' ability to communicate about issues and resolve disagreements), and time together (satisfaction with the quality and quantity of shared interests and leisure time). These four scales can also be combined to give an overall measure of relationship satisfaction (see Table 3.1 for sample items).

Attachment Security. As we discussed in the previous chapter, two factors are critical to individuals' sense of security in their intimate relationships: discomfort with closeness and anxiety over relationships. As the

---

**TABLE 3.1. Sample Items for Assessing
Relationship Satisfaction**

Global Distress
  There are serious difficulties in our marriage.
  My marriage has been disappointing in several ways.
Affective Communication
  There is a great deal of love and affection expressed in our marriage.
  Whenever I am feeling sad, my spouse makes me feel loved and happy again.
Problem-Solving Communication
  Even when angry with me, my spouse is able to appreciate my viewpoints.
  My spouse seems committed to settling our differences.
Time Together
  My spouse seems to enjoy just being with me.
  My spouse likes to share his or her leisure time with me.

name implies, discomfort with closeness measures the tendency to experience discomfort with high levels of intimacy. Individuals high in discomfort with closeness also have difficulty in trusting and depending on relationship partners, and generally prefer to be very independent and self-reliant. Anxiety over relationships reflects concerns about whether partners' feelings of love and commitment are really deep and lasting, together with fears about being rejected or abandoned. We assessed these two aspects of attachment security using the Attachment Style Questionnaire (Feeney, Noller, & Hanrahan, 1994). (See Table 3.2 for sample items assessing attachment, caregiving, and sexuality.)

Spousal Caregiving. Ways of responding to spouses' needs for care and support were assessed using two scales: responsive caregiving and compulsive caregiving. (The items we used were developed by Kunce and Shaver, 1994, but the responsive caregiving scale combined their measures of sensitivity, proximity, and cooperation.) The responsive caregiving scale measures the individual's ability to recognize when the partner needs help and support, as well as the readiness to provide reassurance and physical closeness during these times of need. The compulsive caregiving scale measures the tendency to become over-involved in the partner's needs and problems, and to take undue responsibility for the partner's issues. In Chapter 2, we noted that the optimal style of caregiving involves being responsive to the other person's needs, without becoming over-involved and burdened by them.

Sexuality. In terms of sexuality, we were interested in how partners generally felt about their sexual relationship (rather than how often they performed specific sexual behaviors). For this reason, we focused on two main aspects of sexuality: sexual communication and sexual desire (using items developed by Apt & Hurlbert, 1992; Hudson, Harrison, & Crosscup, 1981; and Wheeless, Wheeless, & Baus, 1984). Sexual communication refers to partners' ability to communicate about their sexual needs and preferences, and to the level of satisfaction with these aspects of communication. The sexual desire scale focused on levels of sexual drive, and the amount of sexual interest and involvement with the partner.

TABLE 3.2. Sample Items for Assessing the Three Systems of Behavior

Attachment
  Discomfort with closeness
    I worry about people getting too close.
    I prefer to depend on myself rather than on other people.
  Anxiety about relationships
    I worry that others won't care about me as much as I care about them.
    I wonder why people would want to be involved with me.
Caregiving
  Responsive care
    I am very attentive to my partner's nonverbal signals for help and support.
    When my partner seems to want or need a hug, I am glad to provide it.
  Compulsive care
    I frequently get too "wrapped up" in my partner's problems and needs.
    I create problems by taking on my partner's troubles as if they were my own.
Sexuality
  Sexual communication
    I tell my partner when I am especially sexually satisfied.
    My partner shows me by the way s/he touches me if s/he is satisfied.
  Sexual desire
    I look forward to having sex with my partner.
    Just thinking about having sex with my partner excites me.

General Psychological Adjustment. As noted earlier in this chapter, the transition to parenthood can be quite stressful; hence, it may produce changes in individual adjustment (i.e., feelings of well-being), as well as in the couple relationship. Psychological adjustment was assessed in terms of three emotional states that are common indicators of the extent of well-being: depression, anxiety, and stress. The depression scale measures symptoms of depressed mood, feelings of hopelessness and pessimism, and difficulty in becoming involved in everyday activities. The anxiety scale focuses on physiological signs of anxiety, such as trembling and rapid breathing, and on the general subjective experience of being worried, anxious, and panicky. (In contrast, "anxiety over relationships," discussed under attachment security, focuses *specifically* on concerns about love, loss, and rejection.) The stress scale assesses the tendency to be tense, irritable, impatient and easily agitated, and to have difficulty relaxing. The three scales (developed by Lovibond & Lovibond, 1995), focus on the individual's

TABLE 3.3. Sample Items for Assessing Individual Adjustment and Coping Resources

Individual adjustment
  Depression
    I felt that life was meaningless.
    I felt sad and depressed.
  Anxiety
    I felt scared without any good reason.
    I experienced trembling (e.g., in the hands).
  Stress
    I found it hard to wind down.
    I found myself getting agitated.
Coping resources
  Self-esteem
    Things usually don't bother me.
    I'm popular with persons my own age.
  Social support
    Members of my family help me out when I need it.
    My friends take me seriously when I have concerns.

experiences over the *past week;* as a result, the scales are useful for detecting changes in adjustment that may be linked to recent events (see Table 3.3 for sample items).

Coping Resources. Given the many demands that new parenthood brings, we were also interested in the resources individuals could draw on to help them deal with difficult or challenging situations. Resources that are helpful in such situations can be either internal (characteristics of the individual), or external (aspects of the physical or social environment), and we were interested in both these types of resources.

First, we assessed self-esteem, because a sense of self-worth and competence can act as a buffer against the consequences of dealing with stressful situations. The measure we used (Coopersmith's Self-esteem Inventory, 1981) assesses the individual's sense of his or her own personal value, as well as the person's perceived value to friends and family members.

Second, we assessed individuals' perceptions of the level of support they could anticipate receiving from the various members of their social network. In other words, we were interested in the extent to which they thought that other people (spouse, friends, and family members) would listen to their concerns, understand their perspective on things, and help them out in various ways. The measure we used was originally developed for a study of social support during pregnancy (Brown, 1986), although it can be applied more generally.

Coping Strategies. Studies of stress and coping suggest that people use three main types of strategies to cope with stressful situations: problem-focused, emotion-focused, and social support-seeking. Problem-focused coping refers to strategies that deal directly with the stressful situation, and aim to solve the problem that is causing the stress. In contrast, emotion-focused coping refers to strategies that focus more on the emotion engendered by the situation, rather than the situation itself. In other words, these strategies aim to reduce the negative emotions, such as anger and anxiety, that tend to accompany stress. The third type of strategy, social support-seeking, combines elements of both problem-focused and emotion-focused coping. That is, individuals may turn to other people either for practical advice and assistance, or for an opportunity to vent their feelings about the situation.

When people respond to items assessing coping strategies, it is important that they have a particular situation in mind; after all, we tend to deal differently with the demands of different situations. Because our main focus was on first-time parenthood, transition couples completed the coping items with regard to their experiences in this area of their lives. (The items were based on the work of Vitaliano, Russo, Carr, Maiuro, & Becker, 1985, but were adapted slightly to ensure their relevance to the transition to parenthood; see Table 3.4 for sample items.) Couples in the comparison group responded to the same items with regard to a recent stressful event of their own choosing.

Parenting Stress. Finally, two questionnaires tapping the stress of being a new parent were included for the transition couples only. The first of these measures (based on the work of Bates, Freeland, & Lounsbury, 1979) was an indirect measure of parental stress, and assessed the parents' perceptions of their infant's temperament. In other words, parents rated how placid or irritable their baby was, and how easy or

TABLE 3.4. Sample Items for Assessing Coping Strategies and Parenting Stress

Coping strategies
  Problem-focused coping
    Came up with a couple of different solutions to the problem.
    Made a plan of action and followed it.
  Emotion-focused coping
    Hoped a miracle would happen.
    Tried to forget the whole thing.
  Social support-seeking
    Talked to someone about how I was feeling.
    Asked someone I respected for advice and followed it.
Parenting stress
  Infant temperament
    How easy is it for you to calm or soothe your baby when s/he is upset?
    What kind of mood is your baby generally in?
  Parenting strain
    To what extent has the arrival of your baby been disruptive?
    To what extent have you experienced difficulty establishing your baby into
      a routine?

difficult the baby was to care for and to soothe; they were also asked to indicate how changeable the baby's moods were, and how many "fussy" periods usually occurred each day.

The second measure of the stress of new parenthood was more direct and more broadly focused, assessing the overall level of parenting strain (Terry, 1988). This measure asked parents how stressful they were finding particular aspects of parenting (e.g., lack of sleep, colic and feeding problems, loss of independence); in addition, parents were asked how much their normal routines had been affected by the arrival of the baby.

Diary Records

Our third method of data collection involved asking spouses to complete diary records about their involvement in common household and baby-care tasks over a period of four days (two weekdays and two days at the weekend). Based on previous studies of household work (e.g., Presland & Antill, 1987), we developed a structured list of tasks, and asked each spouse to complete independent reports of task performance for each of the four days.

The diaries were designed to assess how much time spouses spent on these tasks, the extent to which each task was done by one spouse or shared between them, and how satisfied they felt with their partner's efforts in relation to these tasks. Transition couples were asked to keep records about eight household tasks (e.g., cooking meals, doing the dishes, and cleaning the house) and eight baby-care tasks (e.g., feeding the baby, bathing the baby, and tending to the baby during the night). Comparison couples were asked only about the household tasks, but in all other respects, the two sets of diaries were the same. (The diaries are discussed in more detail in Chapter 9.)

The reason we used diaries for this part of the study is that diary records are particularly useful for obtaining information about specific events that occur relatively frequently over a given period of time. Instead of having to think in general terms about household tasks, and guessing at the frequency with which particular tasks are carried out, participants are asked to record each task as it arises, or at least once each day. This procedure is likely to lead to more reliable and valid data than global estimates made retrospectively. In the case of this study, the diary records also allowed for direct comparisons of work patterns on weekdays and at weekends (when husbands' availability and involvement are likely to be greater).

SUMMARY

This study has several advantages over many studies of new parenthood. We designed the study around the concept of adult attachment, because this stage of the life cycle gave us a unique opportunity to explore changes in the attachment system, and in the related behavioral systems of caregiving and sexuality. The adult attachment perspective provided a solid basis for the research, guiding our focus on particular aspects of the transition to parenthood and our choice of appropriate measures. Both a transition group and a comparison group were included in the study, and these groups of couples were followed over a period of approximately 10 months. These features of the study enabled us to identify any changes specific to the experience of new parenthood. The different methods that we used to collect data complemented each other, providing different kinds of information about the whole process of adjusting to new parenthood.

We also assessed a wide variety of factors related to this transition, giving us a picture both of individual adjustment and of changes in the couple relationship. Finally, collecting data from both husbands and wives provided two different perspectives on first-time parenthood, a domain in which the focus has been primarily on women's experience.

Throughout the following chapters, we attempt to answer a number of important questions about the experience of becoming parents, from an attachment perspective. These questions include:

- How do different couples react to finding out about their first pregnancy?
- What do couples see as the best and worst features of becoming parents?
- How do couples cope with the stress of having a new baby in the home?
- What factors are linked to postnatal depression, and what are its effects on partners?
- How involved are new fathers in helping out with household and baby-care tasks?
- Does parenthood change the attachment network of men and women?
- Why do some couples emerge relatively unscathed from this transition, whereas others struggle to adjust?

FOUR

The Couples

Two different groups of married couples shared their relationship experiences with us. One group were recruited during their second trimester of pregnancy (i.e., between the 14th and 26th week). Because we were interested in following these couples throughout the rest of their pregnancy and the early months of parenthood, we will call them the transition group. The comparison group, on the other hand, consisted of couples who reported that they were not planning to have children in the near future.

DEFINING CRITERIA FOR PARTICIPATION

Both groups were restricted to couples who were in their first marriages and who had no children. These conditions were important for ensuring that the two groups of couples were as similar as possible in terms of their backgrounds (e.g., age and length of marriage) and the current state of their relationships (e.g., satisfaction with couple communication and with the relationship as a whole). This issue of the comparability of the groups is discussed in more detail later in this chapter.

Another reason for restricting the sample to first-time marriages and first-time parents was that we wanted all of the couples in the transition group to be new to the experiences of pregnancy and parenthood. That is, we were interested in their perceptions of the changes that these *new experiences* brought, and the adjustments that they made as a result. Our focus on first-time parenthood also recognizes the fact that bringing home a new baby is a very different experience if there are already children in the home. For instance, first-time parents have to establish new patterns of relating to each other, and learn how to accommodate the many demands of the newborn. On the other hand, the task facing more experienced parents has its own special challenges, such as dealing with older children who may see the newborn as usurping their place in the family.

LOCATING THE COUPLES

At the beginning of the study, there were 107 couples in the transition group and 100 couples in the comparison group. For both groups, a variety of methods were used to advertise the study and recruit couples. For example, the study was advertised through radio interviews, newspaper articles, and paid advertisements both in local newspapers and in magazines specializing in issues around pregnancy and child care. Some couples were recruited through undergraduate psychology courses, in which students are encouraged to act as research participants in order to gain experience of a range of research topics and methods. This latter approach to recruiting does not restrict the sample entirely to students: Usually, only one member of each couple is a student, with the other generally being employed in full-time work. Most couples recruited in this way belonged to the comparison sample, probably because spouses are unlikely to embark on a university degree when their first baby is on the way. We also used a "snowballing" technique to increase the size of the samples; this approach involved asking couples to nominate any friends who met the criteria for participating in the study, and who might be interested in taking part.

To target transition couples more specifically, we also approached a number of health services dealing with prenatal care. These services included women's hospitals, antenatal clinics, and obstetricians' offices. Finally, we contacted several retail outlets specializing in maternity and child-care products, and arranged for posters and leaflets advertising the study to be displayed.

WHAT WERE THE COUPLES LIKE?

By using several different methods of recruitment, we hoped to locate couples who came from a variety of backgrounds. We also hoped that the couples would vary in their evaluations of their marriages, so that our results would not be limited either to those who felt very secure and satisfied with their relationships, or to those who felt very unhappy. To assess whether we had succeeded in obtaining a broad sample, we looked at the characteristics of the couples as they started out in the study. Specifically, we focused on three aspects that might affect the transition to parenthood: background characteristics, relationship evaluations, and individual resources and adjustment.

Background Characteristics

The overall sample of couples varied quite widely in age, with husbands ranging from 21 to 54 years, and wives from 19 to 47 years. The average age was 30 years for husbands and 29 for wives. Similarly, couples varied widely in terms of the length of their relationships, as measured from when they first started dating. One couple had been together for only 12 months, whereas, at the other extreme, one couple had been together for 28 years. Length of marriage ranged from one month to 15 years, with an average length of just over three and a half years.

As well as representing both shorter and longer-term relationships, the couples reported a range of patterns of courtship. Almost two-thirds of the couples had lived together before their marriage. For roughly one-third of these couples, however, the period of cohabitation began relatively late in their relationship, after they had officially announced their engagement. Not all couples had experienced a smooth and untroubled courtship. Almost 20% of them reported that they had had at least one breakup during their premarital involvement. In addition, about 40% of couples had had at least one period of "long-distance" relating, before settling in to married life.

Couples were drawn from a variety of educational backgrounds. At one end of the spectrum, 16 husbands and 9 wives had not completed high school. Nevertheless, highly educated couples were somewhat more likely to volunteer for the study, with about half of the husbands and wives having university degrees. As would be expected, given these high educational levels, the majority of the sample were involved in relatively high status occupations. Professional or managerial positions were held by just over half of the husbands and wives. The remainder were employed in a wide variety of occupations. Just over 10% of the husbands and 20% of the wives were not in paid employment, being either full-time students, homemakers, or currently unemployed. Not surprisingly, most of the wives who were not in paid employment belonged to the transition group, with some of these having given up work quite recently in preparation for the birth of their child.

The couples we recruited were almost entirely of Anglo-European background, with English as their first language. The only exceptions were three couples who were of Indian background, but these couples also spoke English as their first language. Most of the sample were at least nominally Christian, with only a small group professing that they belonged to other religions, and about 20% reporting no religious affiliation. (Appendix B contains more information about the background characteristics of the couples, and the sources of recruitment.)

Relationship Evaluations

We were also interested in seeing how the overall sample of couples evaluated their relationships at the start of the study. To do this, we focused on the four sets of measures assessing aspects of the marriage: relationship satisfaction, attachment, caregiving, and sexuality. Table 4.1 shows the average (or mean) scores on each of these measures, together with the lowest and highest scores obtained.

As this table shows, spouses varied widely in their evaluations of their relationships. While many were quite high in relationship satisfaction, some reported being very dissatisfied and disappointed with their marriages. The measure that we used (based on the Marital Satisfaction Inventory, Snyder, 1979) contains 35 items, each scored as 0 or 1; the total score is simply the number of items endorsed, with higher scores indicating greater satisfaction. Hence, the scores show that many couples endorsed most of these items describing possible sources of satisfaction in their relationships, but one wife was unable to find a single positive feature in her relationship.

Similarly, for the measures of attachment, caregiving, and sexuality, the average scores fell on the positive side of the scales, but were not extreme in this respect. In other words, most couples tended to describe

TABLE 4.1. Average Scores and Ranges on Measures Assessing the Marital Relationship at Time 1				
Measure	**Husbands**		**Wives**	
Relationship satisfaction	30.99	(3–35)	30.94	(0–35)
Attachment				
Relationship anxiety	36.62	(14–62)	37.16	(14–65)
Discomfort with closeness	50.03	(24–83)	45.17	(23–77)
Caregiving				
Responsive care	109.30	(62–144)	114.80	(66–143)
Compulsive care	24.56	(11–43)	25.06	(12–48)
Sexuality				
Communication	126.42	(66–162)	133.74	(61–162)
Desire	78.29	(41–90)	68.23	(25–90)

Note: Actual ranges are shown in parentheses; the possible range of scores was 0–35 for relationship satisfaction, 13–78 for anxiety over relationships, 16–96 for discomfort with closeness, 24–144 for responsive care, 8–48 for compulsive care, 27–162 for sexual communication, and 15–90 for sexual desire.

their couple interactions favorably: They seemed fairly comfortable and secure about their partners' feelings toward them, and they reported strong and satisfying sexual relationships and constructive patterns of caring for the spouse in times of need. However, the scores on each measure spanned a very wide range, indicating that some of the spouses felt quite negatively about these core aspects of their relationships.

Individual Resources and Adjustment

Finally, we were interested in how spouses were faring at the beginning of the study, in terms of their general psychological adjustment (depression, anxiety, and stress), and the resources (self-esteem and social support) that could help them to cope with new situations. Table 4.2 shows the average scores obtained on each of these measures, together with the lowest and highest scores.

The scores show that spouses tended to report quite low levels of depression, anxiety, and stress; in other words, overall, they showed good psychological adjustment. This finding is not surprising, given that these measures assess fairly severe symptoms of distress. Even on these scales, however, the scores varied very widely.

In terms of coping resources, spouses generally reported reasonably high self-esteem, and thought that their various relationships provided them with adequate levels of support. At the same time, there was again a wide range of scores on both of these measures.

TABLE 4.2. Average Scores and Ranges on Measures of Individual Resources and Adjustment at Time 1				
Measure	Husbands		Wives	
Psychological adjustment				
Depression	2.25	(0–19)	2.48	(0–21)
Anxiety	1.28	(0–13)	2.06	(0–17)
Stress	4.90	(0–20)	5.48	(0–21)
Coping resources				
Self-esteem	78.70	(20–100)	78.25	(32–100)
Social support	147.36	(89–198)	157.28	(89–195)

Note: Actual ranges are shown in parentheses; the possible range of scores was 0–21 for each of depression, anxiety, and stress, 0–100 for self-esteem, and 33–198 for social support.

HOW SIMILAR WERE THE TRANSITION
AND COMPARISON COUPLES?

Although it was reassuring to find that our overall sample was reasonably diverse, it was also important to assess whether the two groups of couples were *comparable* at the beginning of the study. In other words, because our research focused on comparing the transition and comparison couples over the best part of a year, we needed to be sure that the two groups started out similar in all important aspects. As discussed in Chapter 1, comparison groups are very important in this type of research, because they help us to distinguish changes that are due to first-time parenthood, from those that are related simply to the passing of time and the normal development of couple relationship.

We first compared the groups on the various background measures: age, length of relationship, length of marriage, history of cohabitation, breaks in the relationship, long-distance relating, education, occupation, and religious affiliation. For wives, there were no differences at all between the two groups. For husbands, on the other hand, there were small differences in levels of education and occupation. Husbands in the comparison group tended to be somewhat more highly educated, and to hold somewhat higher status positions. These small differences probably reflect patterns of advertising and recruitment. Comparison couples were more likely to have heard about the study through newspaper articles or through the psychology subject pool, whereas transition couples were more likely to have heard about it through the public hospital system. Although we tried to recruit transition couples through private obstetricians, this strategy was not as successful as working within the hospital system.

We also compared the groups on the questionnaire measures described earlier in this chapter and detailed in Chapter 3, that is, the four sets of relationship variables (relationship satisfaction, attachment, caregiving, and sexuality), and the measures of individual resources and adjustment. The only area that showed any difference between the two groups was sexuality, and this effect was restricted to the scale measuring sexual communication. Spouses in the transition group were somewhat less satisfied with their communication about sexual issues than those in the comparison group. The difference was quite small, however: Average scores of husbands and wives in the transition group were 124.2 and 130.7 respectively, compared with 128.8 and 137.0 for the comparison group (scores on this measure could range from 27 to 162). It is also important to note that this difference does *not* mean that sexuality was less important to couples coping with pregnancy; in fact, levels of sexual desire did not differ for the two groups. Rather, it suggests that couples in the transition group may have become more focused on communicating about other issues in their lives, such as the progress of the pregnancy and their future plans for their baby.

Overall, then, the transition and comparison couples started out very similar in terms of their background experiences, their relationship history, and their functioning both as individuals and as couples. In other words, we could be fairly confident that any differences between the two groups that we might find later in the study would be due to the experience of becoming parents for the first time.

SIMILARITIES AND DIFFERENCES
BETWEEN HUSBANDS AND WIVES

Our main focus at this first assessment was on checking whether the transition and comparison groups were similar in most respects at the start of the study. However, in describing the experiences of married couples, it is also useful to know whether there are overall differences between husbands and wives. In fact, this issue is quite important, given the widely proclaimed view that men and women are so different that they could have come from different planets! We found both similarities and differences between the reports of husbands and wives, but the similarities were more striking.

Similarities

Husbands and wives saw their relationships as equally satisfying. This finding applied both to the overall scores, and to all four scales assessing specific aspects of satisfaction, such as shared time and problem-solving communication. Husbands and wives were also similar in terms of levels of anxiety about partners' love and commitment, and the tendency to become over-involved (or "compulsive") when caring for the partner in times of need. Finally, with regard to individual resources and adjustment, husbands and wives reported similar levels of self-esteem, depression, and stress.

Differences

On the other hand, there were gender differences in discomfort with closeness, responsive care, sexual desire, sexual communication, general anxiety, and social support. (Tables 4.1 and 4.2 show the average scores for each gender.) Compared with husbands, wives (regardless of group) reported less discomfort with intimacy in their couple relationships. Their caregiving style was more responsive; in other words, they seemed to be more aware of their partner's needs and problems, and more ready to provide comfort. Wives also reported somewhat lower levels of sexual desire, but were more satisfied than husbands with their communication about sexual matters. Finally, wives reported more anxiety in their lives, but tended to perceive higher levels of support from their relationships with partners, friends, and family members.

These gender differences are consistent with many other studies of individual and relationship functioning, and with popular stereotypes of relationship behavior. In particular, they fit with the view that women are more strongly encouraged to seek intimacy, to provide for the needs of others, and to take the major responsibility for maintaining close and supportive relationships. At the same time, the clear finding was that the scores of husbands and wives showed a great deal of overlap on all of the measures, and that any gender differences were small in size.

KEEPING COUPLES IN THE STUDY

Whenever researchers follow a group of people over time, it is inevitable that some participants will drop out. However, researchers tend to be very conscious of the importance of retaining as many of their original sample as possible for the full period of the study. There are generally two major concerns that arise when a large number of people withdraw from a study. First, if the numbers remaining become too small, it can be difficult to detect real differences that exist between groups or across time periods. Second, it is possible that particular types of people may be more likely to drop out. For example, in studying marriage, it is possible that unhappy couples will find the research process more stressful and be more likely to withdraw. If this pattern of withdrawal affects one group more than another, comparisons between the groups will be less valid.

To minimize these problems, it is common for researchers to use a range of methods to encourage couples to remain involved in their projects. In this study, we first pointed out to couples that in terms of the transition to parenthood, they were the "experts"; that is, they were the ones experiencing these issues, and we needed and valued their comments at each phase of the transition. As far as possible, we also tried to make sure that the same interviewer visited a particular couple on each occasion, to build rapport and maintain a sense of involvement. Finally, we kept in touch with couples in between the assessment points, by sending them greeting cards on their wedding anniversaries and when their babies were born.

Rate of Dropout

The overall rate of withdrawal from the study was similar for the comparison group and the transition group. For example, of the original 107 couples in the transition group, 92 couples were interviewed at Time 2 (about six weeks after their babies were born). Similarly, of the 100 couples who started in the comparison sample, 85 were interviewed at Time 2. By the final measurement time, which took place when the babies were about six months old, there were 76 couples remaining in the transition group and 74 in the comparison group. These rates of withdrawal are fairly typical of studies in which couples are assessed over relatively long periods of time.

Reasons for Dropping Out

The main reason that couples did not continue in the study was that they moved without providing us with a forwarding address. This problem is not unusual when the research includes couples going through a major transition, because mobility is likely to be relatively high at these times. Another reason for withdrawal was that seven couples in the comparison group became pregnant during the study. Where the pregnancy occurred at an early enough stage in the research, these couples were invited to join the transition group (two couples fell into this category). Several other couples reported that they were just too stressed by their current circumstances to be able to continue their involvement in the study. This group included one couple who had a baby born 11 weeks premature, and who would have been totally absorbed with the survival of their infant. There was also a small group of couples who were no longer appropriate for the study: one couple in the transition group whose baby was stillborn, and four couples in the comparison group who separated during the course of the study.

Predicting Dropout

To explore whether particular types of couples were more likely to withdraw from the study, we compared those couples who dropped out with those who remained, on all the measures completed at the first assessment (background information, and measures of individual and relationship functioning). Of the nine background factors, only educational level was related to the tendency to withdraw: Those with lower levels of education were somewhat more likely to drop out. Perhaps those with postsecondary education were more familiar with the research process, and more likely to recognize the importance of staying involved.

Similarly, of the various measures of individual and relationship functioning, only relationship satisfaction was related to the tendency to withdraw. This effect applied to overall satisfaction in the comparison group, but only to husbands' satisfaction with relational communication in the transition group. In other words, couples who dropped out of the comparison group were slightly lower in overall satisfaction than other couples in that group, and husbands in couples who dropped out of the transition group reported slightly less satisfaction with their affective and problem-solving communication. As we mentioned earlier, this tendency for less happy couples to withdraw from research may reflect their discomfort with the research process, and their reluctance to subject their relationships to further scrutiny.

SUMMARY

Compared with many studies of first-time parents, the sample we recruited was quite broad. Although the couples were mainly from Anglo-European backgrounds, they included a wide range of ages and relationship lengths. Their relationship histories were also diverse (in terms of patterns of cohabitation, long-distance relating, and breaks in the relationship), and the sample represented a range of educational and occupational levels. From the measures of relationship evaluations, it was clear that some couples felt very secure and satisfied with their marriages, whereas others felt quite insecure and dissatisfied. Similarly, some couples seemed well equipped to cope with stressful situations, whereas others seemed to be much more vulnerable. Having such a diverse sample is important to ensure that the results of the study are relevant to couples in general.

The transition and comparison groups were generally similar at the beginning of the study, and the rate of withdrawal was similar for the two groups. In addition, the factors that affected the likelihood of withdrawal were the same for both groups, and the differences we observed between those who stayed and those who left were very small. These findings increase our confidence in the validity of the comparisons we will make between the two groups of couples over time, and the conclusions we will draw throughout the book about the factors affecting the transition to parenthood.

FIVE

Pregnancy and Plans for Birth

"I nearly fell over! It was a happy surprise, though, because we'd just started talking about kids and I wanted to start having children soon."

Once couples had expressed an interest in taking part in the study, we contacted them by phone and arranged for a research assistant to interview them in their own homes. Conducting these home visits minimized the inconvenience to the couples, and allowed them to be interviewed in a familiar and relatively relaxed setting. The research assistant first chatted with the couple informally, talking briefly about the purpose and procedures of the study, and answering any questions they raised.

The interview itself then took place, and was tape-recorded so that we had an accurate record of spouses' responses. Husbands and wives were interviewed together, as a couple, with the interview usually taking place at the dining room table or in the lounge room. Although all the couples agreed to have their interviews audiotaped, there were a few cases in which technical problems prevented us from obtaining a usable record (100 interviews were recorded successfully).

At this first interview with the transition couples, we were interested in hearing their thoughts and feelings about the pregnancy. Our questions focused on four broad issues: planning and decision making in relation to the pregnancy, reactions to the news of impending parenthood, experiences of pregnancy itself, and plans for the birth and beyond.

PLANNING AND DECISION MAKING

The amount of planning and deliberation that precedes a pregnancy varies, of course, from couple to couple (as we discussed in Chapter 1). For some couples, pregnancy is a totally unexpected event, and one that may be very difficult to accept. For others, it follows a period of thinking and talking about the potential costs and benefits of parent-hood, and the "right" time to start a family.

Planned or Unplanned?

We asked the couples in our study whether they saw their pregnancy as planned or unplanned. As we expected, the answers they gave to this question indicated varying degrees of planning and control. Almost half the couples (49 of the 100 interviewed and recorded) said that they had wanted to become pregnant and had done so at about the time they had planned; 18 couples said that they had wanted a baby but had actually taken longer to become pregnant than they had expected; 17 couples said that they had planned to become pregnant, but not quite as soon as they did; and 16 couples said that they had not really planned the pregnancy at all. (This last group included two couples originally recruited for the comparison group; as we noted in Chapter 4, these two couples had become pregnant unexpectedly, and agreed to share with us their experiences of pregnancy and parenthood.) Overall, then, most of the couples described their pregnancy as planned, although not necessarily for "right now."

Couples were also asked whether the conception had occurred nat-urally, or with the aid of fertility drugs or other intervention. For the vast majority of the couples, conception had occurred naturally. The only exceptions were two couples who reported that they had used fer-tility drugs, and three couples whose pregnancies had resulted from fairly long-term involvement in IVF programs.

Why Start a Family Now?

For those couples who saw their pregnancy as planned to some degree, we were interested in the factors influencing decisions about when to start a family. As we noted in Chapter 1, how couples decide on the timing of first parenthood is still not well understood. The reasons that spouses gave for their decision fell into three broad categories: feeling ready, age, and being established as individuals (spouses could nominate as many reasons as they wished).

Feeling Ready. The most common reason cited was that couples simply felt "ready" for parenthood (49 couples explained their decision in these terms). In other words, these couples did not relate their decision to any specific goals, achievements, or concerns. Rather, they talked in terms of a general feeling of readiness, or a sense that parenthood was appropriate as the "next step" in their relationship. As one husband put it, "it's just the right thing and the right time." This way of thinking generally seemed to reflect a "couple" decision, with both spouses talking in similar terms. One wife expressed the couple's sense of readiness in this way:

We had been going out for so long before we got engaged, we didn't want a long engagement. We just wanted to be married and living together. And then it was kind of the next step to have a family. So that was it—it was kind of a natural progression.

Age. The next most common reason for starting a family centered on concerns about spouses' ages. This issue was raised by 44 couples. In just over half of these couples, both partners mentioned age as an important factor. For the remaining couples, wives were more likely to be the ones who focused on this issue, often referring to the ticking of their "biological clock":

We had to decide whether we wanted to have children, before it was too late. So I suppose the biological clock was a big factor. And not just for me–age was a factor for him too, because he'll soon be in his forties.

As we mentioned in Chapter 4, the age of spouses in this study varied very widely. In this group of new parents, the average age of the wives was 29 years, and the upper age was 42 years; the average age of the husbands was 32 years, and the upper age was 53 years. Given these figures, it is not surprising that many of the couples were aware of age as an important factor in their decision to embark on a family. The following comment from an expectant father highlights the relevance of age at first parenthood, and its implications for progress through other phases of the life cycle:

It's also time for me. I'm 41 years old now, so for me, it's clear that if I'm going to have children, I'm going to have them soon. I don't want to start a family at 45, and I don't want to be fooling around with teenage kids at 65, when I'm going through retirement.

Being Established as Individuals. In describing their reasons for starting a family now, 28 couples talked about specific areas of life in which they had first tried to establish themselves as individuals. These areas were related to finances, education, and careers. In other words, these couples stated that they had now reached a stage where they had achieved their individual goals related to work and study, and felt well equipped to provide for the needs of a family.

Comments about achieving financial security tended to be made by both members of the couple. For example, one wife commented that "our financial situation was a big part of it–making sure our finances were okay." Her husband agreed, adding that "we spent the first part of our marriage sorting out some debts, and after that, we decided we were ready to have kids."

In contrast, issues surrounding career and education tended to be raised by one member, usually the wife. This finding is not surprising, given that women are more likely than men to devote a substantial period of time to the full-time care of their young children. In addition, women are enjoying greater access to higher education and to career opportunities than in the past, and the dual-income family is rapidly becoming the norm. For these reasons, issues concerning women's paid employment are much more salient than they have been to previous generations, and many women prefer to establish a career path before becoming involved in child care. Another issue that was relevant to some couples was the amount of flexibility in the wife's work patterns, particularly if she planned to continue working after the birth:

This seemed like a good time for us to have a baby, mainly because of my working arrangements. My working hours are very flexible, and most of the time I can work from home.

Some spouses had clearly put a lot of thought into how to juggle the demands of parenthood and career. For example, the following comment shows how the timing of parenthood can be influenced both by educational goals, and by plans for the wife's eventual return to the workforce:

To be able to stay home and look after the children until they go to school means that we had to work out the best time to have them. And that time was now, while I'm still in the fifth year of my degree. So by the time I'm back looking for work, I'll still be in my early 30s – not closer to 40, which is a bit late to start trying to get back into the workforce.

Multiple Reasons. Of course, there is usually no single factor that determines when couples decide to become parents, and many of the couples we interviewed mentioned a number of reasons for their decision. For example, one husband talked about age, education, and finances, commenting that "we decided to wait until we were a bit older, and had finished university, and become a bit financial." Similarly, other spouses linked factors such as age and education to their sense of personal readiness ("it was about age and maturity really").

REACTIONS TO THE NEWS

In this interview, we next asked couples to describe their reactions to the discovery that they were going to become parents. We asked how they had felt when they had first found out, and also how they were feeling now (in the second trimester of the pregnancy).

Initial Reactions

Couples reported a wide range of initial reactions to learning of the pregnancy. We classified these reactions as either

- negative (I was distraught; I thought "Oh, no! What am I going to do about this?")
- mixed or neutral (I was happy in one way but also worried; I just wasn't sure what to think about it)

- positive (I was excited about it; I was pleased by the news)
- extremely positive (I was jumping around for joy; I was over the moon—just ecstatic!)

Spouses' initial reactions to the news were generally favorable. Forty-three wives and 50 husbands reported reactions that were classified as positive, and another 18 wives and 14 husbands described reactions that were extremely positive. However, 34 wives and 28 husbands reported mixed or neutral reactions, and 3 wives and 3 husbands reported having had negative feelings. Overall, then, husbands and wives seemed to have been equally happy to learn of the pregnancy.

One of the interesting points that emerged during the interviews, however, was the relatively large number of couples in which the husband and the wife reported rather different initial reactions to the pregnancy. There were 25 couples in which we classified the husband and wife as having reacted differently. Three couples showed particularly marked differences in spouses' initial reactions, with only one partner being at all pleased by the news. For example, one expectant mother commented:

Shocked. Yes, I was shocked. And we drove home from the doctor's office with me saying, "It's your fault! It's your fault! It's your fault!" It was anguish. And I didn't sleep for the next two nights.

At the same time, her husband had been so pleased by the news that he had been "grinning from ear to ear," despite the "bruises all over my arm from where she kept hitting me!"

Conversely, in another couple, only the wife had reacted positively to the prospect of becoming a parent. She said that, for her, the pregnancy had come as "a happy surprise." In contrast, her husband reported having been so upset and worried that he was "just white," and "put off" his food.

Although these two examples were among the most extreme in terms of different reactions, they raise important issues about spousal agreement and disagreement. When each partner reacts quite differently to the pregnancy, one (or both) is likely to feel disappointed, misunderstood, or unsupported. Given the highly emotional nature of issues concerning pregnancy and parenthood, partners may also find it difficult to communicate constructively about their differences, especially if they do not feel secure and confident in their relationship. In this way, differences in reactions may make it much more difficult for couples to cope with the changes they are facing at this time.

Current Reactions

We also asked couples to describe their current feelings about their pregnancy. The most common reactions were positive in tone (reported by 63 wives and 61 husbands). The reactions of the remaining wives and husbands were neutral/mixed (13 wives and 9 husbands), and extremely positive (6 wives and 8 husbands). None of the spouses reported that they still felt unhappy about the idea of becoming parents. Interestingly, comparison of these figures with the initial ones suggests that emotional reactions to the news of pregnancy become more *moderate* over time. In other words, the current reactions were less likely than the initial ones to be negative, but also less likely to be extremely positive.

This moderation in feelings is likely to reflect a number of processes. Initial reactions (whether positive or negative) tend to reflect the "novelty" of this important piece of news (e.g., "I walked around with a big smile on my face for two weeks"); hence, the intensity of the feelings is unlikely to be maintained. In cases where the first reaction was extremely positive, the tendency for this feeling to moderate over time may also be explained in terms of the sharpening reality of the experience of pregnancy (as we discuss shortly), and growing awareness of the demands of parenthood. On the other hand, where the initial reaction was negative, spouses who decide to go ahead with the pregnancy need to work at coming to terms with the situation. Their increasing positivity may reflect both a genuine acceptance of the pregnancy, and a need to report emotions that "fit" with their decision. In other words, feeling positive about the pregnancy may help to justify the decision, both privately and to other people.

It is interesting to note that there were only 13 couples in which husbands and wives differed to any degree in their current reactions to the pregnancy. This finding suggests that spouses' feelings about parenthood also tend to *converge* over time, probably as a result of the mutual discussion and sharing of experiences that take place throughout the pregnancy. This convergence did not apply to all couples, however. Although the three couples who reported very different initial reactions had come to see the situation in similar ways, marked differences were currently evident in two couples who had initially responded similarly. For example, in one of these couples, both partners reported having initially been "shocked" and "dumbfounded" by the news. Although the wife reported that she was now "rapt" in the idea of parenthood, her husband still found it "bizarre" and "unreal," and admitted that he had not yet been able to "make a solid link to the idea." Again, these different reactions may make it more difficult for partners to be understanding and supportive of each other.

Predicting Reactions to the News

Why do some prospective parents react to the news of pregnancy with elation, whereas others feel quite distraught? As a first step towards exploring this question, we related the reactions to reports of whether the pregnancy was planned or unplanned. Not surprisingly, negative and neutral reactions to *first* hearing the news were more common among couples who described the pregnancy as unplanned (i.e., either not planned at all, or not planned for this point in time). Just over half the spouses who saw the pregnancy as unplanned reported negative or neutral/mixed feelings about it, whereas such feelings were mentioned by fewer than one-quarter of those who had planned to become parents. However, whether the pregnancy was seen as planned or unplanned was not related to *current* reactions.

We were also interested in whether reactions to the pregnancy could be linked to the questionnaire measures of individual and couple functioning completed at this first phase of the study. In particular, we focused on the measures of general psychological adjustment (depression, anxiety, and stress), relationship satisfaction, and attachment security. The only finding for *psychological adjustment* was a link between husbands' adjustment and wives' initial reactions to the news: Higher levels of depression, anxiety, and stress in husbands were all associated with more negative reactions on the part of wives.

Links between initial reactions to the pregnancy and evaluations of the *couple relationship* were more consistent, applying both to relationship satisfaction and to attachment security. Husbands who had been less pleased to learn of the pregnancy felt more dissatisfied with their marriages, and more insecure (i.e., more anxious about their partners' love and commitment). Wives' reactions were even more closely tied to the state of the couple relationship: Wives had been less pleased to learn of the pregnancy if they felt uncomfortable with high levels of intimacy, if either they or their husbands felt dissatisfied with the marriage, and if either they or their husbands felt anxious about issues of love and commitment in their relationships.

To sum up these findings, the questionnaire measures were linked to spouses' reports of their initial reactions to the pregnancy, but not their current reactions. We have already mentioned that the current reactions were much less varied, and this fact probably explains why they were unrelated to individual and couple functioning. Husbands' initial reactions were linked only to their own marital satisfaction and relationship anxiety, but wives' reactions were linked to husbands' psychological adjustment, and to the marital satisfaction and relationship anxiety of both self and partner.

Because spouses' initial reactions to the pregnancy had to be assessed retrospectively, we have to be cautious about inferring patterns of cause and effect. On the one hand, variables such as stress, depression, and relationship anxiety may *result from* feelings of distress about pregnancy and impending parenthood. On the other hand, it is equally likely that stress, depression, and relationship anxiety *contribute to* the distress that some people experience when they learn they are to become parents. Wives, in particular, seem to be sensitive both to their own doubts and anxieties about their relationships, and to concerns about their husbands' relationship issues and general emotional state.

EXPERIENCES OF PREGNANCY

The next part of the interview focused on spouses' actual experiences of pregnancy. In this section, we asked wives to talk about the progress of their pregnancy, and then invited couples to discuss any unanticipated events or experiences.

Progress of the Pregnancy: Physical and Emotional Well-Being

First, the wives were asked how their pregnancy was progressing. The most common response (made by 57 wives), was that they were experiencing some problems, but that these problems were simply the "typical" difficulties of pregnancy (e.g., "morning sickness," "mood swings," "tiredness," "no energy," "feeling vague and forgetful").

Despite the widespread nature of these "typical" problems, another 28 wives said that their pregnancy was going very smoothly, and that they had not experienced any difficulties at all. At the other extreme, 15 wives reported quite severe problems. These problems included serious illness, anxiety, and depression, and in most cases, physical and emotional problems tended to occur together. One expectant mother described her experiences in this way:

I had morning sickness 24 hours a day, from when I was 6 weeks pregnant right through to 18 weeks. For us, "morning sickness" was all day, every day, and every night. That whole period was sleepless, and very depressing.

Another woman had experienced particularly severe nausea, which resulted in her being hospitalized for most of the early part of the pregnancy:

I ended up in hospital on a drip, because I got morning sickness so badly. I lost about 10 kilograms. I could not keep a thing down, not even water. When I was admitted to hospital, I cried because I was worried that maybe the baby might have died, or that something really bad was going to happen.

As these examples clearly illustrate, pregnancy brought unexpected concerns and difficulties for some couples. We were interested not only in these very difficult experiences, but also in other aspects of pregnancy that spouses might not have anticipated. For this reason, we asked couples whether there had been any "surprises" in relation to their experience of pregnancy.

Surprises

Although many of the couples in the sample had been planning parenthood for some time, almost all of them mentioned one or more things that had surprised them about the experience of pregnancy. The majority of these things were positive (pleasant) or neutral, in tone.

Pleasant or Neutral Surprises. The most common response was that spouses were surprised by the number of physical changes that the pregnancy had produced (this type of comment was made by 47 couples). In other words, couples tended to focus on the changes that were taking place in the wives' bodies. Surprise at the extent of physical change is reflected in comments such as "It's not just about getting fat!," and "I've been surprised by what pregnancy actually does to the body; it's a complete change, and some of the things you just don't expect." Many couples mentioned changes in sensory experience (especially sense of smell) and dietary tastes. For example, some wives noted that they could not stand the taste of coffee any more; others mentioned that they could not handle raw meat because of their heightened sense of smell. One wife summed up the various changes in this way:

What's been surprising to me is all the things you don't want to eat any more or can't eat any more, and all the smells you don't want to be near, and just how much the baby can kick you.

In several couples, both husbands and wives discussed these kinds of physical changes; overall, however, wives were more likely to mention them. This finding is easy to understand, given that wives have more personal and direct experience of these changes. In fact, some husbands may have felt that it was not their place to raise these issues, or that comments about bodily changes might appear to be negative or critical.

The next most frequent comment concerned a sense of wonder over the sheer fact of "new life." In other words, many couples were surprised by the enormity of the realization that they had created a new being, and that this being was "growing and developing inside." This issue was mentioned by 30 couples, with husbands and wives being roughly equally likely to raise it. Moreover, as the following comment shows, the sense of wonder at the existence of the unborn child helped unite partners, and make them both feel involved in the pregnancy.

It really kicked in for me when my wife had that first ultrasound. Actually seeing the ultrasound, and hearing a heartbeat. It all sort of clicked then. I thought "Oh yes, I am a part of this," whereas before I hadn't felt like that.

Similarly, one of the wives expressed surprise at her husband's fascination with their unborn child:

I've been surprised at how keen and excited he is, and how much it's changed him! He comes home from work, and wants to feel my stomach. And he's been talking to her too—saying things like "When are you going to come out?"

Twenty-five couples reported being surprised at how pleasant they were finding the whole experience of pregnancy. That is, in these couples, both husbands and wives reported that the wife seemed to feel unexpectedly well, or that she had "that healthy glow." For example, one expectant mother said that she was really enjoying being pregnant, and her husband agreed with this comment, noting "she just keeps going through this big beaming stage."

For 22 couples, the amount of help and support received from other people constituted a pleasant surprise. This support was sometimes emotional in nature (e.g., when others reacted very positively to the news of the pregnancy), and sometimes more tangible (e.g., being given baby clothes, or other items for the nursery). As one woman put it:

Now that I'm having a baby, all the women want to come and see me, and want to know how it's going. And people with kids want to see you more. And just the generosity of people–we've been given clothes and toys, and well wishes and nice thoughts. That has surprised me.

This issue of help and support from others was often discussed by both members of the couple, but when it was raised by only one person, this was almost always the wife. The greater importance of social support for the women in this sample probably stems from two factors. First, pregnancy clearly creates more immediate demands and difficulties for women than for men. Second, women generally place somewhat more emphasis on emotional support and intimacy than men do, and hence are likely to be very aware of the role of supportive relationships.

Unpleasant Surprises. Not all couples reported that pregnancy brought "nice" surprises, however. Thirteen couples said that they were surprised to learn about all the things that could potentially go wrong, and that these had become a source of concern. One expectant father put it this way: "I pretty much expected most of it, I suppose, apart from all the things that can go wrong, both before and after, and how that makes you worry."

The major focus of concern was the possibility of losing the baby, and in particular, the awareness that the early period of pregnancy is critical in this regard. One wife, for example, commented on how surprised she was at the depth of her concern over things that could go wrong. Another couple commented that they would relax only when the baby was old enough to survive if it was born early, and this meant that they were not going to relax until about the 32nd week!

Although concerns about the early period of pregnancy are quite well founded, some reports of "surprising things" (in terms of things that can go wrong) were less rational. In fact, some of the comments pointed to spouses having internalized misinformation and "old wives' tales." For example, one wife was worried because she had been told that she should not hang out the washing or stretch up to reach high filing cabinets at work, in case the baby became strangled with the umbilical cord.

The other unpleasant surprise reported by several couples concerned a perceived lack of support from others, or experiences of negative interactions with others. Nine couples raised this issue. One expectant mother, for example, said that she was sick of comments about her physical appearance and bearing, such as "Look, pull your shoulders back and walk like this." Similarly, another woman expressed her resentment at people's tendency to criticize and interfere:

I'm so sick of their nagging. "Don't pick that up." "You can't do this." "You shouldn't be doing that." And I'm thinking to myself, "I can do it while I'm still capable – just leave me alone!"

It is interesting to note that these comments about negative interactions contrast with those of the couples we discussed earlier, who were surprised by the high levels of supportiveness they had encountered. Clearly, the responses of other people are important throughout this time of adjustment, and these findings highlight the varying experiences of couples in this regard. Of course, even well-meaning comments and advice can be a source of strain and concern, as illustrated by the case of the woman who was told that she should not stretch to reach things. Again, as was the case with comments about supportiveness, wives were much more likely than husbands to mention the *lack* of support from others.

PLANS FOR BIRTH AND BEYOND

Finally, we were interested in couples' plans for the future, in terms of their options for the birth itself, their approach to juggling the demands of parenthood and careers, and any plans to have more children.

Couples' plans for the birth itself were largely traditional. That is, almost all of the couples were planning for the birth to take place in hospital. Of the remainder, six couples had chosen a birthing centre, and only one had decided to have a home birth.

In terms of juggling parenthood and careers, we asked both husbands and wives about their plans for taking time off from work, either before or after the birth of the baby. In considering their answers, it is important to note that 10 of the wives had already given up paid employment in preparation for the birth, although they were still in the second trimester of pregnancy. In addition, two wives were working from home, and saw no need to take formal time off, and another eight were studying (rather than in paid employment). Of the couples where the wife was employed outside the home, only five wives reported that they were not planning to take any time off work before the baby was born. Of the remainder, the amount of time to be taken off before the birth ranged from 1 week to 14 weeks, with most wives planning to take off between 4 and 6 weeks (32 wives answered in this range).

Wives' plans for working outside the home after the birth were very varied. Sixteen wives reported that they did not plan to return to work in the foreseeable future, 21 planned to undertake full-time work, and 60 planned to work on a part-time or casual basis. Of those who were planning a return to work, the amount of time to be taken off after the birth ranged from four weeks to one and a half years, with the most common response being one year (22 wives planned to take one year off work).

Given that men are tending to become increasingly involved in the care of their young children, we were also interested in husbands' plans for balancing work and child-rearing. In this sample, none of the husbands were planning to take time off before the baby was born (this issue did not arise for nine of the husbands, because these men were not currently in paid employment). Thirty-one husbands reported planning to take some time off after the birth, but the period of time was generally quite short, ranging from one week to eight weeks. Clearly, then, couples in this study generally saw the wives as adopting the role of primary caregiver.

Our final question at this interview concerned couples' plans to have more children. We realized that these plans might well change over time, but we were interested in their ideas about the future of their family. The large majority planned to have more children, and husbands and wives almost always agreed about this issue. Based on the wives' reports, 73 couples said that they definitely wanted to have more children, 14 were unsure, and 5 said that they did not want any more children.

SUMMARY

In terms of their plans for the birth and for spouses' roles as homemakers and providers, the couples in this study were generally quite traditional. In other respects, however, this interview revealed marked differences in their approaches to pregnancy and parenthood. For some, the pregnancy had been carefully planned, and timed to fit with spouses' educational and career goals and their general sense of readiness in the relationship. For others, the pregnancy was not planned, and in some cases, the news had been quite distressing. Consistent with our view of the transition to parenthood, it seemed that a secure and satisfying couple relationship was an important factor in helping couples adjust to this phase in their lives. Experiences of pregnancy also varied widely: Some couples reported that they were pleasantly surprised by the ease of pregnancy and by the support they were receiving, but others reported severe problems related to physical and emotional health. In the next chapter, we take a further look at couples' varied experiences, focusing this time on the first weeks of parenthood.

SIX

Couples' Experiences of Birth and New Parenthood

"Our everyday talk just isn't there any more, because suddenly all the focus is on the baby. And although that brings a lot of joy, you also start to notice those things that have dropped away."

About six weeks after their babies were born, we again visited the transition couples in their homes. As on the first occasion, we interviewed each husband and wife as a couple, and tape-recorded the discussion (92 couples were interviewed at this second phase of the study). This interview focused on two broad issues: how the couples had coped with the labor and birth, and how they were reacting to the early days of parenthood.

LABOR AND BIRTH

In this interview, we directed the first three questions about the experience of labor and birth primarily at wives. We asked them to talk about the length of their labor, the types of pain relief used, and the extent of surgical intervention. These questions were designed to allow wives to share their experiences, and to give us some indication of the relative ease or difficulty of the birth.

Ease or Difficulty of Birth

Not surprisingly, wives' answers to these questions revealed widely differing experiences. The number of hours in labor ranged from 1 to 48, with about half of the wives reporting labors of 11 hours or more. The huge range of answers to this question undoubtedly reflects not only the variability of labor itself, but also the difficulty in defining the start of "labor," without information from the attending health professionals. In other words, some wives may equate the onset of labor with the first contractions, whereas others may restrict the term to the most intense part of the birth process.

A relatively small number of wives (11) reported that they had used only natural methods of pain relief, such as massage and warm baths. Fifteen reported that their strongest method of pain relief was either nitrous oxide or pethidine, but the majority of the women (roughly 60%) had been given epidural anaesthetic. Four wives had been given general anaesthetic, to facilitate the delivery of babies at risk of foetal distress. For one-quarter of the births, no surgical intervention had been required. Forty-four percent of women reported relatively minor procedures (such as episiotomies), and 31% had had cesarian births. Thirteen of the babies were born at least three weeks before term, with the most premature baby arriving seven weeks early.

Expectations versus Experiences

Once we had obtained this basic information about the birth, we invited both husbands and wives to talk about how their experiences of labor had compared with their expectations. (All the husbands had been present at the birth of their babies). Most of the couples (more than 70%) said that the labor was different from what they had expected. Interestingly, however, there was little clear pattern to the departure from expectancies.

On the negative side, 14 wives and 7 husbands said that the labor had been harder or longer than they had expected. Another comment made by some husbands and wives (17 spouses in total) was that they were surprised at how helpless, or lacking in control, they had felt during the birth. In addition, 13 wives commented that the birth had been more painful than they had expected. (Although husbands were quite involved in talking about the labor and birth, they were clearly hesitant to voice opinions about the level of pain involved; they may have thought that it would be presumptuous for them to do so, given their inability to experience the pain directly.)

On the other hand, a substantial number of spouses reported unexpectedly positive experiences of labor and birth. Twenty-two wives and 11 husbands said that the labor had been shorter or easier than they had expected, and 4 had found it less painful than expected.

The following comment from one of the wives illustrates her positive attitude to labor and birth, and her satisfaction with the experience:

When I was pregnant, I got sick of all the terrible labor stories, and people trying to scare me. I thought "No, I won't think like that, I want to experience this for myself." And like – it wasn't a breeze, it was hard work, but it was fine.

The husbands' presence during labor and birth had been important both to them and to their wives. One woman, for example, said:

He was the first one to calm the baby down, and that was really special to me – the fact that he was able to help deliver her, and then give her a cuddle when she stopped crying.

Similarly, husbands talked about the experience of the birth as "very exciting" and "the best thing," and described themselves as having been "overwhelmed" and "awestruck." Several husbands commented proudly that they had been asked to "cut the cord," and one described his pleasant surprise at the amount of involvement he had had during the labor and birth:

I was far more involved than I thought I would be. I thought I would just sort of sit to one side, and give her a little pat on the shoulder every now and again. But the doctor and the nurse had me right in there in the middle of it, saying, you know "Hold this leg! Do this! Do that!" And that was really good.

EXPERIENCES OF PARENTHOOD

During this interview, we were particularly interested in hearing spouses' reactions to these early days of parenthood. To focus the discussion as much as possible, we asked couples to tell us about their "worst" or most challenging experiences, and about their "best" or most positive experiences.

Worst Experiences

Most couples were able to nominate a couple of aspects of parenting that they considered the "worst," or most challenging. Issues that were raised by at least five couples, listed in order of decreasing frequency, were

lack of sleep	48
not knowing what to do	35
restricted lifestyle	33
feeling "disconnected" from infant	13
concern over household tasks	10
lack of couple intimacy	10
lack of social support	6
dirty nappies	6
contradictory advice	6

Lack of Sleep. Given the many and persistent demands made by newborn infants, it is not surprising that the most common problem that couples talked about was lack of sleep, and the related feelings of exhaustion and tension. The pervasive effects of lack of sleep are vividly portrayed by one wife, who said:

It's being constantly tired. Just permanently. I mean, you know, you just never catch up really. You're just always tired. Like you could always stop what

Page

you're doing and go and have a nap, just anywhere, any place, you could fall asleep – just so tired.

Another wife described the problems that lack of sleep posed not only for herself, but also for her husband who had to cope with full-time paid employment:

At night time when the baby cries, you know I think, "Well, he has to go to work." And I feel responsible to shut this child up, you know. And he – he's like got a pillow over his head, and I'm like thinking, "Oh, gee," and I'm feeling like a zombie.

For both husbands and wives, then, lack of sleep emerged as a problem that often led to frustration, short tempers, and difficulty in functioning effectively at home and in the workplace. As one husband put it, everything in these early weeks of parenthood was done "through a veil of tiredness."

Not Knowing What to Do. The next most common complaint concerned "not knowing what to do" with the infant. This complaint focused not only on the practicalities of learning how to care for the baby, but also on the emotional trauma for the parents when they felt unable to comfort the infant. These points emerge clearly in the following exchange between husband and wife:

w: For me, the worst thing is when she's crying and you don't know what's wrong.
h: Yes, that's what I was about to say.
w: Not being able to – like, you feed her and she still cries, and you get wind up and she still cries, and you change her and she still cries, and you sort of think – you're cuddling her and she's still crying. And it's that feeling of helplessness, not being able to say "What's wrong?" and have them answer you. And it just tears at your heart when you can't get them to stop. Yes, to me, that is the worst thing.

As couples talked about this issue, it became clear that parental fear and anxiety about "what to do" for the baby can be quite diffuse and generalized, as seen in this wife's comments:

I think it's the fear. I'm just so terrified that something's going to happen to him, you know. Like, you never have one relaxed moment. There are different levels of it. I mean, you relax because you can enjoy being with him when he's happy. But you're still worrying that "Oh, look, his eye's turning; oh, is that okay?" The worst part is that I just don't have a minute – not a minute free of worrying about him, and you know, just everything – like for the rest of his life. I mean, I worry in years. I'm worrying about the next 100 years.

Another point that emerged was that for quite a lot of couples, concerns about "what to do" centered largely on feeding the baby. For example, one wife stated:

I suppose the hassles with her feeding, to start with, were more of a concern for me. But since that's been worked out, that's fine. I mean I don't have – I don't have any qualms about not breastfeeding her. I'm not that "Oh, gosh, breast is best" and all that sort of thing, but I suppose that's probably – that was the biggest challenge for me to start with.

In discussing the issue of feeding the baby, some couples commented on the need to *learn how*. In other words, breast-feeding does not necessarily "come naturally."

It hasn't been too bad, but it's just – I don't know – you know how you see dogs and cats feeding their babies – and you see on TV – you see pigs feeding their piglets and they make it look so easy. I don't know – it's just something to me that, breast-feeding a baby, like as a human, it wasn't something that came naturally to me. It wasn't something you just "Okay, let them lie there and suck." It's not that easy.

Before we leave the issue of breast-feeding, it is important to point out that for some mothers, in particular, this issue can be a very emotional one. A strong desire to do what is best for the baby can mean that the practicalities of feeding take on highly emotional overtones, as seen in the next comment:

I feel really strongly about the benefits of breast-feeding. But I spent two of the last four days in tears, thinking I'm going to have to go to bottle-feeding. So that's probably the worst for me. The lack of sleep isn't as stressful as the breast-feeding.

In summary, then, quite a few couples felt awkward and confused during their first weeks of parenthood. Although many of them had read books and articles on parenting and talked to other people about their experiences, they often felt that caring for their infant involved a "very steep learning curve," and that much of the learning occurred as a result of "trial and error."

Restricted Lifestyle. The next issue that surfaced in couples' complaints about parenthood concerned the restrictions that the new infant placed on their lifestyle and their everyday activities. The need to organize the baby, and all the objects needed for the baby's routine, is highlighted in the following quote from one of the new mothers in the study:

Your lifestyle is just completely changed. I mean L would ring me up and say "Let's go out shopping." And I'd say "Oh, hang on, I've got to feed B, and this, and this, and this; oh, she's sick now, I don't want to bother." And, like she'll come down and pick me up and something. Takes me 45 minutes to pack her bag and get me ready and just do all those things like that. Which doesn't piss me off or anything, but it's just a whole completely different thing. You used to just walk out the door and not have to worry about anything. Now there's prams and strollers. And bottles and water and this and that and something else and – oh – better bring a change of clothes, better bring a washer, better bring this, better bring that, you know – oh, is it going to be cool in the air-conditioning? – better bring a blanket. And then I walk out the door and I'm completely, you know – I'm still in my pyjamas or something.

Rather than feeling totally helpless in the face of these organiza-tional demands, a few wives talked about how extra time and planning can help minimize this problem. In fact, the demands of parenthood had actually driven one woman to become *more* punctual than she had been in the past!

I'm actually on time when I go places now. Before, I just didn't – I'd always be 15 or 20 minutes late. Now, I'm on time, because if someone says "I'll meet you at one-thirty," you sort of work back and think, "Right, now – it takes me an hour to do this, and that, and that." So you start getting ready like at ten o'clock, to meet that one-thirty appointment.

Feeling "Disconnected." A smaller number of spouses reported con-cerns about feeling "uninvolved" with their new infant, or not being able to relate to it as they might have hoped. Although some husbands reported that they had little feeling for the baby at this point in time ("I can't really get emotional about it"), the strongest concerns about this issue were raised by wives. In other words, wives were no more likely than husbands to be feeling "disconnected," but for wives, this feeling was brought into sharp relief because of their day-to-day responsibility for the care of the child. For some wives, this feeling of disconnection had been quite short-lived:

At first, I couldn't have said that I loved her. I thought she was okay, and everyone said how nice she was, and how good it was to have her and everything, and all that.

Even in the earliest days, however, feelings of this kind may raise doubts in the mother's mind about her suitability as a parent. One new mother expressed such doubts this way:

I felt really funny toward him. I had no sense that I loved him, and I was really worried by that. I thought "I'm going to make a terrible mother," because I just don't feel anything for him at this stage.

At the time of this second interview, a few mothers were still grappling with feelings of disconnection, although it seemed that these feelings were abating slowly:

I find it hard being alone in the house with the baby. I find it hard to believe I had the baby. Yeah – not quite connected to it. Feeling all these things that I didn't expect to feel – resentment, rage. Yes, I mean before I really got to know her, I sort of found it really hard when she screamed and just – just the sound of it just went straight through me.

Concern Over Household Tasks. Several couples talked about how difficult it was to get household tasks done. As one new mother said, "trying to do the housework is another thing – it's just impossible." Although this issue was usually raised by the wives, the content of the discussions highlighted the potential implications for both spouses:

w: The worst thing is the sharing, or rather the *non-sharing,* of the responsibilities – like getting up in the night and doing things like that. And things not getting done around the house because you haven't got time to do them, and somebody expects you to do them.
h: Somebody?

This exchange shows how feelings about the performance of household tasks are tied up with spouses' expectations of each other, and with issues of sharing and equity. But spouses' expectations of *themselves* are also important, as wives' own high standards for housework sometimes contribute to difficulties in this area:

I'm finding it a bit difficult because I'm usually pretty independent. And now I'm having to rely on my husband a lot and also being excused for things that, you know, are normally the woman's job. You know – like dishes being done and the house being cleaned. I still feel like I should be able to do it. And if it's not done, I feel like I've failed a little bit.

As we saw in Chapter 1, the demands of balancing child care, house-work, and paid employment can push couples towards more traditional patterns of division of labor. Many couples are quite keen to share the responsibilities of new parenthood and other household tasks, but this sharing can be difficult to implement in reality. One new father noted that despite mutual discussions with his wife, and his best intentions of role sharing, this arrangement simply did not seem to have "worked out." In another couple, the wife was quite concerned about the unexpected direction that division of labor was taking in the home:

The biggest thing that has caused me to have a short fuse at times is when I've felt like I'm the parent, and the responsibility has got a bit lopsided. And that we're becoming more like the traditional family, I suppose, where the woman brings up the baby and the man makes the money. And yeah – that's not what we wanted, because that's not what we were achieving.

Lack of Couple Intimacy. For some couples, the "worst" part of parenting was not directly related to their interactions with their new baby, or to patterns of household work. Rather, they were concerned about how their relationship with their spouse was suffering as a result of the demands of child-rearing. This concern over a lack of couple intimacy is reflected in the following exchange between husband and wife:

w: I think the other thing I've found hard is not having enough communication as a couple. Because suddenly you've got something that is crying at you, and you need to feed it and you need to change it. Like we went through four weeks of not having a conversation. And it's like you go "How's work?" "Good." And that – that's your whole conversation for the evening.
h: Grunt, grunt. [laughter]
w: And that was it, and I found that really hard. Because we always talked and we always had very open communication. And to suddenly get to the point where you can't just sit down and talk over your day and things like that, I find that really hard.

Similarly, other spouses talked about how much they were missing "having time for each other," and "just being us." They saw this reduction in couple time as a definite source of stress in their marriage.

Spouses' comments also tended to confirm the popular stereotype that parenthood brings decreased intimacy not only in terms of limited time and conversation, but also in terms of sexual contact and other displays of physical affection. One husband commented:

Our relationship has changed so completely. I mean, we used to sort of cuddle and kiss each other, and be quite touchy, and stuff like that. We've done virtually none of that. Certainly that's all gone out the window.

A similar point of view was put forward by one of the wives, who named "interrupted cuddles" with her husband as the worst aspect of parenthood. Of course, levels of physical intimacy are affected by spouses' feelings of fatigue, as well as by the sheer lack of time. As one new mother put it:

But when there's a baby there, especially when you've been coping with the baby all day, and then you're both tired as well…

Some couples found themselves resenting this decrease in marital intimacy. In fact, one of the new mothers talked about how much she was missing the shared couple time, and commented that she felt as though the baby was "an intruder" who came between herself and her husband.

Lack of Social Support. For couples who mentioned a lack of social support, complaints focused either on the *absence* of support, due to the physical distances between family members, or on the stress caused by *difficult interactions* with friends or family. The absence of family members tended to create a lack of both emotional and tangible support. For example, one new mother lamented the lack of family members with whom the emotions linked with new parenthood could be shared:

The worst thing is being away from Mum; not having family around you. I was in hospital, and my husband went home to an empty house with all those feelings and whatever.

The following comment from a new father focuses more on the practical help that family members might have been able to provide:

We don't have any family support here at all. So there's no grandmas to come around and help load the washing, or bake a couple of lasagnas to put in the freezer, or anything like that.

A very different source of difficulty in interacting with others was the perception that "people take over from you." In other words, some spouses reported that friends or family members tried to dictate how the baby should be cared for, or that they imposed too much on the couple at this busy time. The negative effects of some interactions with well-meaning family members are vividly illustrated in this comment:

I sent my family home [laughter]. It was far too traumatic with them here. I mean, I'm probably not the easiest person to get along with at the best of times. But having someone who is so much older than me and such a different person to me, I found it extremely difficult – to the extent that I came close to strangling H's mother on occasions, I really did. She constantly fussed over me – you know, and wouldn't leave me alone – which was driving me mad.

Similarly, the following exchange between husband and wife highlights the strain that can result when friends and family members make too many demands on new parents' hospitality:

w: The worst thing is just trying to cope with all the visitors.
h: Yes. Either they just pop in for a quick beer, or they stop by and drink tea all night. And then we have visitors that come over and they end up staying the night and things like that.

Dirty Nappies. Given the pervasive nature of many of the parenting problems raised by couples (e.g., lack of sleep; confusion over infant care), it is not really surprising that few couples mentioned "changing dirty nappies" as the worst part of parenting. However, some new parents clearly felt strongly about this task, as shown in the following comment:

The worst thing is nappies – especially when they're toxic. Having the baby handed to you while you're having a shower going – she's had a toxic nappy, and you have to wash her off.

Contradictory Advice. Finally, some couples talked about the confusion generated by the contradictory advice they had received on child care. Although we coded this as a separate concern, contradictory advice is likely to add to couples' sense that they do not know what to do to take the best care of their child (discussed previously). For example, one new father said:

If we went on advice from other people, so to speak, we would have been told "She's only crying"; "It's bad habits"; "Leave her in the cot"; you know. But anyway, it's just a matter of learning and finding out, because there's so many different opinions as to what the right thing to do is.

Interestingly, the conflicting advice that couples complained about did not always come from listening to different friends and family members. The following exchange shows how one couple had had repeated contact with a particular group of health professionals, and had been given different advice about their baby's problem on each occasion:

H: The worst thing about us not knowing is, and if there's any nurses listening to this – get your act together! Every time you speak to somebody, it's a different thing. "Now use Multigen." Oh no – first it was "Use these wet drops." "Don't use these wet drops." "Use those wet drops." "Don't use those wet drops." "Use Multigen." "Don't use Multigen." "Use prune juice." "She's too young for prune juice." "Go back to the sugar and water again." And that's where we started from!

W: Brown sugared water; that's all.

H: She's actually gone through five remedies, to get back to where we were again.

W: And everybody tells you a different thing.

H: The thing about it is – what bothers me, is that we're calling the same phone number and getting different answers every time!

One of the points that emerged from the comments on contradictory advice is that, as we suggested earlier, this problem can compound the feeling of "not knowing what to do." In the following comment, a new mother describes how her confusion and concern over breast-feeding was exacerbated by the contradictory advice she was given in hospital:

I was going to say, the biggest challenge for me was breast-feeding. That was like climbing a mountain and – you know, that was a huge challenge. Like every day, "Am I going to make it? Am I going to be able to do it?" The nurses were helpful, but every single one of them said something different. There was a lot of confusion and they didn't necessarily – each nurse on each shift wanted you to do it her way. So that if you met up with her four shifts later, you're sort of thinking frantically, "What was it that she said?" And then you'd do something, and she'd go "No, no, you don't do it that way, you don't do that."

Nothing about Parenting Is Bad! Before we leave the topic of "worst experiences," it is important to note that five couples said that they could not identify anything bad about being a parent. These couples reported that they had found parenting very easy and enjoyable ("really pure textbook and quite straightforward"), or that they had "taken to it like ducks to water." Of course, one reason why parenting is easier for some couples is that their babies are less difficult or demanding. One new mother noted:

She's not one of these babies that constantly screams. The people next door actually said to my mother, who lives down the road "Has she had the baby yet?" [laughter] And my mother said, "Yes, the baby's been there for a few weeks now." And they said, "We've never heard her cry."

Similarly, one new father commented that there was nothing about parenting that did not please him. He then added that "the worst part of parenthood is being away, at work!"

Best Experiences

On the other hand, *all* the couples we interviewed were able to identify aspects of parenting that they considered the "best." Again (as for the "worst" experiences), almost all couples raised a couple of issues at this point in the discussion. Issues that were raised by at least five couples, again listed in order of decreasing frequency, were

baby smiling	45
just having the baby	31
responsive interaction	25
seeing the changes	23
being together as a family	11
baby recognizing parents	11
increased closeness to spouse	10
relationships with others	7
creating life	7

Baby Smiling. Common wisdom suggests that the early weeks of infant care can be difficult for parents, because they see little direct reward for their effort and involvement; all of this changes, however, when the baby begins to smile. The new parents in our study certainly seemed to agree with this perspective, with "the baby smiling" heading the list of "best things." Both husbands and wives were clearly captivated by their infants' smiles. For instance, one mother commented:

Giving us big gummy smiles. They're gorgeous. He's only just started in the last 10 days, I suppose, giving us a genuine smile. It's not a wind smile. And you tickle his chin and he just gives you this great big smile.

Similarly, one of the fathers talked about how good it was to see his baby's smile, even in the earliest hours of the morning:

Seeing her smiles. She watches you walk into the room and she smiles, and in the morning – at three o'clock in the morning when we're feeding her, she laughs at you.

Just Having the Baby. About one-third of the couples talked about the "best side" of parenting in very general terms. For example, one new father had trouble expressing his feelings in words, and finally observed that "well, you get a baby out of parenthood – she's wonderful!" A similar difficulty in expressing the joys of new parenthood was noted by one of the mothers:

You can't describe it. The minute I saw him, the minute he was born, I don't know what it is. I can't put it into words. I've thought about it a lot, but it's just – this is my child and this is – you know – wanting to care and protect and love.

Other parents who focused on "just having the baby" talked in terms of "a miracle," "just his whole being," "just his existence," and "just having the cute little thing." For these parents, then, it was the very existence of the child that was so pleasing, rather than any single specific aspect. This feeling was described particularly clearly by one of the couples who had been trying to fall pregnant for a long time, and who had eventually done so as a result of IVF procedures. The wife said that she found herself doing "all the boring things" that new parents tend to do, like "just looking at their fingers and toes and just seeing how beautifully they're made." Her husband agreed with this sense of wonder at having the baby, saying that "after sixteen years, we were holding the desire of our hearts."

Responsive Interaction. For other parents, however, the biggest joy came from interacting with the baby, and seeing the baby respond to them. One couple expressed this thought in the following way:

н: The response.
w: Yeah, the response is really nice. And he tries so hard to talk to you. You know, after a bath, he says "ah" and "oo" a lot, and watches my lips and just so intently; you can see that he's trying to copy my lips – it's really sweet. And you know that they're looking at you and trying to take it in.

This type of mutual interaction was seen as immensely rewarding by both husbands and wives, and these spouses explicitly talked about the contrast between the first few weeks of parenting (when the baby was largely nonresponsive), and their more recent experiences:

The best thing? That she's started to interact. Up till then, it's all pretty much a one-way track – feeding and changing and she doesn't know you. Well, she may know you, but she doesn't respond. But as soon as she responds, you can sort of look at her for hours and play with her – it makes such a big difference. There's sort of an interaction there.

Similarly, another new parent contrasted her infant's current responsiveness with the earlier experience of a "blank face." As this example suggests, the specific kinds of responses that parents commonly talked about were the baby following things visually, and watching people or objects in a more focused way. The emphasis on these responses from the baby is similar to that of the parents who waited eagerly for their baby's first smile.

Another recurring theme in these descriptions was the parents' awareness that the baby responded to their attempts to soothe and pacify them. In other words, parents felt pleased and proud that they were able to comfort their infants when they showed signs of distress:

I usually just get her up and feed her, and then we just lie in bed together for a while. That's nice, and she really responds to that, because she's so calm. Especially if she's really upset and you go to change her and she starts screaming or something, and you try all of this and sometimes you're desperate and then – I just put her into bed with me and she just calms instantly. She just relaxes; you can see her whole body relax, and that's really good.

The sense of mastery that this kind of experience gives new parents is highlighted in the following comment from one of the mothers:

It's really a base level of being proud and thinking that I can do this, and that it's worked out. And I know that I can stop him crying. Like if he's upset or whatever, I can stop him, at this age. That's quite a powerful feeling, that I can satisfy everything that he needs at the moment, and that – it won't last for that long, though [laughter].

Seeing the Changes. Given how quickly babies grow and develop, it is not surprising that several couples reported a lot of pleasure in watching their babies' development. One new mother noted that "just watching the changes is amazing." The changes that parents mentioned included the baby making new sounds, new facial expressions, and new kinds of movements. One mother said that she could now see "a whole little personality that she's developing."

For some parents, then, the best part of parenting was simply *watching* their babies develop and change. These parents commented that the changes could be seen from one week to the next, or even that they could see something new "each day." Watching these changes gave parents a sense of the infant's "progress."

For some parents, however, the pleasure came not only from watching the changes, but also from knowing that their own care and involvement was making those changes possible. One mother, for example, after describing her baby's development, noted that "you know that she's developing, and that you're helping her by stimulating all the different things in her."

Being Together as a Family. Several couples talked about the joys of that "family feeling." This feeling was about enjoying being together, doing things together, and generally having good times together. One new father stated that there were two best things about parenthood: having his wife, and having his baby. In other words, being able to share time, activities, and experiences created that "family feeling."

For one couple, the emerging sense of family was symbolized by their first experience (as parents) of Mother's Day, and the new mother's cards and gifts were seen as taking on a special importance in this regard. When this issue was discussed, the husband was quick to point out that "Father's Day is coming up not too far away!"

The sense of unity that the term *family* implies was highlighted by one couple, who saw this as an important issue. The husband commented at one point that "I look at the baby and think, you know, 'That's my family', and she's thinking that back at us." Although this latter comment probably overestimates the baby's ability to reason and to reciprocate feelings, it clearly reflects the importance of family to the father concerned. Another wife talked about how comfortable she and her husband were with the thought of being a family, and how thankful they were that this anticipation had now become a reality.

Baby Recognizing Parents. These comments about the sense of family bring us to the next point, which concerns the experience of the baby recognizing the parents. This aspect of parenting is similar to "baby smiling" and "responsive interaction," in that all of these aspects focus on the beginnings of mutual exchanges between parent and child. Again, the perception that the baby recognizes the parents, or realizes "who they are," tends to make the parents feel special and powerful. As one woman described it:

I was in the coffee shop and the woman said, "he wants his mum," and she handed him to me. As soon as he got in my arms he stopped crying, and I thought like "I'm his mum," and it was like "oh, he knows who I am," and he just snuggled into my neck, and it was like "wow, he really knows me!"

In other words, some of the pleasure that parents derived from their baby recognizing them reflected their growing sense of competence and mastery of the parenting role. One mother noted how good she felt when her baby was crying and "you pick her up and she stops crying because she knows who it is."

Increased Closeness to Spouse. It is interesting to note that although some couples were concerned about the baby "coming between" them (as we saw under "Worst experiences"), others reported the opposite reaction. That is, they felt closer to their spouse than they had before the birth. For example, one new father agreed when his wife commented on their increased closeness, saying,

Yes, there's definitely something special there in our relationship that wasn't there before. I can't really explain what it is, but there's just something between the two of us that's a little bit different.

Similarly, one of the wives described this feeling of intimacy very succinctly when she commented:

I think it's brought the two of us closer together. Sometimes we lie in bed with her between us, and we just look at each other and go "Oh!" [laughter].

The increased closeness that some spouses reported seemed to stem from the shared experience of parenting, especially when husband and wife tried to work together to perform tasks and make decisions. One wife suggested that parenthood had brought them together in "a different kind of way – it's very much like a partnership now." In other words, these spouses had responded to the extra demands that the new baby made by working as a team and relying more closely on each other.

Relationships with Others. In their discussions of the best things about parenthood, some spouses focused on improved relationships with people close to them. For example, one wife commented:

I've found that it's given my mother access to communicate with me on another level. Whereas before we had problems communicating as mother and daughter, now it's mother, daughter, and granddaughter. It's like we've got a third area to discuss.

Similarly, another wife talked about the eager reactions of various family members to the arrival of the baby, and the sense of family cohesion that this created:

The most amazing thing is to see the grandparents and the way they respond and react to her. Well, both sets – the whole focus is on her – they adore her. And the nieces and nephews, they range in age from 6 to 14, and seeing their reactions was just delightful. They all came to the hospital and they all made her cards and drew her pictures and brought presents they had made. And when she came home, they all wanted to come over as soon as possible to see her. It's just lovely to see how they've welcomed her.

Some couples noted that their friends and work colleagues had also been very helpful and involved. One woman said that she and her husband had spent days writing out "Thank-you" notes to those who had helped them in some way; she appreciated the gestures others had made, because they showed "how much we mean to other people."

Other couples described a more general social response that came with parenthood: The baby attracted the attention of just about everyone, and caused "grins on everyone's faces." For example, one woman stated:

You meet lots of people. In fact, it's surprising how many people you meet. People just stop you in the shopping center or the street, and ask you "How old is she?" And we think that's really good.

It would be naive, however, to suggest that all members of the social network are equally keen to greet the arrival of the baby and become involved with it. One husband suggested, instead, that the changes that occurred in relating to other people were quite complex. This couple now felt closer to some people, but more distant from others, because of their new interest in their baby and child-related topics in general:

I seem to be able to talk to people with kids a lot easier. Like you can relate to what they are talking about more. I used to talk to friends who had children and think "You're boring; I won't talk to you any more." But now I can understand why, because your whole life just revolves around your child. But we're finding that some of our friends, we're just bored with them now, or they're bored with us. But before we had the baby, they used to be really close.

Creating Life. Finally, a number of couples described the major highlight of parenthood as their sense of creation. Put another way, their focus was on the wonder of what they had made or achieved. This feeling was variously described as "just seeing the final product that we had made," "seeing the outcome," and "knowing that we brought this little person into the world." One father reported that it was a strange (though wonderful) feeling, to "see something of yourself replicated." Similarly, one mother reported that she was still having difficulty believing that "we actually made him."

For some spouses, the significance of this act of creation lay in the sense of continuity that it provided. One father commented that it was important to know that "if something happens to you, there's somebody that's got a part of you." Another father expressed this reaction quite eloquently:

This is the afterlife that actually exists. It's your genetic material continuing on in some way. You can think all you like about that; it's "wonderful," in the proper sense of the word.

Men, Women, and New Parenthood

Before we leave our discussion of this second interview, it is important to note that some couples saw men's and women's experiences of parenting as quite different. For example, in the following exchange, the husband describes the infant as "boring," and suggests that she will become more interesting as she grows up. Moreover, when his wife disagrees with this assessment, he seems rather dismissing of her point of view:

H: As an object, she's very uninteresting and boring, and she cries a lot and she demands a lot. But you know, you think of all the great things that she's got ahead – you know, all the fun times, like teaching her how to walk and her first bicycle, and having birthdays. She doesn't interact very well now.
W: But she does! She does!
H: Yeah, but that's what W sees.

This husband went on to acknowledge, however, that his wife spent much more time with the baby than he did, and that she might see things that he missed. Women's greater day-to-day involvement in the tasks and processes of child care is further illustrated in this exchange between another husband and wife:

H: We haven't taken too much notice of her milestones and things like that.
W: Oh, we have!
H: We haven't been writing them down.
W: I have!
H: Have you?
W: It's in my diary at the moment.
H: Great! [laughter].

In another statement about men's and women's roles as parents, one of the mothers expressed what she saw as the unfairness of the situation: Her role involved a lot of hard work and basic caregiving, whereas her husband seemed to have all the fun!

You breastfeed for an hour, and then you change them, and then you dress them, and all that sort of stuff. Then I think "I'll let H do some parenting," so I let him look after the baby and I'll do other things. So then he gets to play with him. So at first I was feeling like "Oh, I don't get to play"; like, you know, I get to do all the basic care needs. But now he's awake a bit more often, so I do get to play with him [laughter].

Another wife echoed this thought about the hard work involved in mothering, but expressed more strongly her dissatisfaction with her husband's attitude:

Today, the baby cried and cried and cried and cried. And I'm thinking, "H is getting home at five o'clock"; so I had the bath and everything ready, waiting for him to get home so I could just go "Great, give me some time; get myself together." But it didn't happen. When he got home like at twenty past six, I just lost the plot. And then H was saying "Well, I need time," because actually he stayed back and had a beer with the boys. And he said "Well, I need my time," and then it was like "Well, what about *my* time?" And "You don't realize how hard it really, really is."

One husband clearly acknowledged the disparity of the gender roles. That is, he agreed that it was "easy" for him, because he was not home very much to be affected by the baby's demands or the lack of routine. As we saw earlier in this chapter, however, holding rigid expectations about gender roles (which jobs are "women's work") is likely to make the adjustment to new parenthood more difficult. Several couples noted that it no longer made sense for them to think in these terms: If the woman was doing the bulk of the child care, the husband had to take on extra responsibilities around the house. (We explore these issues in more detail in Chapter 9, which focuses on the diary-based reports of household work.)

Given that many couples recognized the need to negotiate new patterns of household work, it is important not to overstate the different perspectives of men and women, or to assume that these differences are destined to cause lasting problems for couples. In addition, as the following comment from one father indicates, some couples were already succeeding in working through their initial differences, and coming to a deeper understanding of parenthood:

When B was first born, I used to get really pissed off, because nothing would get done. And I would be just "What have you *done* today?" And I thought "What are you *doing*? How hard is it?" I just thought "How hard could it be?" – you know, you just feed him and put him down to sleep, and then you go and do your stuff. And then Saturday afternoon, I had him for three hours. I put him down and had to walk away for a minute, because I felt like I could have thrown him through the front door or something. He just wouldn't sleep and he was – and now I just go – "I just couldn't do it."

SUMMARY

Couples' reports of the first few weeks of parenting revealed a wealth of different perspectives. Their comments on the "best" and "worst" aspects of parenthood highlight the complexity of their experiences. In fact, the interviews suggest that the experience of new parenthood is something of an enigma, in which sheer drudgery is mixed with high emotion. This enigma was nicely captured by one of the mothers:

It's a bit hard to explain, isn't it? I mean, technically speaking, a day is shuffling around, no sleep, wiping up vomit and pooh, cleaning her up and trying to bathe her, and trying to calm her down, and trying to get her to sleep, and then trying to feed her, and trying to ... But it's okay, because she's gorgeous.

The content of the interviews, while focusing to a large extent on the new babies, highlights the role of the couple relationship. As the quote at the beginning of the chapter shows, the arrival of the baby brings new joys and discoveries, but also changes the day-to-day interactions between husband and wife. For several couples, the worst aspects of parenting were the loss of couple intimacy (in terms of both conversation and sexual contact), or concerns over inequity and lack of sharing of responsibilities. Conversely, for other couples, the best aspects of parenting were the sense of being all together, as a family, or the feelings of increased closeness to the spouse. In short, among the descriptions of the babies and the ups-and-downs of infant care, it was quite common for couples to raise issues about their relationships. These issues would almost certainly have been raised more often, had we not asked couples to focus on their very "best" and "worst" experiences. Spouses' spontaneous comments about partners' availability, dependability, support, and understanding fit with our overall focus on the importance of a secure and comfortable couple bond during this transition period.

SEVEN

How Does New Parenthood Affect Couples?

> "Forget the idea that baby and I are a team, or that I'm the boss. She's the leader. And the rules change all the time, and I'm not advised that they're going to be changed."

At the second assessment, which took place about five months after the study began, both groups of couples again completed questionnaires reporting on their relationships and their general psychological adjustment. In addition, the new parents (whose babies were then about six weeks old) reported on the amount of stress associated with parenthood, and the strategies they were using to deal with the demands of parenting. In this chapter, we explore four aspects of these reports: changes occurring since the first assessment; overall differences between groups and genders; links between attachment security at the beginning of the study and current relationship quality and adjustment; and patterns of stress and coping among new parents.

CHANGES SINCE THE FIRST ASSESSMENT

A central issue in this longitudinal study was the extent to which the couples changed between the first and second assessments. We were interested in tracking any changes in their relationships, as well as in their psychological adjustment. Hence, at the second assessment, we examined responses to the core questionnaires that the couples had now completed twice: relationship satisfaction, attachment, caregiving, sexuality, and general psychological adjustment.

In looking at scores across the two assessments, we were particularly interested in measures on which the transition and comparison groups showed different patterns of change. More specifically, we were looking for areas in which the transition couples changed between the first and second assessments, but the comparison couples did not. As we mentioned earlier (see Chapter 1), this kind of outcome would indicate that new parenthood had a marked impact on couples, over and above any changes that would be expected just from the passage of time.

At this stage, we found limited evidence for different patterns of change. In fact, most of the variables we measured (attachment, caregiving, sexuality, and psychological adjustment) were quite stable over the five-month period, for both transition and comparison couples. Similarly, overall scores on relationship satisfaction did not change over this period for either group. However, we did find change that varied according to group for two of the four aspects of relationship satisfaction: time together and global distress.

Time Together

As we noted in Chapter 3, the "time together" scale assesses partners' satisfaction with the quality and quantity of shared interests and leisure time. The patterns of change for this measure were quite complex, being somewhat different for husbands and wives, and are graphed in Figure 7.1. As the figure shows, new mothers reported that they had become less satisfied with the quality and quantity of shared couple time; in contrast, new fathers and comparison couples showed virtually no change from the first to the second assessments.

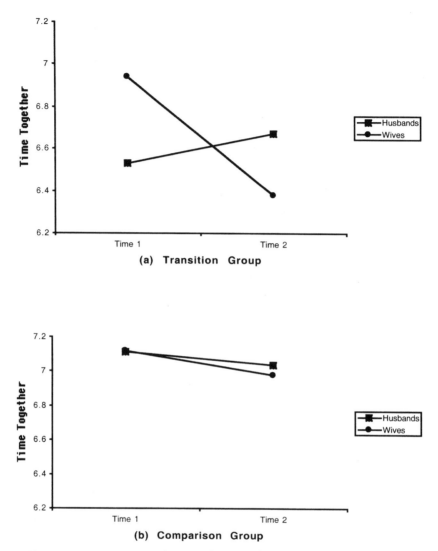

Figure 7.1. **Mean scores on time together according to group, gender, and time.**

It is not surprising that the new mothers perceived limited opportunities for quality time with the partner. After all, they were now
busy taking care of the demands of the baby, as well as doing the bulk
of other household tasks. (In Chapter 9, we present detailed information from the diary records about how tasks were allocated and performed in these families.) In fact, the loss of shared leisure time is a

common source of complaint among new parents, as we discussed in Chapter 1.

It is interesting to note that the new fathers did *not* report a similar drop in satisfaction with time together. Almost all these husbands were working outside the home, and their interactions with adults outside of the family setting may have helped act as a buffer against feelings of isolation and dissatisfaction. In addition, as some new mothers mentioned during the interviews (see Chapter 6), husbands' involvement with their babies often focused on "play" activities, rather than on basic chores; fathers may have tended to see these activities as an enjoyable part of shared couple time. Of course, wives' dissatisfaction with time together is still potentially problematic, and may even be compounded by the fact that their husbands were seeing the situation rather differently.

Global Distress

The other aspect of satisfaction that showed differential change for the two groups was global distress. Overall, scores on global distress were very low; this is usually the case with studies of intact relationships, because these items describe quite strong feelings of dissatisfaction and disappointment with the relationship. Interestingly, however, new parents reported *less* global distress at the second assessment than at the first, whereas husbands in the comparison group reported *more* global distress and wives showed no change (see Figure 7.2). In other words, although most studies have pointed to declines in relationship satisfaction associated with the arrival of the first baby, this finding highlights the fact that *positive* changes can also occur.

The small increase in global distress for comparison husbands may be due to the general trend, even for happy couples, to experience some disenchantment with their relationships over time (though it is not clear why this change would be restricted to husbands). As researchers such as Miller (1997) have pointed out, many factors can contribute to disenchantment. These factors include misplaced expectations of the partner (over a long period of time, partners' current eccentricities and past weaknesses are gradually revealed), the loss of illusion (negative partner behaviors invariably accumulate, counteracting any tendency to idealize the partner), and reduced effort (active

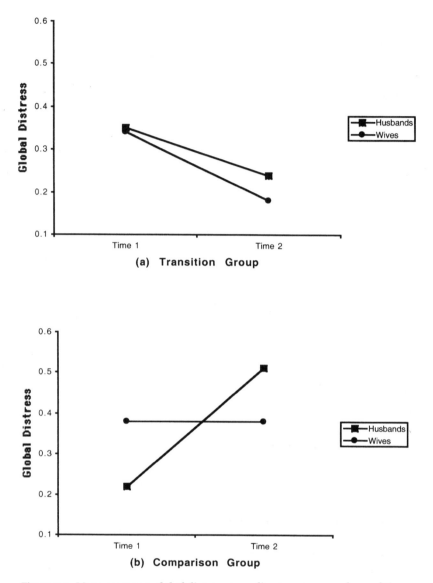

Figure 7.2. Mean scores on global distress according to group, gender, and time.

efforts to impress partners and gain their approval are difficult to maintain over time). For new parents, on the other hand, these factors may
be much less salient than their sense of elation and shared achievement. As a result, the period following the birth may be one in which

couples view the relationship with their partner as particularly happy and rewarding.

DIFFERENCES BETWEEN GROUPS AND GENDERS

For all of the remaining measures, the two groups of couples showed little change over the five-month period. However, we were also interested in looking at overall differences between the two groups and the two genders.

Differences Between Groups

At this second assessment, the transition and comparison groups differed in one respect only: satisfaction with their sexual communication. (Similarly, at the beginning of the study, this was the only difference between the two groups; see Chapter 4.) Specifically, couples in the transition group reported being less satisfied, on average, with their communication about sexual issues.

For the transition couples, then, it seems that both pregnancy and the demands of caring for a new baby tended to inhibit sexual communication. As we saw in Chapter 1, it is fairly common for couples to report a lessening of sexual activity and enjoyment during pregnancy and for some time after the birth. Many issues related to sexuality can arise or intensify throughout this period, including concerns about the partner's sexual satisfaction, uncertainty about one's own sexual attractiveness, physical discomfort during intercourse, and general fatigue. In western countries, couples tend to resume intercourse around six to eight weeks after the birth of the baby, but both mothers and fathers often express concerns about possible sexual problems at this time (von Sydow, 1999). In other words, many couples in the transition group would not have resumed sexual activity by this second assessment, and some of these couples probably found it rather difficult to talk about this situation.

Gender Differences

At the second assessment, men and women differed on several measures. Women (regardless of group) reported less discomfort with intimacy in their couple relationships. Their style of caregiving within the marriage was more responsive (i.e., showing more awareness of the partner's needs and more readiness to provide comfort), but also more compulsive (with a tendency to become over-involved in the partner's problems). Women also reported less sexual desire, but more satisfaction with their sexual communication. Finally, women reported more stress in their lives.

Most of these gender differences were also evident at the beginning of the study (see Chapter 4), with the exceptions being compulsive caregiving and stress. As we mentioned in the earlier chapter, the pattern of differences was consistent with other studies comparing the relationship experiences of men and women, and with the argument that women are socialized to pursue emotional intimacy and to act as the caretakers of relationships. At the same time, it is important to bear in mind that the differences between men and women were small, and that there were no differences in the various sources of relationship satisfaction, or in relationship anxiety, general anxiety, or depression. In short, the perspectives of men and women showed more similarities than differences.

LINKING ATTACHMENT SECURITY WITH RELATIONSHIP QUALITY AND INDIVIDUAL ADJUSTMENT

In Chapter 2, we suggested that attachment security is central to the style of relating that couples develop. Based on previous experiences with caregivers and other relationship partners, individuals gradually develop "mental models of attachment." In other words, they develop a set of expectations about other people and about the rewards and costs associated with close relationships. These expectations shape the way they approach their relationships, including how comfortable they feel with intimacy, and how anxious they are about issues concerning love and commitment.

For this reason, we were interested in the links between initial scores on the attachment dimensions (i.e., scores obtained at the beginning of the study) and later reports of couple and individual functioning. That is, we wanted to know whether attachment security affected the way that couples were faring later in the study, especially in the context of the transition to first-time parenthood.

We found that the attachment dimensions were clearly linked to both individual and couple adjustment. That is, secure attachment was associated with better psychological adjustment, and with more constructive and satisfying styles of relating to the spouse. This pattern was generally similar, irrespective of whether couples were dealing with new parenthood or not. (See Appendix C for more information about these associations.)

For both husbands and wives and for both groups, these links were particularly pervasive for the *"anxiety over relationships"* dimension of attachment. Specifically, there was support for links between anxiety over relationships and

- greater adjustment difficulties
  - more depression
  - more anxiety
  - more stress
- less effective style of caring for the spouse
  - less responsive care
  - more compulsive care
- less satisfaction with the marriage
  - less overall satisfaction
  - less satisfaction with time together
  - less satisfaction with problem-solving communication

In addition, for both new fathers and comparison husbands, anxiety over relationships predicted lower scores on sexual desire and sexual communication. Overall, these results suggest that basic insecurities about love and commitment contribute to adjustment problems for the anxious individual, and difficulties for the couple relationship.

By contrast, only two findings for the "discomfort with closeness" dimension of attachment tended to be consistent across gender and group: Discomfort with closeness was linked to less responsive caregiving, and to dissatisfaction with sexual communication. By definition, individuals who are uncomfortable with closeness generally prefer not to depend on others, or to have others depend on them. When this preference for independence and self-reliance is very strong, it is likely to interfere with the ability to "tune in" to partners' physical and emotional needs.

Given that the links between attachment dimensions and other measures generally applied to both groups, it seems that attachment security helps to foster a sense of well-being and more constructive patterns of interaction, regardless of whether couples are going through this particular adjustment period. This finding does not rule out the possibility that insecure attachment becomes more problematic when people face stressful events. Although the transition to parenthood is a time of change, only a minority of couples find it extremely stressful, or regard it as a serious threat to their relationships; for most, new parenthood is a time when partners look forward to sharing the joys and challenges of what is, after all, a "joint project." Attachment security is likely to have especially strong effects in situations that are highly stressful, or seen as threatening the relationship. Indeed, this claim is supported by previous studies comparing responses to major and minor conflicts, and by some of our findings concerning postnatal depression (reported in the next chapter).

STRESS AND COPING IN THE TRANSITION TO PARENTHOOD

A striking feature of the literature on first-time parenthood is the changing view of this transition. As we pointed out in Chapter 1, early studies usually portrayed the transition as a time of crisis, whereas that view has been challenged by more recent (and more sophisticated) research. Nevertheless, parenthood clearly brings new challenges, and for this reason, we wanted to explore parents' reports of stress and coping. We were interested in their overall perceptions of these issues, and in possible differences between mothers' and fathers' experiences. Finally, we were interested in the effects of attachment security on perceptions of stress and coping.

How Stressful was New Parenthood?

When the babies were about six weeks old, we asked the parents to describe the temperament of their infants, and also to report on the amount of strain associated with parenthood. The measure of infant temperament assessed fussiness, irritability, and the variability of the baby's mood. The measure of parenting strain was broader in focus: It assessed a range of common problems of infant care, such as lack of sleep, feeding problems, and uncertainty about the baby's health and progress, together with the amount of change required to partners' "normal" routines. (See Chapter 3 for sample items.)

Both these measures showed that parents' perceptions of stress varied enormously. For example, scores on the measure of infant temperament could range between 8 and 56, and in this sample, spanned virtually that entire range (from 10 to 55). Some parents (9 husbands and 11 wives) described their babies as easy to handle in every respect, but at the other extreme, some (4 husbands and 1 wife) saw their babies as irritable and extremely difficult to manage.

This wide variability in parents' perceptions of their babies' temperament was supported by the interviews that we conducted at about the same time (these interviews are discussed in detail in the previous chapter). On the one hand, some parents described their babies as "good, very easily managed," "very good – doesn't cry or get upset a lot," "great, not a whiner at all," "a dream of a baby," and even "so good – just perfect!" On the other hand, a smaller number of parents reported that their babies were "very tense," or "very irritable."

Results for the measure of parenting strain also showed the huge variability in parents' perceptions. Scores on this measure could range between 3 and 81, and couples' responses again spanned most of this range (from 10 to 72). Some parents (14 husbands and 8 wives) said that they had experienced almost none of the problems listed on the questionnaire, or had experienced them but not found them at all difficult to deal with. On the other hand, a similar number (8 husbands and 10 wives) reported having experienced almost all of the problems, and having found them quite difficult to manage. Not surprisingly, parents who rated their babies as more difficult in temperament reported more strain than other parents.

Men, Women, and the Stress of Parenthood. For both infant temperament and general parenting strain, there was widespread agreement in the reports of mothers and fathers. In other words, when one spouse reported that the baby was difficult to manage, or had required a great deal of adjustment to normal routines, the other usually described the situation in similar terms.

Despite this high level of agreement within each couple, mothers and fathers tended to differ in their *average* perceptions of parenting stress. With regard to infant temperament, mothers rated their babies as slightly easier to manage than did fathers (with average scores of 25.13 and 26.59, respectively). In contrast, however, mothers rated parenting as more stressful than did fathers (with average scores of 34.84 and 30.09, respectively).

Although these two findings might seem at odds with each other, they can both be understood in terms of women's greater involvement in the day-to-day care of their infants. At this stage of parenthood, most of the mothers in this sample (more than three-quarters) were providing full-time care for their infants. In addition, of those husbands who had taken some time off to support their wives after the birth, almost all had now returned to work. The slight difference in evaluations of infant temperament, then, probably reflects the fact that the mothers had had more contact with their babies, and more experience at trying to understand their needs and pacify them. At the same time, given their role as primary carer, it is not surprising that these mothers would be more aware than their husbands of the demands and disruptions caused by the new arrival.

How Did Couples Cope with the Demands of Parenthood?

As we discussed in Chapter 3, there are many different ways of coping with stressful events. Coping strategies are usually considered to fall into three broad classes: problem-focused coping, emotion-focused coping, and social support-seeking. Problem-focused strategies represent attempts to deal directly with the stressful situation (e.g., coming up with a number of solutions to the problem; following a plan of action). The aim of these strategies is to remove, or at least reduce, the source of stress. Emotion-focused strategies focus on the emotions evoked by the situation, rather than the situation itself (e.g., trying to forget the situation; engaging in self-blame). The aim of these strategies is to reduce the fear and anxiety that are often associated with stressful events. The third type of strategy, social support-seeking, involves turning to other people for help. The emphasis can be either on practical assistance (e.g., seeking advice from people who have relevant knowledge or experience) or on emotional support (e.g., sharing feelings with friends or family members).

Emotion-focused coping is generally regarded as the *least effective* type of strategy, because it does not directly address the problems that cause the stress. Of course, there are some situations (such as war) in which people have almost no control over the source of stress. In these situations, emotion-focused coping may be useful in helping individuals to deal with their sense of anxiety and helplessness. Usually, however, stressful situations can be improved to some extent by making use of support networks and by taking appropriate courses of action.

In this study, our focus was on the coping strategies that new mothers and fathers reported using to deal with the stresses of parenthood. (Unlike these couples, not all of those in the comparison group were facing a common stressful event; hence, it would be very difficult to understand the reasons behind their particular patterns of coping.)

Men, Women, and Coping Strategies. New mothers rated themselves as using all three coping strategies to a greater degree than did new fathers. Again, this finding can be understood in terms of the mothers' involvement as primary caregivers. In other words, these mothers were responsible for most aspects of the infants' daily care, including feeding, bathing, changing, and soothing. As a result, they would encounter a range of parenting issues and problems that might call for a range of different solutions.

Both mothers and fathers reported fairly low levels of emotion-focused coping; that is, they tended to report either not using these strategies at all, or using them only occasionally. On average, fathers reported "occasional" use of the various strategies classified as either problem-focused or support-seeking. Mothers also reported "occasional" use of problem-focused strategies, but said that they engaged in "quite a bit" of support-seeking.

Overall, then, the single most common type of coping strategy was *mothers' support-seeking*. As we noted earlier in this section, support-seeking can take many different forms, including talking about one's feelings, accepting sympathy and understanding, and obtaining practical advice from friends, family members, or professional people. Hence, support-seeking is clearly relevant to dealing with the different tasks and pressures of new parenthood.

Attachment, Stress, and Coping

In Chapter 2, we noted that the concepts of stress and coping are quite central to attachment theory, because different attachment styles are thought to reflect the different ways that individuals have learned to cope with stressful situations. Based on this argument, we expected that attachment security (as assessed at the beginning of the study) would be linked to important aspects of stress and coping. Specifically, we expected that men and women who felt more secure about their relationships would

- perceive themselves as having more resources to draw on
- find the demands of parenthood somewhat less stressful
- engage in more effective coping strategies.

Attachment Security and Coping Resources. Although stressful situations are taxing, they also represent a challenge, and part of that challenge involves drawing on the various resources that are available. As we discussed in Chapter 3, these resources can be either internal (such as a sense of self-worth and competence), or external (resources in the physical or social environment, such as friends and family members).

The measures we took at the beginning of the study clearly linked attachment security with greater coping resources. That is, for both husbands and wives, discomfort with closeness and anxiety over relationships were linked to lower self-esteem and perceptions of less availability of social support; the link between relationship anxiety and low self-esteem was particularly strong. These findings fit with attachment theorists' claim that our sense of security (or insecurity) is closely tied to our ideas about how competent and lovable we are, and how dependable and trustworthy other people are.

Attachment Security and the Stress of Parenthood. Support for the link between attachment security and the stress associated with new parenthood was more limited. Specifically, there was a weak link between fathers' relationship anxiety and their reports of greater parenting strain. In other words, fathers who tended to worry about their couple relationships found parenting slightly more stressful than other fathers. This higher level of stress is easily understood, given that the arrival of the infant changes the day-to-day interactions between partners, and reduces the time and energy available for attending to each other's needs and concerns.

Of course, the amount of stress associated with new parenthood is affected by a myriad of factors, and it would be naive to expect any single factor to account for the different perceptions held by different individuals. We have already seen that infant temperament (or "difficulty") was related to parenting strain. Other factors likely to be relevant include the amount of experience that parents have had in dealing with young babies, the quality of advice and support they receive, their financial resources, and so on.

Attachment Security and Coping Strategies. There was considerable support for the idea that parents who were secure in their relationships would engage in more effective forms of coping (i.e., problem-focused coping and support-seeking, rather than emotion-focused coping). Attachment dimensions predicted both support-seeking and emotion-focused coping (but not problem-focused coping).

More specifically, low levels of support-seeking were reported by mothers who described themselves as uncomfortable with intimacy; high levels of emotion-focused coping were reported by mothers who were anxious about their relationships, and by fathers who were either uncomfortable with intimacy or anxious about their relationships. (These findings are discussed more fully in the next section.) Overall, then, attachment insecurity was most strongly linked with emotion-focused coping, a form of coping that generally has little effect on reducing levels of stress.

A Model of Attachment, Stress, and Coping. So far, we have seen that attachment security was related to fathers' perceptions of parenting strain, and to mothers' and fathers' reports of coping resources and coping strategies. Together, these findings suggest a possible interplay among attachment, stress, and coping, as shown in Figure 7.3.

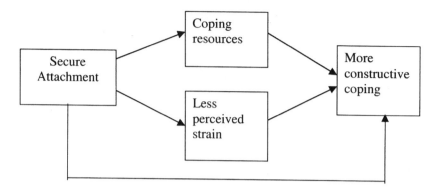

Figure 7.3. Model of attachment, stress, and coping.

The model shown in this figure contains two main propositions. First, the coping strategies that new parents adopt are affected by their attachment security, the availability of coping resources, and the level of stress they are experiencing. Second, the effects of attachment security on coping strategies may be explained, at least in part, by its links with coping resources or stress. For example, individuals who are very anxious about their relationships may see themselves as inadequate and other people as offering little support; in turn, these perceptions of limited resources may lead them to resort to emotion-focused coping.

We tested this model using a technique called structural equations modeling. In testing the model, we extended the results reported so far, by including the characteristics of *both* partners. That is, we asked how the coping strategies adopted by one spouse might be affected by the attachment security of both partners, and by both partners' resources and levels of parenting strain. Including the characteristics of both partners recognizes the mutual interdependence that is a hallmark of marriage: The behavior of one spouse is often affected quite strongly by the thoughts, feelings, and actions of the other.

In terms of understanding how spouses coped with parenthood, we found that the model was useful for predicting support-seeking and emotion-focused coping. Again, the findings for problem-focused coping were quite weak, and will not be discussed further.

Although the model was useful for understanding the factors related to *support-seeking*, it seemed that coping resources were not important in this regard. In fact, only husbands' level of parenting strain and wives' attachment security proved relevant. When husbands were more stressed by parenting, *both* partners engaged in more support-seeking. This finding suggests that husbands' stress adds to the overall difficulty of the adjustment, prompting husbands and wives to call on the advice and support of others.

Wives who felt uncomfortable with intimacy were *less* likely to seek support from others. This finding is not surprising, because people who are uncomfortable with high levels of intimacy prefer to be independent and to "keep to themselves." Nevertheless, as we noted earlier in this chapter, mothers generally reported that support-seeking was their preferred way of dealing with the demands of parenthood. Given the overall importance of support-seeking to new mothers, those who are reluctant to ask for help may find the pressures of parenting quite taxing.

On the other hand, when wives were uncomfortable with intimacy, their husbands were *more* likely to seek support from others. It seems that the self-reliant and somewhat distant behavior of these wives may encourage their husbands to seek advice and support in their broader social network. Conversely, when wives were anxious about their relationships, their husbands were *less* likely to report seeking support from others. Perhaps these husbands felt a need to focus on reassuring their wives and dealing with their concerns, rather than on interacting with members of their wider social network. These links between wives' insecurity and husbands' coping highlight the impact that one partner's issues and concerns can have on the other (as we noted earlier, spouses are "interdependent").

The findings for *emotion-focused coping* provided even stronger support for the model of stress and coping. Wives' emotion-focused coping was predicted by their own level of parenting strain, their own perception of available support, and their own sense of insecurity (both discomfort with closeness and anxiety over relationships). However, two links in the model were particularly strong: the effects of parenting strain and relationship anxiety. Wives engaged in *more* emotion-focused coping if they felt highly stressed or very anxious about their relationships (see Figure 7.4 for a summary of the findings, and see Appendix C for additional details of the tests of the model).

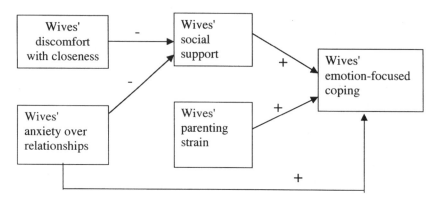

Figure 7.4. Factors predicting wives' emotion-focused coping.

Both high levels of parenting strain and high levels of relationship anxiety are likely to make new mothers feel quite vulnerable. By definition, when parenting is seen as very stressful, mothers are encountering a range of difficult problems and having to make major adjustments to their usual routines. Similarly, when wives are very anxious about their relationships, parenthood may raise serious questions about the impact of the new arrival on the couple relationship. These situations are likely to engender feelings of distress and vulnerability, and emotion-focused coping represents an attempt to deal with these negative emotional states.

Husbands' emotion-focused coping was predicted by their own and their partner's sense of insecurity (both discomfort with closeness and anxiety over relationships), as well as by both partners' coping resources and own level of parenting strain (as summarized in Figure 7.5). Although the overall picture is relatively complex, two particularly strong findings again emerged. First, husbands' relationship anxiety was strongly predictive of their low self-esteem, and hence of their involvement in emotion-focused coping. Second, husbands' level of parenting strain was also strongly predictive of their tendency to use emotion-focused coping. These effects of husbands' parenting strain and relationship anxiety are similar to those for wives.

In short, highly stressed and insecure spouses tended to use more emotion-focused coping, a response that is presumably driven by their more negative emotional state. Unfortunately, as we have already

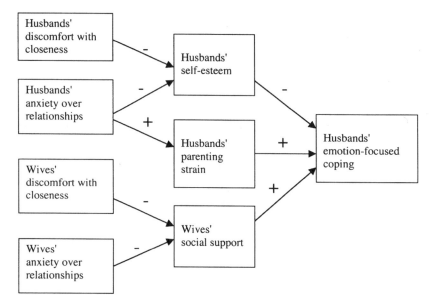

Figure 7.5. Factors predicting husbands' emotion-focused coping.

noted, emotion-focused coping often has little effect on reducing levels of stress. After all, a difficult situation is not usually altered by strategies such as trying to forget the whole thing, hoping for a miracle, engaging in self-blame, or keeping others from knowing about the extent of the problem. In Chapter 11, we look at this issue of the consequences (for individuals and their relationships) of the different coping strategies.

SUMMARY

When the babies were six weeks old, comparison of changes occurring since the first assessment showed few differences between the new parents and the childless couples. The exceptions were two aspects of relationship satisfaction: New mothers showed a drop in satisfaction with time together, but on the other hand, new mothers and fathers showed a drop in global distress (i.e., they were less likely to report general feelings of unhappiness in their relationships). These findings fit with common wisdom, which points to new parenthood as a time of both joys and challenges.

Responses to the challenges were varied, with new parents differing widely in their reports of general well-being, couple relationships, stress, and coping. Attachment security was a useful predictor of these aspects of adjustment. Discomfort with closeness was linked to less responsiveness to the spouse's needs, more dissatisfaction with sexual communication, and, for new mothers, reluctance to seek support from others. Anxiety over relationships played an even stronger role: This aspect of insecurity was linked with less adaptive ways of responding to the partner's needs and problems, lower relationship satisfaction, more depression, anxiety, and stress, and more emotion-focused coping. Clearly, some new parents were struggling with personal adjustment problems, as well as changes to the couple relationship. In the next chapter, we look more closely at a group of new mothers who were grappling with feelings of depression and inadequacy.

EIGHT

Dealing with Depression

Depression was another important issue that emerged from both interview and questionnaire responses when the new parents' babies were about six weeks old. At this point, some of the mothers acknowledged that they were having considerable difficulty with feelings of gloom, pessimism, and hopelessness. In this chapter, we focus on the experiences of these women. We wanted to understand the nature of the problems they were experiencing, to examine the factors that might be linked to their depression, and to see how they were faring at the end of the study.

POSTNATAL DEPRESSION

Studies of new mothers suggest that postnatal depression is not a rare phenomenon; in fact, between 8% and 15% of women may be affected by this problem (O'Hara, 1997). Although the defining characteristic of postnatal depression is "dysphoric" (or depressed) mood, this mood state is usually accompanied by other symptoms, such as extreme fatigue, strong feelings of guilt, and disturbances of sleep and appetite. A diagnosis of postnatal depression usually requires that these symptoms be present over a reasonable period of time, and affect the woman's ability to function effectively (O'Hara, 1997).

These diagnostic criteria highlight the scope of the problems associated with postnatal depression. When a new mother cannot function effectively, there are serious implications for her own adjustment, for the care and management of the baby, and for the couple relationship. In addition, the very concept of postnatal depression runs counter to popular images of motherhood, which focus on positive emotion, "maternal instinct," and the unfailing provision of care. In fact, as researchers have pointed out, feelings of depression can be particularly devastating at this point in the life cycle, because a woman and her family expect joy and happiness to be the order of the day, rather than sadness and despair.

What causes women to become depressed after childbirth? In attempting to answer this question, researchers have examined the role of a wide range of factors, including:

- background factors (e.g., level of education, financial resources)
- early experiences in family of origin (e.g., difficult relationship with own mother)
- personal adjustment difficulties (e.g., prior depression)
- biological factors (especially hormonal factors linked to the postdelivery period)
- obstetric factors (complications related to the delivery)
- infant factors (especially infant temperament)
- stressful life events (e.g., unemployment, illness in family members)
- aspects of the couple relationship (e.g., relationship dissatisfaction)
- lack of social support (from partner, friends, and family).

The main conclusion drawn from this research is that *no* single factor has received unambiguous support as a cause of postnatal depression. Nevertheless, some factors do appear to be much more important than others. There has generally been little support for the role of background and obstetric factors, and studies of relationship experiences in the family of origin have produced mixed findings. In contrast, there is a fair degree of support for the role of personal adjustment difficulties, infant temperament, and stressful life events (especially those events that have a direct impact on the mother's ability to care for her baby, such as severe illness in a dependent family member). Even stronger evidence exists for the importance of relationship factors, both within and beyond the marriage: Postnatal depression is more likely to occur when mothers receive little support from partner, friends, and family members, and when their marital relationship is marked by conflict or dissatisfaction (Murray & Cooper, 1997; O'Hara, 1997).

Because most of these factors were measured in our study, we were able to assess their relevance to depression in this sample of new mothers. In addition, we were interested in assessing the role of attachment insecurity, which has been largely neglected in the literature on postnatal depression.

IDENTIFYING DEPRESSED MOTHERS

To identify mothers who were suffering from depression, we examined scores on the depression scale that was completed at the second assessment. As noted when we described the measures in Chapter 3, instructions for this scale ask respondents to describe their feelings and concerns *over the past week*. That is, the items are designed to measure recent mood states, rather than the individual's typical or characteristic mood. For this reason, the scale can be quite useful for picking up changes in adjustment that may be linked to recent events.

At the same time, it is important to point out that the measure we used (the Depression Anxiety Stress Scales, or DASS; Lovibond & Lovibond, 1995) was not specifically designed to measure postnatal depression. This is because we needed the measure to be relevant to both men and women, to both transition and comparison couples, and at all three phases of the study. (As part of a separate study, some of the new mothers in our sample volunteered to complete another measure, the Edinburgh Postnatal Depression Scale. Of the 41 mothers who did so, five showed significant levels of postnatal depression. However, because we assured the women that data from the two studies would be kept totally separate, we could not link their scores back to those from our own study.)

As we discussed in Chapter 4, the items on the depression scale of the DASS deal with fairly severe symptoms of distress, and as would be expected in a normal sample, spouses in our study generally obtained fairly low scores. Further, overall levels of depression were similar for husbands and wives, for transition and comparison couples, and for the first and second assessment points.

Nevertheless, we were able to identify, among the new mothers, a group who were grappling with feelings of depression. Specifically, the researchers who developed the DASS have published normative data that allow individuals to be placed into one of five categories, depending on their scores on the depression scale: normal, mild depression, moderate depression, severe depression, and extremely severe depression. Using these criteria, 12 of the new mothers had scores that fell outside of the "normal" range. Of these women, seven were categorized as mildly depressed, three as moderately depressed, and two as extremely severely depressed. (It is important to note that members of the research team informed all participants about appropriate sources of counseling and other support, and that some participants used these ongoing services.)

DEPRESSION AND REPORTS OF NEW PARENTHOOD

One method that we used to investigate the experiences of these depressed women was to return to the interviews conducted six weeks after the birth of their babies, to see how they described their experiences of new parenthood. Four important points emerged from the interview material.

Husbands' Expressions of Concern

First, the high levels of maternal depression were evident from husbands' concerns about their wives' emotional states, particularly in the case of the severely depressed mothers. For example, in the most severe case of maternal depression, the husband interrupted the discussion of the "best part of parenthood" to raise his concerns about his wife's condition.

H: This probably isn't answering the question, but I – well, I'm not so much worried about this little one, because I think I can handle that. I'm worried – I'm much more worried about my wife – the way she's coping – *whether* she's coping, and stuff like that.
W: I'm not coping!
H: Like I think that, like the crying baby, I can deal with. It doesn't really worry me. Or it did worry me for the first couple of days, but then you get used to it. So dealing with the child, that's okay – but a crying wife is a bit harder to deal with.

Similarly, the husband of the other severely depressed mother expressed considerable concern about how his wife was coping with the demands of parenthood:

I worry more about my wife – her health, and also the big lifestyle change. And you know, she has always been one who really needs her sleep, and to see her getting her sleep broken and all. Like, all of that worries me, just in terms of making sure that she gets through each day and is all right for looking after the baby. So there have been quite a few changes that I have had to make personally, in terms of things I do around the house. So those are my two main concerns right now – my wife and my baby – and just working with what has to be done and keeping things going.

In line with the points made earlier in this chapter, this husband's expressions of concern highlight the complex problems that postnatal depression can create. When the mother has primary responsibility for infant care, but finds it difficult to function effectively, there are implications for *all* members of the family.

Multiple Difficulties

The second point to emerge from the interviews was the large number of difficulties, or "worst things," that these depressed wives reported in relation to parenting. (As we noted in Chapter 6, most couples raised only one or two issues when they were asked about the worst part of parenting.)

In the first extract above, we saw that the mother who was the most severely depressed explicitly noted that she was "not coping." In addition, she suggested that there were five "worst aspects" of parenting. The difficulties that this mother raised were as follows:

- lack of sleep ("not getting enough sleep – you just can't prepare for the fact that you're going to be awake every few hours")
- not knowing what to do to care for the baby ("just knowing how to deal with her; for instance, she only has little five-minute snoozes during the day and they say that's not enough for a newborn, but what can I do about it?")
- receiving contradictory advice ("I've got so tired of contradictory advice from people; it seems like I just have to make up my own mind about things")
- restrictions to lifestyle ("we used to just pack up whenever we felt like it and go to a nice restaurant, maybe once a week; and even little things, like trying to write a letter to a friend or something – you just can't do it")
- concerns over household tasks ("when the baby's asleep during the day, that's the only time I get to try to do things – but then you spend most of your day running around doing things for her").

Similarly, the other mother whose score on the depression scale placed her in the "extremely severe" category talked explicitly about "getting depressed." She commented that new parenthood had been "one big hell of a shock," and her husband expressed a similar reaction to the experiences of the first few weeks ("I thought it was hell, actually").

This mother went on to identify four of the difficulties that were commonly seen as "worst things": not knowing what to do, feeling "disconnected" from the baby, restrictions to lifestyle, and lack of social support. Further, in terms of social support, this mother raised both of the issues that seemed to give rise to feelings of being unsupported by others (see Chapter 6 for further discussion of these issues). That is, she was bothered not only by the absence of close family members ("I would have liked Mum to be here day and night, and I suppose I needed a bit more support"), but also by the presence of people who seemed to be trying to take control ("people who take over from you, and that sort of thing").

In addition, this highly depressed mother talked about two "worst things" that we did not discuss in Chapter 6, because they were mentioned so infrequently in the sample. First, she talked about the problem of increased conflict between herself and her husband ("we find that we're fighting more now, more than ever"). Second, she commented on the financial strain associated with parenthood ("and God, the money you need; even the little things; like we wonder how people that haven't planned for it can possibly do it").

Intensity of Problems

The third point raised by the interview material was that the depressed mothers not only reported a range of difficulties in their parenting, but also tended to see these difficulties as quite overwhelming. For example, one of the depressed mothers, when discussing the problem of lack of sleep, talked about how she had tried to force the baby to sleep, and commented: "I forced her so many times, I was going out of my mind." She also said that she was trying to look forward to a time in the future when "we're all sane again." Other mothers in this group talked about "it's been just awful – just feeling absolutely frantic," "having a lot of panic," "feeling deranged," "being just so terrified," and "it's very overwhelming because you just have no control."

These descriptions reveal the sense of helplessness that these mothers tended to feel, and the intensity of their fear that things would "go wrong." One mother worried every time her baby cried, because "I've heard a lot of stories about babies convulsing and having fits when they get too hot and when they get sick." Of course, one feature of depression is the tendency to expect the worst, and to see relatively normal events as potential catastrophes.

The Role of Lack of Sleep

The final point to emerge from the interviews was that the specific complaints raised by the depressed mothers were generally similar to those raised by other mothers, with the exception of lack of sleep. In other words, depressed and nondepressed mothers were equally likely to talk about such problems as not knowing what to do to care for the baby, and feeling the restrictions to lifestyle (although mothers who were very severely depressed mentioned a greater number of these problems).

In contrast, although many couples in the sample mentioned lack of sleep as the "worst thing," this issue was *more* likely to be raised by depressed mothers than by others. In Chapter 6, we saw how sleep deprivation was often associated with shortness of temper, and with difficulty in functioning effectively at home and at work. Hence, it is not surprising that lack of sleep and feelings of exhaustion are part of the constellation of problems that depressed wives tended to report. However, it is difficult to draw conclusions about patterns of "cause-and-effect" here. As we have already mentioned, lack of sleep is likely to create difficulties in everyday functioning, which may contribute to feelings of depression; at the same time, depression can also exacerbate sleeping difficulties. In fact, a vicious circle may develop, in which depression and sleep deprivation are bound up together.

This problem of disentangling the causes and effects of depression applies more generally. For instance, we have seen the breadth of difficulties that some of the new mothers were attributing to parenthood, but is not easy to explain *why* these mothers were having such a difficult time. Superficially, it seems that women who face a larger number of problems in their early weeks of parenting are more likely to experience depression. However, it is equally plausible that high levels of depression cause these mothers to see many aspects of parenting in a negative light. In other words, depression can *stem from* difficult experiences, but can also cause experiences to *seem* more difficult: When we are feeling "down," even minor problems can appear insurmountable. In a later section of this chapter, we address the question of the causes of depression in more detail.

Postnatal Depression and Postnatal Blues

Before we leave the interview material, it is important to note that the highly depressed mothers were *not* the only ones who talked about having felt unhappy or tearful. Some of the other mothers described such feelings, but reported that they were quite short-lived (e.g., "I was really teary in the evenings for the first week, when I couldn't work out what he needed and he wouldn't settle down.") For these couples, the temporary feelings of edginess and depression were something that they could already look back on and laugh about:

I had a bit of postnatal depression for about two days. It was a few weeks ago, and you know, I was just like "Boo hoo!" And then I was over it. [laughter]

Such reports of occasional tearfulness in the first few days of parenthood were relatively common, and quite different from the ongoing and diffuse depression that the smaller number of mothers reported. In other words, compared with postnatal depression, the condition known as postnatal blues is milder, more transient, and more common (O'Hara, 1997). Given the wide variability in emotional responses to parenthood, we were interested in identifying factors that might explain why some mothers experienced more severe depression than others.

WHAT FACTORS CONTRIBUTED TO DEPRESSION?

To gain a better understanding of factors that contribute to depression in the early weeks of motherhood, we turned to both questionnaire and interview data. Our general approach involved a technique called discriminant analysis, which looks for measures that discriminate between different groups of people. In this case, we were interested in comparing two groups: one consisting of the 12 mothers with "higher than normal" depression, and one consisting of all the other new mothers. We used this technique to address a number of questions related to the possible causes of depression.

Psychological Adjustment

The first question focused on levels of psychological adjustment at the start of the study. We wanted to see whether the mothers who were depressed *after* the birth had already been experiencing adjustment difficulties (depression, or other negative emotional states) *before* the arrival of the baby. In other words, we wanted to check whether the depression reported by these mothers was due simply to chronic adjustment problems.

To check this possibility, we compared the two groups of mothers in terms of their initial scores on the three scales of the DASS (depression, anxiety, and stress). There were no differences between the scores of the depressed and nondepressed mothers during the second trimester of pregnancy, suggesting that the adjustment difficulties that the former were reporting had developed quite recently. Further, their levels of depression could not be explained as a response to husbands' chronic adjustment difficulties: Their husbands were not unusually depressed, stressed, or anxious at the start of the study.

Interestingly, when we carried out a similar analysis for the women in the comparison group, we found a very different result: Those who were highly depressed at the second assessment had also been highly depressed at the beginning of the study. This finding suggests that the factors associated with wives' depression (at Time 2) were different for the transition and comparison groups. In particular, depression tended to reflect preexisting adjustment difficulties in the case of comparison wives, but not in the case of new mothers. Rather, depression in mothers seemed to be linked, at least *indirectly*, to experiences related to birth and parenthood.

Social Support

Our second question concerned the levels of social support that were available to the women. Based on previous studies, we thought that the depressed mothers might have felt that there was little support available to them from partners, friends, and family members. However, this was not so; in fact, depressed and nondepressed mothers reported similar levels of social support at the beginning of the study.

Feelings about the Pregnancy

Our third question was whether the depressed mothers, or their partners, had been unhappy about some aspect(s) of the pregnancy. In other words, was their depression linked to an unplanned or difficult pregnancy?

To answer this question, we compared the responses of the two groups to several questions asked during the first interview: whether the pregnancy was planned or unplanned, whether it was progressing normally, and how the husband and wife had reacted to finding out about the pregnancy (both initially, and at the time of the interview). Again, there were no differences between the scores of the two groups.

Factors Related to the Birth and the Infant

A fourth possibility was that the depressed wives had experienced particularly difficult births, or had unusually difficult babies, and that the physical and emotional stress of these experiences had contributed to their unhappy emotional state. To check this explanation, we first compared the responses of the two groups of mothers to relevant questions asked at the second interview: number of hours in labor, extent of pain relief used, extent of surgical intervention required, whether the labor had proceeded as expected, and whether the baby was born before term. Again, these measures did not differentiate the two groups.

To assess the role of infant characteristics, we compared the ratings of infant temperament completed by depressed and nondepressed mothers, and by their partners, six weeks after the birth. Interestingly, depressed mothers rated their babies as difficult to manage, but their husbands did not. As we saw in the previous chapter, however, mothers and fathers generally agreed in their assessments of their babies' temperament. Hence, it seems that the depressed mothers' assessments of their babies as "difficult" might be due, at least in part, to their negative mood. In other words, seeing the baby as difficult might be a *consequence* of depression, rather than a *cause* of it. An alternative explanation is that these babies *were* very difficult to handle, and that the fathers were so uninvolved in child care that they failed to recognize the difficulty. However, the diary data (detailed in the next chapter) did not support this explanation: Husbands of the depressed women were just as involved in baby-related and general household tasks as other new fathers. In short, we cannot conclude that infant temperament was an important factor contributing to postnatal depression.

Relationship Factors

Having found little evidence of preexisting depression, lack of support, unwanted pregnancy, and difficult birth as major causes of maternal depression, we turned to a consideration of couples' relationships. That is, we asked whether the marital relationships of the depressed mothers might be more troubled than most. Because we wanted to identify factors that *contribute* to depression during the transition to parenthood, we were particularly interested in the relationship measures taken at the beginning of the study. (As we saw with the results for infant temperament, a link between depression and other variables is difficult to interpret, if these variables are measured at roughly the same point in time.)

We investigated this issue by comparing the two groups of mothers in terms of their own and their husbands' scores on key relationship variables: overall marital satisfaction, and the two aspects of attachment security (discomfort with closeness, and anxiety over relationships). The two groups differed, but only in terms of the women's anxiety over relationships. Wives who were depressed six weeks after the birth had reported significantly higher relationship anxiety than other wives at the beginning of the study (with average scores of 45.60 and 36.43, respectively). In other words, they had reported a tendency to worry about their partners' love and commitment, and about the strength and stability of their relationships.

It is important to keep in mind that these wives were *not* particularly depressed at the beginning of the study, despite having felt insecure about their relationships. Overall, these findings suggest that anxiety over relationships, *when coupled with* a major transition such as first-time parenthood, may predispose some women to become depressed. As we suggested in Chapter 2, then, the effects of insecurity may become more apparent when people face challenging situations. (In Chapter 7, we noted that attachment security tended to predict better individual and couple functioning, regardless of whether couples were facing new parenthood or not. However, as the present findings show, it was only in the context of parenthood that insecurity triggered depression in women who showed "normal" adjustment at the start of the study.)

THE COURSE OF DEPRESSION

Given the difficulties the depressed mothers were experiencing, a crucial question is how they and their partners were faring at the end of the study. According to previous studies, postnatal depression often lasts for several months; in addition, some women experience ongoing symptoms, although these symptoms are usually less severe than in the period following the birth (O'Hara, 1997). Of course, where symptoms are severe or long-lasting, professional help becomes important, and a variety of treatment methods are available, ranging from music and massage therapy through to more traditional forms of counseling and therapy (Cooper & Murray, 1997; Field, 1997).

To look at the outcomes for depressed mothers in our study, we examined the questionnaire responses obtained when the babies were about six months old (these data from the final assessment are considered in more detail in Chapter 11). We used the same method as before to compare the groups of depressed and nondepressed mothers, focusing this time on two key issues: psychological adjustment and relationship quality.

Adjustment Outcomes

Our first question concerned levels of psychological adjustment. In other words, were these women still feeling depressed at the end of the study, or had their scores returned to their initial "normal" levels? And how were their husbands affected by the situation?

Unfortunately, the adjustment outcomes for these women and their partners were not good. At the final assessment, they continued to report more depression than the other mothers. In addition, they were now reporting higher levels of stress than other mothers. Equally important, their husbands were reporting high levels of anxiety (general anxiety, as measured by the DASS), although they had not done so at the beginning of the study, or when the babies were six weeks old. These findings are summarized in the upper section of Table 8.1. Of course, in evaluating these outcomes, we need to keep in mind that the babies were still only six months old at the end of the study; further follow-up would be needed to assess long-term outcomes.

Relationship Outcomes

Our second question concerned the outcomes for couples' relationships. That is, given that insecure attachment seemed to be linked to the onset of mothers' depression, we wanted to see whether these marital relationships became more secure once the spouses had settled into parenthood.

Measure	Couples with Depressed Wives	Couples with Nondepressed Wives
TABLE 8.1. Adjustment and Relationship Outcomes (Time 3) for Couples with Depressed and Nondepressed Wives		
Psychological adjustment		
Wives' depression	6.22	2.42
Wives' stress	11.44	5.76
Husbands' anxiety	2.89	0.87
Couple relationships		
Wives' anxiety over relationships	46.89	36.19
Wives' discomfort with closeness	53.89	44.71
Husbands' anxiety over relationships	44.44	35.03

Again, unfortunately, the outcomes for these couples were not promising. At the end of the study, wives in this group continued to report fairly high levels of relationship anxiety, and were now also reporting high discomfort with closeness. Further, their husbands were reporting high levels of relationship anxiety, although they had not done so earlier in the study. (See the lower section of Table 8.1.)

In other words, the wives were now reporting a more general sense of insecurity in their relationships, and the husbands now seemed to share their wives' concerns over issues of love, commitment, and the stability of the relationship. Although these couples were still reporting reasonably high levels of relationship satisfaction, it would be surprising if their increasing sense of insecurity did not eventually impact on their evaluations of the relationship.

DEPRESSION AND RELATIONSHIP PROCESSES

Collectively, these findings suggest that the depression experienced by some new mothers is best understood as part of an ongoing *process,* which clearly affects both husbands and wives. For wives who tend to worry about whether their partners really love them and whether their relationships are strong enough to withstand challenges, the arrival of the first baby seems to be quite a difficult time. This finding is not hard to understand: The attachment bond between husband and wife has to accommodate the new arrival, and the changes in relating that accompany this event may seem threatening to those who are not confident of their partner's feelings.

Earlier in this chapter, we saw that depressed mothers find many aspects of parenting difficult, are likely to expect the worst, and are often overwhelmed by feelings of panic and lack of control. Their husbands seem to be well aware of their wives' fragile emotional states, and are generally eager to help, but their situation is not easy either. In the following extract, one husband describes the strain he has been under, as he has tried to deal with demands at home and at the workplace:

H: There are expectations at work, related to my position. There are a few people at work – the older guys – who have said to me "You leave the baby for your wife to look after." You know: "You're the one earning the income," and whatever. And that's the way it was – I mean, they're older, and that's the way it was for them. And they don't understand – but I can't leave W if she's a mess.

W: Thanks!

H: Let me finish – I mean if she stays up all night, and gets up, and the next day she's dealing with the baby all day, it really knocks her around. So I'll help in the middle of the night. But it has been tough at work, because I'm not getting as much sleep, so I'm not as alert as I was and I can't do as much.

In our discussion of stress and coping (in the previous chapter), we noted that in very close relationships, such as marriage, partners are highly interdependent. In other words, each person's thoughts, feelings, and actions have a strong impact on the other. Of course, this interdependence can be a great benefit to partners, as they are able to share their experiences and rely on each other for comfort, support, and understanding. At the same time, it also means that negative thoughts and emotions are often shared. In fact, depending on the way that spouses communicate their own concerns and respond to those of the partner, negativity can actually intensify.

This is likely to have been the case for some of these depressed mothers and their partners. By the time the babies were six months old, the mothers reported feeling quite stressed, and were also anxious and uncomfortable about key aspects of their relationships (love, commitment, and intimacy). At this point, their husbands also reported feeling anxious, both in terms of general feelings of anxiety, and in terms of inse-curities about their relationships. This kind of cycle, in which the reac-tions of one partner affect the adjustment of the other, can also be seen in the next chapter, in which we relate the diary reports of household work to spouses' feelings about themselves and their relationships.

SUMMARY

A number of the new mothers in this sample were feeling very depressed in the weeks following childbirth. Their feelings of depres-sion and inadequacy were evident from the interviews we conducted, as well as from the structured measure of depression. These mothers reported finding many aspects of parenthood difficult and stressful, and tended to worry a great deal about things that might go wrong. Levels of depression were not related to women's prior adjustment, to feelings about the pregnancy, or to birth complications. On the other hand, the depressed mothers were more anxious about their relation-ships at the beginning of the study, suggesting that the combination of insecurity and the stresses of parenthood may trigger feelings of depression. At the end of the study, these mothers were still feeling depressed and insecure, and their husbands were also reporting a sense of insecurity. Again, these results highlight the key role of a secure couple bond in the transition to parenthood: When one partner feels insecure, there are likely to be implications for the spouse and for the functioning of the relationship.

NINE

Men, Women, and Household Work:
The Diaries

"The worst thing is the sharing, or rather the nonsharing,
of the responsibilities – like getting up in the night and doing
things like that."

One of the most consistent findings from studies of new parenthood concerns the importance of the allocation and performance of household tasks. As we discussed in Chapter 1, new parents often report that they had not fully anticipated the amount of work involved in parenthood, or the difficulty they would experience in maintaining equitable and nontraditional patterns of domestic work.

Similarly, when couples in the transition group were asked about the "worst part" of parenting (see Chapter 6), several spouses raised issues concerning the division of household labor. These issues often centred on the different expectations and roles of husbands and wives. For example, one new father noted that the reality of parenthood had come as quite a shock to him, because he had expected to be greeted by a clean and organized household when he came home from work at the end of each day:

I used to spend every holiday at my cousins' farm, and I suppose it gave me this false impression – that I would go out to work, come home, and everything would be spotless; there'd be food on the table waiting for me, and all that type of thing. So the first week after the baby was born, I used to get really angry, because nothing would have been done.

Wives' own high standards for housework also created difficulties for some new parents. As one new father said of his wife:

She just won't slow down. She's trying to do everything, and she won't sleep when the baby sleeps during the day. But it's a question of balancing things, and I think you have to set some priorities – like it doesn't matter if the floor doesn't get cleaned.

The diaries that couples completed for this study allowed us to examine these issues of roles and task performance in greater depth. As we described in Chapter 3, spouses were asked to keep individual diaries over four consecutive days from Friday to Monday, detailing their involvement in various household and baby-related tasks. They were asked to indicate how much time they spent performing each task on each day, and whether the task was carried out alone, or together with the spouse. They also rated each task in terms of whether they thought that the amount of effort that the spouse expended on the task was fair, or should be increased or decreased. All spouses were asked to report on the following eight household tasks:

- Cooking meals
- Taking care of bills/banking
- Washing and hanging out clothes
- Doing the grocery shopping
- Doing the dishes
- Cleaning the house
- Doing the gardening
- Ironing clothes

In addition, a list of eight baby-related tasks was included in the diary records that were given to spouses in the transition group. (As we outlined in Chapter 3, the babies were about three months old at the time the diary records were completed.) The baby-related tasks were as follows:

- Changing the baby
- Feeding the baby
- Bathing the baby
- Putting the baby to sleep
- Preparing bottles, food, etc., for the baby
- General care of the baby (playing, comforting)
- Tending to the baby during the night
- Tending to baby's medical needs (taking baby to doctor, clinic, or chemist)

The diaries were completed by 83 husbands and wives in the transition group, and 76 husbands and wives in the comparison group. As we noted earlier, the diary records required couples to provide a number of ratings for each household and baby-related task for each of the four days. For those couples who were already feeling very pressured by the various demands on their time, this requirement may have seemed rather daunting. However, couples were very conscientious about recording their involvement in the various tasks; only one couple failed to return the diary records, but went on to complete the remainder of the study.

AMOUNT OF TIME SPENT ON TASKS

A major purpose of the diary records was to allow us to document the amount of time that couples were spending on household and baby-related tasks. This information helps us understand how couples were juggling the various demands on their time.

Total Time Spent on Household Tasks

The first question we wanted to address was whether the total amount of time spent on household tasks over the four-day period differed according to group (transition versus comparison) and gender. (At this stage, because we wanted to compare results across the two groups, we could focus only on general household tasks.)

We found that, overall, new parents spent significantly more time doing household tasks than did comparison couples. In addition, overall, wives spent more time on household tasks than their husbands did. Finally, we found that new mothers spent a *particularly* large amount of time on these tasks (even when the effects of group and gender, as just discussed, were taken into account). These findings are shown in Figure 9.1.

This finding is not totally surprising, given that the majority of women in the transition group (more than two-thirds) were not working outside the home at this point in time. When new mothers care for their children on a full-time basis, there is likely to be an expectation that they take on extra responsibility for the running of the home. In fact, data on patterns of household work suggest that when wives become parents, their hours of unpaid work increase by as much as 90% (Bittman, 1991).

Similarly, husbands' lesser contribution to household tasks may be explained, in large part, by their greater involvement in paid employment. As Figure 9.1 shows, for the comparison group (where both spouses were generally in full-time paid employment), there was a relatively small difference between the contributions of husbands and wives.

Another way of examining the link between husbands' paid employment and their work around the home is to compare patterns of household work on weekdays with those at weekends, when husbands'

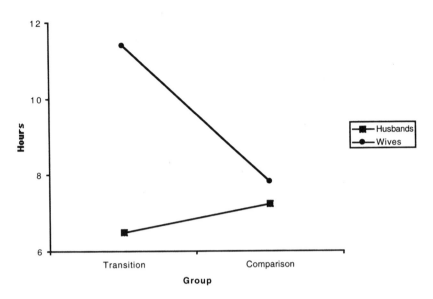

Figure 9.1. Total hours spent on household tasks according to group and gender.

availability is usually much greater. When we looked at the weekend records only, we found no difference between transition and comparison couples in time spent on household tasks, but overall, wives were still doing more housework than husbands. In contrast, the results for the weekday records paralleled those for the four-day period as a whole: Time spent on household tasks was higher for new parents and for women, and particularly high for new mothers (see Table 9.1).

Total Time Spent on Baby-Related Tasks

For the new parents, we were also interested in the extent of difference between mothers and fathers in the total amount of time spent on baby-related tasks. Overall, across the four-day period, mothers spent much more time on these tasks than fathers did (with averages of 37.95 hours versus 12.73, respectively). This difference applied both on the weekdays and at the weekends, although it was somewhat smaller at the weekends (see Table 9.2).

These findings certainly support the claim that mothers who provide full-time care for their young children also take primary responsi-

TABLE 9.1. Total Hours Spent on Household Tasks by Transition and Comparison Spouses	
WEEKEND	
Transition group	
Husbands	4.15 hours
Wives	5.30 hours
Comparison group	
Husbands	4.22 hours
Wives	4.72 hours
WEEKDAY	
Transition group	
Husbands	2.32 hours
Wives	6.09 hours
Comparison group	
Husbands	3.00 hours
Wives	3.10 hours

bility for the general running of the home. New mothers in this study reported spending more than 12 hours each day on infant care and other household tasks. Given this heavy load of routine domestic work, it is easy to see why some of these mothers were rather unhappy about the decline in "quality couple time" (see Chapter 7).

Parenthood and Time on Tasks: Different Approaches?

Although the general trends we have discussed so far point to the effects of group (comparison versus transition) on patterns of household work, it is important to acknowledge the wide differences *within* each group. We were particularly interested in focusing on the group of

TABLE 9.2. Total Hours Spent on Baby-Related Tasks by Transition Spouses	
WEEKEND	
Husbands	7.74 hours
Wives	18.42 hours
WEEKDAY	
Husbands	4.99 hours
Wives	19.53 hours

new parents, and looking for different types of couples, in terms of the relative contributions made by husbands and wives.

To examine this issue, we used a technique called cluster analysis. The analysis was based on the relative contributions of fathers and mothers to household and baby-related tasks (i.e., the ratio of number of hours spent by the husband, to number of hours spent by the wife). Cluster analysis identifies subgroups marked by particular patterns of scores, and pointed to three different groups of couples among our sample of new parents.

In the first group (consisting of 22 couples), husbands were quite involved with baby-related tasks; that is, their involvement with the baby was not much less than that of their wives. They were slightly less involved in household tasks, but still spent almost two-thirds as much time as their wives did on these tasks. In the second group (26 couples), husbands were very heavily involved with household tasks, and actually did just as much as their wives in this area. However, they had relatively little involvement in baby-related tasks, spending about one-quarter of the time that their wives did on these tasks. Finally, in the third group (33 couples), husbands were doing much less work than their wives on both types of tasks (about one-quarter to one-third of the hours spent by wives).

These results are interesting because they show that husbands differ not only in their general readiness to contribute to domestic work, but also in the *type* of work they are prepared to perform. In particular, the domestic arrangements of the second group of couples suggest that some husbands, while wanting to support their wives at this time, may not feel comfortable about being heavily involved in caring for the baby. Of course, the division of labor adopted by couples also reflects the preferences of the wives, some of whom may see baby care as primarily their own domain.

Time Spent on Specific Tasks

We also wanted to look at the amount of time spent on the specific tasks that we sampled, especially in terms of differences between men and women. For comparison couples, only four of the eight household tasks showed a gender difference: Wives spent more time cooking meals, washing and hanging out clothes, and cleaning the house, but husbands spent more time gardening. Not surprisingly, the results for these four tasks are in line with traditional notions of what constitutes "woman's work" and "man's work."

For new parents, gender differences in contributions to household tasks were even more marked, with husbands and wives differing in their amount of involvement in all eight tasks. Again, the specific effects were generally in line with traditional gender roles: Wives spent more time on every task, except for gardening. The stronger gender difference among new parents fits with the findings of other studies (see Chapter 1), and can be explained in terms of both expectations and experience. We have already mentioned that full-time child care and homemaking responsibilities tend to be seen as a "package deal"; in addition, when faced with the extra demands of parenting, partners often fall into a pattern of each doing "what they know best."

In terms of infant care, wives in the transition group spent more time than their husbands on all eight tasks. The difference in men's and women's contributions to these tasks is illustrated in Figure 9.2, which shows the total number of hours spent on each task across the four-day period.

As this figure shows, the *relative* contributions of fathers and mothers differed across the eight tasks. In general, these differences tend to be accounted for by practical considerations, such as who is usually available to meet a particular need. For example, the largest disparity was for "feeding the baby," reflecting the fact that most of the new mothers were still breast-feeding their infants at this point. Taking the baby to the doctor or clinic was another task done mostly by mothers, presumably because these visits usually take place during times when fathers are likely to be at work. On the other hand, fathers tended to have a greater input into the "general care" of the baby, a category that included playing with the baby and providing comfort when needed. This finding is in line with other research showing that fathers often spend more time playing with their infants than doing baby-related "chores."

Time on Tasks: Summary

Overall, then, the measures of "time spent on tasks" suggest that parenthood tends to increase the gender division in domestic work, as

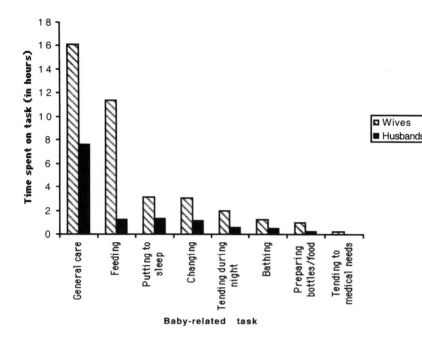

Figure 9.2. Time spent by new mothers and fathers on baby-related tasks.

spouses contend with the many pressures on their time. This response to parenthood has been reported by several other researchers (see Chapter 1). It is also illustrated by the interview material presented in Chapter 6; for example, one new mother regretted the fact that she and her spouse were becoming like the traditional family, "where the woman brings up the baby and the man makes the money." At the same time, we have seen that couples facing first-time parenthood differ in their approaches to domestic work, with some husbands being much more involved than others.

SHARING OF TASKS AND RESPONSIBILITIES

Generally, then, despite women's greater involvement in baby-care and other household tasks, husbands in this study were clearly taking on significant responsibilities around the home. Given this finding, we were interested in looking more closely at the extent of task *sharing* within couples.

We examined this issue from two perspectives: first, in terms of joint responsibility for tasks (i.e., where both spouses contributed to the same tasks), and second, in terms of joint activity (where spouses actually performed tasks together, as a couple). It is important to note the difference between these two ways of looking at how couples share tasks. Joint responsibility indicates that husband and wife both performed a given task, such as cleaning the house, at some point in the four-day period. However, they would not record this task as "shared," or joint activity, if the husband did his share of housecleaning on Saturday, while the wife did hers on Friday and Monday.

Joint Responsibility

We measured the amount of joint responsibility for tasks by tallying the number of tasks that had been performed by both the husband and the wife, at some time during the four-day period. Hence, for each set of tasks (household and baby-related), scores for joint responsibility could range from 0 to 8.

Both transition and comparison couples showed substantial joint responsibility for the eight household tasks. The average number of these tasks performed by both spouses was 4.10 in the transition group, and 4.40 in the comparison group (these numbers were not significantly different). Overall, about two-thirds of couples reported having shared at least four of the eight tasks. In fact, these figures undoubtedly underestimate the overall extent of joint responsibility, because our definition required that a given task be performed by both spouses *within* the four-day period covered by the diary records.

Among new parents, joint responsibility for the eight tasks of infant care was even more evident. The average number of tasks shared during the four-day period was 4.73, and more than 80% of couples reported having shared at least four of these tasks. Again, these figures probably underestimate the overall extent of joint responsibility. For example, very few couples reported any involvement in tending to the medical needs of the baby, simply because the babies were generally quite healthy. For this reason, the amount of "joint responsibility" was negligible for this task, although husbands and wives would be very likely to cooperate in this area if the need arose.

Joint Activity

As we mentioned earlier in this chapter, spouses were asked to indicate whether each task was carried out alone, or together with the spouse. In providing this information each day, they were told that if any part of the task was done together on that day, then they should record that task as "shared." Based on this information, joint (or collective) activity was defined as the number of tasks that were done *together* by husband and wife.

For the full sample of couples, the average number of household tasks performed together over the four-day period was 3.78 (out of a possible total of 32). This number is fairly low, partly because several couples (about 10%) reported *no* collective performance of household tasks. Again, however, there was wide variation in the sample, with some couples reporting up to 14 tasks performed together over the four days.

Collective performance of household tasks was lower for new parents (with an average of 3.24 tasks over the four-day period) than comparison couples (average of 4.36 tasks). This finding again supports the idea that parenthood leads to increasing separation of household duties. The lower levels of collective activity can be easily understood, given that one spouse needs to be tending to the new baby for much of the time.

This point brings us to the issue of collective performance of baby-care tasks. Among the new parents, an average of 7.38 collective baby-related tasks (out of 32) were reported over the four days. Very few couples reported no collective involvement in infant care, and some couples reported up to 20 tasks performed together over this period. In short, for new parents, collective involvement in domestic chores was likely to centre around the needs of the infant.

EVALUATION OF SPOUSES' EFFORT

In describing men's and women's involvement in domestic work, a crucial question is how satisfied partners are with each other's task performance. We know from the figures already presented that husbands spend less time performing chores around the home than wives do. However, if wives see this lower input as justified by the extra time that husbands devote to paid employment, they may be quite satisfied with this situation. Consistent with this argument, previous research has found that mothers often report seeking a sense of *fairness,* rather than equal sharing of household tasks (e.g., Goodnow & Bowes, 1994; Wolcott & Glezer, 1995).

To examine this issue, we used two measures, both based on individuals' ratings of their spouses' effort: perceptions of unfairness or inequity (the absolute difference between partners' current and desired effort), and desired spousal effort (taking account of whether more or less effort was desired from the spouse).

Perceptions of Unfairness

Scores on the measure of perceived unfairness could range from 0 to 2, where 0 indicates no unfairness and 2 indicates a great deal of unfairness. For household tasks, spouses generally saw each other's overall effort as reasonably equitable, with the average score on this measure being 0.29. Men and women did not differ on this measure, and neither did transition and comparison couples. For baby-related tasks, perceptions of unfairness were even lower, with an average score of 0.19. Again, men and women did not differ in their perceptions of unfairness.

Earlier in this chapter, we described three types of couples among the sample of new parents, defined by the extent of husbands' involvement in domestic chores: Some husbands were heavily involved in ordinary household tasks, some focused their involvement on baby-related tasks, and others showed low levels of involvement across both types of tasks. Rather surprisingly, neither husbands nor wives in these three groups differed in their perceptions of unfairness for household tasks.

They did differ, however, in their perceptions of unfairness for baby-related tasks: When husbands showed low levels of involvement across *both* types of tasks, husbands and wives tended to acknowledge this inequity (with an average score of .30). Put another way, both husbands and wives saw husbands' low involvement as somewhat unfair, although we have no way of telling from our data whether the husbands were prepared to remedy the situation.

Interestingly, spouses in the other two groups showed very low scores on perceptions of unfairness for baby-related tasks (around .12). In other words, it did not seem to matter whether husbands contributed to general household chores or to infant care; as long as they were making a substantial effort in *one* area, spouses accepted the situation as fair. Again, this finding emphasizes that there is no one "right way" for couples to negotiate home duties. In addition, it seems that couples are usually able to look at each other's contribution in terms of "the bigger picture," rather than focusing on dissatisfactions in one area.

Desired Spousal Effort

For desired spousal effort, scores could range from –2 to +2, where positive scores indicate a desire for the spouse to increase their effort, scores near zero indicate satisfaction with current effort, and negative scores indicate a desire for decreased effort. For every household task except gardening, these scores differed for men and women (regardless of whether they were in the transition or comparison group). In each case, husbands wanted their wives to either *decrease* or *maintain* their current effort, whereas wives wanted husbands to *increase* their effort. Although this gender difference was consistent across seven out of eight tasks, we need to acknowledge that the average scores were very small. In other words, consistent with our findings for perceptions of unfairness, the average amount of desired change was small.

For three of the eight household tasks (bills and banking, doing the dishes, and gardening), there were also differences between the transition and comparison couples. For each of these three tasks, the comparison couples wanted spouses' involvement to remain much as it was, whereas the new parents reported wanting a small increase in the spouse's effort.

The most interesting finding for household tasks, however, was that the difference between husbands' and wives' perceptions of effort was stronger for new parents than for comparison couples. This pattern applied to five of the eight tasks: washing and hanging out clothes, doing the grocery shopping, doing the dishes, cleaning the house, and ironing the clothes. In other words, new parenthood seemed to *accentuate* husbands' tendency to see their wives as "doing too much," and wives' tendency to see their husbands as "not doing enough." Of these two "pushes for change," however, wives' was somewhat stronger: New mothers clearly wanted their husbands to become more involved in household chores, particularly those that are typically seen as "woman's work."

Perhaps men are somewhat reluctant to take on these tasks, partly because the tasks are not seen as falling within the traditional male role, and partly because men do not see themselves as competent to perform them. Of course, these two reasons for avoiding particular tasks are closely related: Competence comes with experience, and if husbands are not performing these tasks regularly, they are unlikely to gain the skills. For some couples, there is also the problem of women having high standards for household tasks, and displaying dissatisfaction when the tasks are not performed to their liking (Emmons, Biernat, Tiedje, Lang, & Wortman, 1990).

In the area of baby care, there was a significant difference between husbands' and wives' perceptions of effort for all eight tasks. Again, in every case, husbands wanted their wives to *decrease* their involvement in infant care, and wives wanted husbands to *increase* their involvement. For this set of tasks, these two "pushes for change" were roughly equal in strength. It is important to note, however, that the gender difference was most pronounced for the more challenging or unpleasant aspects of infant care: tending to the baby in the night, changing the baby, and putting the baby to sleep. Interestingly, although these less pleasant tasks were the ones for which wives particularly wanted more effort from their spouses, they were not the tasks that husbands were performing least (according to Figure 9.2). Rather, it seems that when tasks are less pleasant, any differences in spouses' inputs are salient and can become a source of complaint.

Overall, then, across both kinds of tasks, we see that husbands tend to want their wives to put in less effort and wives want their husbands to put in more effort. This result suggests, rather ironically, a simple solution to the dissatisfaction with spouses' effort: If husbands became more involved in getting the work done, their wives could reduce their own effort. Of course, many factors prevent this approach from being a simple or universal "solution." For example, competing demands on men's time affect their availability for doing things around the home, and traditional expectations of role performance support this division of labor. In addition, as we suggested earlier, women's high standards for performance of household and baby-related tasks are also likely to be relevant, especially if the spouses differ in terms of their standards for cleanliness and tidiness, and ideas about the amount of attention babies actually need.

DOMESTIC WORK AND ADJUSTMENT TO NEW PARENTHOOD

Another important issue that we wanted to address from the diary reports was the link between task performance and adjustment to new parenthood. In other words, we wanted to know how task performance during this transition period impacted on the individual and the couple. To examine this issue, we linked the diary reports to the questionnaires that the new parents completed both at the beginning of the study, and at the end (other results from the final assessment are presented in Chapter 11).

The first clear finding was that questionnaire measures of individual and couple adjustment were linked to the diary reports of *perceptions of unfairness,* but not to the reports of time spent on tasks. (We go on to explore the impact of perceptions of unfairness throughout this section.) In other words, we see again that the crucial issue is not the actual amount of time that spouses put into household and baby-related chores, but rather, whether the extent of their effort is seen as fair or unfair.

The second consistent finding was the importance of *husbands' initial feelings* about themselves and their relationships. When husbands were depressed, and when they were insecure or dissatisfied with their relationships at the beginning of the study, they were more likely to perceive domestic work patterns (household *and* baby care) as unfair. In addition, when husbands were depressed, anxious, or dissatisfied with their relationships at the beginning of the study, their *wives* were more likely to perceive domestic work patterns as unfair. In contrast, wives' initial feelings about themselves and their relationships did not predict either partner's perceptions of unfairness. (Appendix C provides further details of the associations between diary reports and questionnaire measures.)

We also found that the adjustment measures taken at the *end* of the study were related more strongly to *husbands' perceptions of unfairness* than to wives' perceptions. When husbands saw domestic work patterns as unfair, they became more stressed over the course of the study, and their wives became more stressed, depressed, and anxious, and more dissatisfied with their relationships. These negative outcomes were associated most strongly with husbands' perceptions of unfairness in the area of baby care. Although wives' perceptions of unfairness were less consistently linked to outcome measures, one important finding emerged: When wives saw their husbands' involvement in baby care as unfair, those husbands became more anxious about their relationships (i.e., more insecure) over the course of the study.

These findings suggest that the division of labor plays a very important role in the transition to parenthood, and also point to the delicate interplay between husbands and wives. Although husbands' perceptions of unfairness were predicted only by their own psychological adjustment and relationship evaluations, wives ended up being deeply affected by this state of affairs. This situation is summed up in Figure 9.3.

Similarly, wives' perceptions of unfairness were predicted by their husbands' psychological adjustment and relationship evaluations, and had implications for husbands' later feelings of security. This situation is illustrated in Figure 9.4.

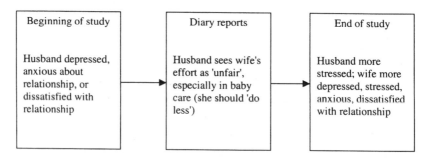

Figure 9.3. Links between husbands' perceptions of unfairness and partners' reports of individual and couple functioning.

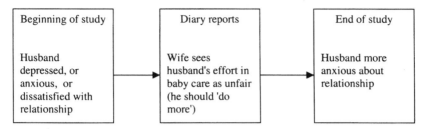

Figure 9.4. **Links between wives' perceptions of unfairness and partners' reports of individual and couple functioning.**

Overall, we have seen that the strongest and most consistent finding was the negative effect of *husbands' perceptions of "unfair" patterns of infant care.* For this reason, it is interesting to speculate about what these husbands may have been doing that contributed to their own feelings of stress and to their wives' increasing levels of depression, stress, anxiety, and relationship dissatisfaction. We know that husbands generally wanted their wives to decrease their effort on baby-related tasks. Hence, it seems that husbands who felt quite strongly about this issue may have been missing the shared couple time and intimacy that they had before the birth of the baby (as we discussed in Chapter 6). That is, they may have felt rather neglected, as though the baby had usurped their special position in their wife's affections. These husbands may have complained about their wives' constant involvement with the baby, or they may have responded to the situation by withdrawing from their wives, leaving them feeling unsupported. Such behaviors are likely to result in wives' feeling quite vulnerable, given that they have primary responsibility for the care of their young baby.

On the other hand, when wives felt strongly about their husbands' limited contribution to infant care, those husbands became more insecure about their relationships by the end of the study. That is, they felt more anxious about their partners' love and commitment and about the future of the relationship, possibly because they felt threatened by their wives' dissatisfaction. This finding highlights the *malleability* of attachment style. In other words, although attachment security seems to be a relatively stable characteristic of the individual, it can be affected by important events, especially those that occur within intimate relationships. Similarly, in the previous chapter, we saw how women's postnatal depression was associated with increased insecurity for both partners. Such findings support our initial assumption that the transition to parenthood is a crucial time in the history of a marriage.

SUMMARY

When we discussed the interview conducted shortly after the babies were born, we saw that issues concerning the performance of household tasks and the sharing of responsibilities were a central concern for some couples. It seemed that, depending on how these issues were handled, new parenthood could either bring couples closer together, or drive them farther apart. The results presented in this chapter support these claims. Couples who managed to share the load did so in different ways, and the actual amount of time spent on tasks was much less important than spouses' perceptions of fairness and unfairness. Where one partner (especially the husband) was dissatisfied with the other's contribution, there were negative consequences for both spouses and for their relationship. It is important to keep in mind, however, that what spouses see as fair and unfair depends on their views about gender roles, their personal standards for task performance, and their expectations about their ongoing relationship and the support it should provide.

TEN

Couples' Changing Attachment Relationships

"After the baby was born, I did feel different. Like we're a family,
and the love's split three ways now."

A central theme of this book is the importance of attachment relationships, that is, close relationships that play a special role in meeting
needs for comfort and emotional security. In this chapter, we explore
the nature of couples' attachment relationships throughout the transition to parenthood. We focus on two broad issues related to attachment
bonds. First, we look at the importance of attachment relationships
with spouses, friends, and family members, including comparisons
across the two groups of couples and across the three major phases of
the study. Second, for transition couples, we examine the development
of the new parents' sense of attachment to their babies.

RELATIONSHIPS WITH SPOUSES, FRIENDS, AND FAMILY MEMBERS

As we noted in Chapter 2, there has been a growing recognition by relationship researchers that needs for comfort and security are universal, and evident at all stages of the life span. In other words, both children and adults have "attachment figures," who play a special role in their lives. For this reason, we asked couples to name their attachment figures (or "most important people") at each of the three main assessment points. We were interested in finding out which people they saw as central to meeting their needs for comfort and emotional security, and how this attachment network might change across the transition to parenthood.

The Measure

To explore this issue, we used the items of the WHO-TO questionnaire (based on the work of Hazan & Zeifman, 1994). This measure assesses the four aspects of attachment behavior discussed in Chapter 2: proximity-seeking (wanting to be close to a particular person), separation distress (feeling upset at the thought of being away from them), secure base (being involved effectively in daily tasks and activities, and confident in the person's dependability), and safe haven (turning to the person for reassurance and comfort in times of stress). The items of the WHO-TO, and the attachment behaviors they measure, are listed below.

Who is your favorite person to have fun or relax with?	Proximity
Who would you turn to first if you felt upset about something?	Safe
Who do you think will always "be there" for you?	Secure
Who is the one person you really hate to be away from?	Separation
Who do you want to talk to or be with when you're feeling down?	Safe
Who is the person you know you can always count on?	Secure

Who would you miss the most if you had to be away for a while?	Separation
Who is the first person you'd tell if you were worried about something?	Safe
Who is the person you most like to spend time with?	Proximity
Who is the person you'd be most excited to see after being away?	Separation
Who do you know would help you out if you were really in need?	Secure
Who do you just like to be around?	Proximity

Proximity = proximity seeking; Safe = safe haven;
Secure = secure base; Separation = separation distress.

Which Relationship Partners Serve as Attachment Figures?

Our first step towards understanding couples' attachment network was simply to examine all the responses that couples gave to these items, across the two groups and the three measurement times. There were a total of 39 different responses, showing the wide range of people that were important in the lives of these spouses. However, only four responses occurred frequently: spouse, parents, friends, and, for transition couples, the new baby. (The remaining responses covered various family members, such as sisters, brothers, nephews, nieces, aunts, uncles, and grandparents, together with occasional responses of "God," "myself," and in one case, "drugs").

One of the questions we wanted to examine concerned the *range* (or breadth) of attachment figures; in other words, the number of different people the spouses turned to for comfort and security. For each participant and at each of the three assessments, we tallied the number of different attachment figures named across the set of 12 items. This number ranged from 1 to 5 (at all assessment points). On average, spouses named between one and two attachment figures each time they filled out the items. As we discuss next, these low scores reflect the dominant pattern of relying primarily on the spouse as an attachment figure.

In this section, to allow comparison of the main response patterns across the two groups of couples, we focus on attachments to spouse, parents, and friends. At each assessment, we obtained three scores for each participant, reflecting the importance of these various "targets" of attachment. These scores were simply the number of items on the WHO-TO (out of the possible total of 12) for which the particular target was named as "most important person." These measures reflect the relative importance of the different attachment figures. In other words, in this context, attachment refers to the *importance* of particular persons in meeting one's needs for comfort and security, rather than to the amount of discomfort or anxiety involved in the relationship.

The strongest single pattern to emerge from these scores was the central importance of attachment to the *spouse*. For both transition and comparison couples, and at all measurement times, spouses received by far the greatest number of nominations as key attachment figures. In fact, across the set of 12 items, the average number of times the spouse was named as "most important" ranged from 8.4 to 10.9.

This finding supports previous research demonstrating the special characteristics of marital relationships. For example, Argyle and Henderson (1985) showed that spouses played a unique role in providing their partners with emotional support, shared interests, and instrumental rewards (such as advice, property, and shared work). Of course, the tendency to rely on one's spouse for feelings of security can be explained partly in terms of the sense of commitment that is central to the marriage contract, and partly in terms of practical issues, such as the proximity and availability of the spouse.

Parents ranked next in order of importance as attachment figures. They were nominated at much lower rates than spouses, however, with the average score generally being less than one. Friends were also nominated by many spouses, but the average score was again very small (usually around 0.3).

These findings reflect the typical development of attachment patterns across the life span. As we discussed in Chapter 2, previous research has documented systematic changes in the attachment network from childhood to early adulthood, involving a gradual shift away from reliance on parents and towards reliance on peers (Hazan & Zeifman, 1994). Important peers can include both friends and romantic partners; however, as stable romantic relationships develop, partners become increasingly central as attachment figures. In fact, those who are involved in romantic relationships of two years' duration or longer tend to rely almost exclusively on their partners for all their attachment needs.

Differences Due to Gender, Group, and Time

Although reliance on partners seems to be the norm in established couple relationships, the extent of this reliance may be affected by factors such as gender and family structure (e.g., childless couple versus parents). In line with this suggestion, a gender difference emerged consistently in the nominations of attachment figures. Although husbands and wives agreed in their overall rank ordering of attachment figures (spouse, followed by parents, followed by friends), husbands named their spouse slightly more often, and their parents and friends slightly less often, than did wives.

This gender difference fits with previous research. For example, many researchers have suggested that the friendships of women are more intimate than those of men, in terms of dimensions such as self-disclosure and emotional support. In addition, there is some evidence that married women stay in closer touch with their parents than married men, and feel a greater sense of support from them (Noller & Feeney, in press). For married men, the spouse is often the single close confidante and source of support.

Another interesting finding concerns the patterns of attachment figures across the two groups. Transition and comparison couples reported similar patterns of attachment relationships at both the first and second assessments. At the end of the study, however, new parents named their spouse and friends less often, and their parents more often, than did comparison couples. This difference between the two groups was more pronounced for wives than for husbands, as shown in Figure 10.1. (Because friends were nominated at very low rates, only the results for spouse and parents have been graphed.)

Given that these group differences were evident only at the final assessment, it is not surprising that the two groups of couples showed different patterns of change across the course of the study. In fact, comparison couples responded similarly to the WHO-TO items at all

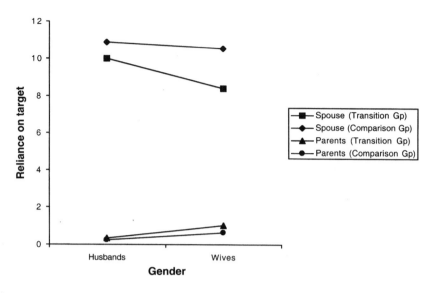

Figure 10.1. Nominations of spouse and parents as attachment figures at the end of the study, according to group and gender.

three times. In contrast, members of the transition group showed small but significant changes in their naming of attachment figures: Transition couples (especially wives) reduced their nominations of the spouse as the study progressed, and transition wives increased their nominations of friends and parents. The changes were most marked between the second and third assessments; in other words, they occurred after the baby had been home for some time. Changes in transition wives' reports of attachment figures are shown in Figure 10.2 (again, because friends were nominated at very low rates, only the results for spouse and parents have been graphed).

Because these changes were restricted to the transition group, we can be confident that they are linked to the experience of parenthood, rather than to some general trend in marital relationships. The shifts in the attachment network can be understood in terms of the major focus of couples' time and energy during the early months of parenting. The arrival of the infant is likely to increase the contact and involvement that new mothers and fathers have with their own parents; grandparents can be a very important source of advice and support, and most

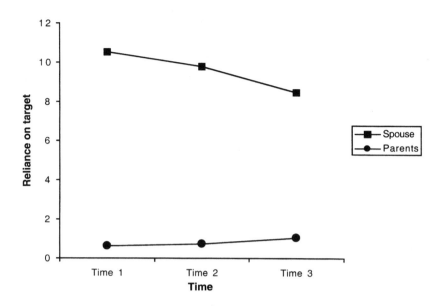

Figure 10.2. Transition wives' nominations of spouse and parents as attachment figures at each assessment time.

want to be actively involved with the new arrival. At the same time, as we saw in Chapter 6, babies impose considerable restrictions on parents' lifestyle, and tend to reduce the amount of time available for socializing with friends. It is not surprising that these changes affected mothers more than fathers, given that mothers in this sample were the primary caregivers. As we discuss next, for new parents, the lower rate of naming the spouse is likely to reflect the emergence of the baby itself as a target for attachment behavior.

ATTACHMENT TO BABY

In this study, we did not include any direct measure of the attachment bond between parent and child. (An observational measure known as the Strange Situation is commonly used to assess the security of the infant's attachment to the caregiver, as discussed in Chapter 2; this measure is quite complex, however, and is not appropriate for use with very young babies.)

Rather, we used two very different methods of assessing parents' sense of attachment to their new baby. First, we looked at transition couples' responses to the WHO-TO, this time tallying the number of items for which the baby was named as "most important person"; this procedure provides an index of the importance of the baby as an attachment figure. Second, we examined the transcripts of the interviews conducted six weeks after the birth, focusing this time on spouses' comments about their responsiveness to their babies (in terms of emotional involvement and responses to the infant's needs and signals). This focus fits with previous research, which shows that parents' responsiveness is crucial to the quality of the attachment bond that forms between parent and child. Using both these methods, we were interested in exploring the variability in new parents' responses to their infants, and also in tracing the development of their sense of attachment to the baby.

Importance of the Baby as an Attachment Figure

Before we discuss the results for the WHO-TO measure, it is important to review what this measures does. It defines attachment figures as the *most important persons,* in terms of giving *the respondent* a sense of comfort and security. In other words, the focus is on the relationship making the adult, rather than the infant, feel secure. So, failure to name the baby on this measure does *not* mean that spouses did not welcome the baby, or that they were not caring for the infant appropriately; rather, it means that they were not seeing the baby as central to their own sense of security.

Initial Assessment. At the beginning of the study, when couples first completed this measure, they were in the second trimester of their pregnancy. At this stage, given our definition of attachment figures, we expected to find very low levels of attachment to the baby. Again, this does not mean that expectant parents are disinterested in their babies, or unconcerned about their well-being. In fact, previous research suggests that some expectant mothers and fathers feel quite attached to their unborn babies, in terms of experiencing strong emotions towards them and being preoccupied with thoughts of them (Condon, 1993).

With regard to the items of the WHO-TO, it seemed possible that expectant parents might report some concern over loss and separation (separation distress); however, it seemed very unlikely that they would report a sense of being able to "count on" their unborn infants (secure base), or being able to share their concerns with them (safe haven).

Responses to the questionnaire confirmed these expectations. Only five spouses named the baby in response to any of the WHO-TO items at this first assessment. Interestingly, this small group of spouses included only one wife, who named the baby for 2 of the 12 items. Four husbands named the baby as "most important person" for either one or two items. All of these positive responses were to items assessing separation distress (see Table 10.1 for numbers of wives and husbands naming the baby in terms of separation distress and proximity seeking at each assessment.) In other words, some spouses were already beginning to sense the extreme distress they would feel if they were to lose the baby or be separated from it.

Second Assessment. By about six weeks after the birth, the baby had taken on a more important place in the attachment network. Although just over half of the new mothers did not name the baby as an attachment figure, 37 mentioned the baby for one to three items, and one mother named the baby for seven of the items. New fathers were somewhat less likely to name the baby as an attachment figure. About two-

TABLE 10.1 Numbers of Wives and Husbands Naming the Baby in Terms of Separation Distress and Proximity Seeking at Each Assessment

Item	First Assessment		Second Assessment		Third Assessment	
	Wives	Husbands	Wives	Husbands	Wives	Husbands
Separation distress						
hate to be away from	0	2	29	15	38	26
would miss the most	1	2	29	16	45	28
most excited to see	1	2	31	21	43	34
Proximity seeking						
have fun with	0	0	2	3	10	5
like to spend time with	0	0	13	10	17	10
just like to be around	0	0	0	0	0	0

thirds of them did not name the baby at all; 16 mentioned the baby for one to three items, and 9 named the baby for four or five items.

This slight gender difference was reflected in the average number of items for which the baby was named as *most important*. These scores were 1.11 for wives, and .73 for husbands. Although these scores might seem low, it is important to note that even at this very early stage of the child's life, the baby was already seen as a more important attachment figure than were parents and friends.

At the same time, most nominations of the baby as an attachment figure still reflected the focus on separation distress (see Table 10.1). In other words, six weeks after the birth, many mothers and fathers were saying that the baby was the person they would miss the most, and most hate to be away from. However, proximity seeking was also starting to emerge as an attachment function: Several spouses said that the baby was the person they most liked to "spend time with" and "have fun with."

Given that almost half of the new parents were starting to think of their baby in attachment terms, we were interested in seeing whether perceived importance of the baby as an attachment figure was linked to the quality of the marital relationship. Previous studies of the links between different close relationships suggest two main possibilities in this regard (Noller, Feeney, Peterson, & Sheehan, 1995). First, perceiving the baby as an attachment figure might be associated with a *more* secure and happy couple relationship; in other words, a secure marriage might serve to foster feelings of attachment to the child. The other possibility is that perceiving the baby as an attachment figure might be associated with a *less* secure and happy marriage; that is, some parents might turn to the baby for their attachment needs, to compensate for a distant or troubled relationship with the spouse.

To address this question, we correlated the number of items for which the baby was named as *most important* with three key measures of the couple relationship: the two dimensions of attachment security, and the overall measure of marital satisfaction. Husbands' naming of the baby as an attachment figure was not related to these measures, but for wives, naming of the baby was associated with lower scores on the attachment dimension of anxiety over relationships. Similarly, we were able to show that wives who named the baby for three or more of the WHO-TO items were significantly lower in relationship anxiety (with an average score of 31.33) than those who named the baby for one or two items (average of 37.04) and those who did not name the baby at all (average of 38.24).

Although wives' naming the baby as an attachment figure was linked to level of relationship anxiety as measured at the same assessment point, it was not related to initial scores on relationship anxiety. For this reason, we are not able to draw any firm conclusions about cause-and-effect. However, it does seem that, for wives at least, a greater sense of security in the marriage tends to go along with a stronger sense of attachment to the baby. Wives who are very confident of their partner's love and commitment may be less concerned about how the new baby might affect the marital bond and, conversely, their growing sense of attachment to the baby is likely to foster the general "family feeling" that several couples described during their second interview (see Chapter 6).

Third Assessment. At the end of the study, when the infants were six months old, importance of the baby as an attachment figure had continued to rise. Although one quarter of wives and more than 40% of husbands were still not nominating the baby as an attachment figure, roughly half of the parents named the baby for one to three items, and 16% named the baby for between four and seven items. As can be seen from Figure 10.3, the gender difference in perceptions of the baby as an attachment figure had increased somewhat from the second assessment.

The WHO-TO items that were endorsed at this stage were primarily the same as those endorsed shortly after the birth (see Table 10.1). In other words, spouses were still describing their attachment to the baby in terms of the person they would miss the most, and most hate to be away from, and the person they most liked to "spend time with" and "have fun with." The rise in average scores, then, reflects the growing number of spouses reporting these feelings, rather than the addition of any extra attachment behaviors.

This finding is not surprising; as noted earlier, it is both appropriate and common for parents to want to spend lots of time with their offspring, but inappropriate for them to regard the young child as someone they can "count on" or share their problems and concerns with. Rather, the parent's role is to provide *the child* with these attachment

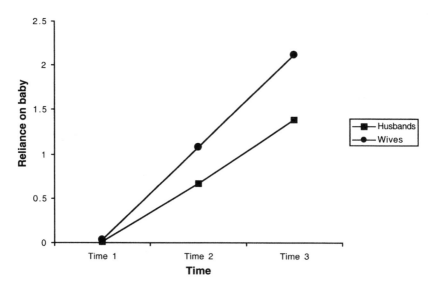

Figure 10.3. New mothers' and fathers' nominations of baby as an attachment figure at each assessment time.

features of secure base and safe haven. It is interesting to note, however, that infants rapidly become attachment figures for many parents, and in fact, rank second in importance only to the spouse.

Responsiveness to Baby

As mentioned earlier, we also turned to the interview data for evidence of attachment to the baby. In doing this, we focused on reports of different levels of parental responsiveness. That is, we were interested in parents' comments about their emotional involvement with the child, and their responses to the child's signals of distress. These comments are of interest because strong emotions are seen as a key feature of attachment bonds, and attempts to nurture and care for infants are at the very heart of the attachment system. Again, it is important to note that these comments give us *indirect* evidence of the development of a sense of attachment.

Pregnancy and Emotional Responding. The first point of interest is that at the second interview, a couple of wives commented that the pregnancy had not afforded their husbands much of a chance to feel involved with the baby. For example, one wife commented:

When she was in the womb, I mean he could enjoy her, but only from an external perspective. Because, you know, I was the one who was fortunate enough to be carrying her. It was wonderful, because I could feel the kicks and all that kind of stuff. He was always on the outside, and couldn't have that relationship with her. So you know, I think that nine months is really valuable.

These comments are only partly consistent with the questionnaire measure of attachment figures (WHO-TO), which suggested that husbands are just as likely as their wives to report a sense of potential loss and separation from the baby at the prenatal stage. On the other hand, the diverse responses to the WHO-TO measure at the second assessment (in terms of the extent to which the baby was named as an attachment figure) paralleled the differing ways that couples talked about their relationships with their babies during the second interview.

From Disconnection to Strong Involvement. When we described new parents' best and worst experiences of parenthood (see Chapter 6), we noted that some spouses reported feeling emotionally "disconnected" from their infants. Although the questionnaire measure of "attachment-to-baby" (WHO-TO) was not designed to assess bonding difficulties, it is interesting to note that all of the spouses who reported these ongoing feelings of disconnection obtained low scores on that measure at the same point in time.

In Chapter 6, we gave several examples of comments from mothers who were struggling to feel loving and involved towards their babies. The following comment from a new mother provides another example of this difficulty in engaging with the baby:

I sort of feel like I've borrowed him from somewhere. So I'm still not used to him. Probably when he's sort of happy – I like him when he's happy, obviously. But for me, because he doesn't look like me – he looks like H – it's just like it's his baby, and it's not my baby, if you know what I mean.

For other spouses, "disconnection" was reflected in a general lack of emotional response to the baby. For example, the following exchange between husband and wife highlights the husband's limited emotional response:

H: The best thing about parenthood? I don't know. He's not been alive long enough to probably comment on it that much. It's all right. But it hasn't affected me, I don't think.

W: Oh great! Lovely!

H: Oh well – I didn't reject him or anything.

Similarly, another husband explicitly stated that he was unable to "get emotional" about the baby. Interestingly, a number of spouses who reported a lack of connection with their infants talked about how they thought this situation would improve in the future, when the baby was more active and able to do more things. For example, one mother said:

It's hard now, because he's not really doing anything. I mean, you think he smiles, but it's only wind. I think after the next couple of weeks, it will be all right.

Similarly, one new father suggested that he would "connect" more to his daughter when she became more mobile and more sociable:

I think it will be better when she gets a bit bigger. And – yeah – when she can talk and walk and things like that – run around the yard, and help Daddy water the garden and all that.

In contrast to these various examples of disconnection, other parents talked about their very strong emotional responses to their babies. For instance, one father said that his "heart soared" when his baby smiled at him, and, conversely, that the baby's crying was like "a tearing at my heart." Another report of strong emotional responding was provided by a new mother. In the following comments, she gives a clear description of her distress at the thought of being separated from her baby, right from the very first day:

To me, she's just perfect. To have it all there, I can't describe the feelings. I mean they were – they were trying to take her away in the hospital, the first night. She was – she slept with me in the bed, and then the second night, they kept trying to persuade me to take her into the nursery, so that I could have a night's sleep. You know, the concern being that I'd lost nearly three litres of blood, and that I needed a lot of rest.

We see, then, that new parents differ widely in terms of their reports of emotional responsiveness. To some extent, these differences may reflect more general differences in people's emotional experience and expression: The father who commented that he could not "get emotional" about the baby explained this in terms of his being generally "not the type to get emotional about things." For other new parents, strong emotional responses to the baby set in at different points in time. Some mothers reported that their "maternal feelings" had become apparent several days, or even several weeks, after the birth. And in the following comment, we see how differences in responsiveness can be evident within couples, as one new mother describes how her husband is generally more responsive to the baby's needs and signals:

It sort of opens up a whole new ball game. Because you know, we've been married for 9 years, so it's just been – altogether, it's been something like 16 years. Just two people, and then you've got this extra person in the house. And H is more honed in, I think, more so than me, and that seems a bit funny to me. Like we can sit in the lounge, and he'll say "Oh, that's B crying," and I'll go "Oh, is it?" You know, "Oh, it is too!" So he is just tuned in a bit more, more likely to jump up and go to attend to her. Whereas I'm sort of watching TV and getting involved in whatever, and think "Oh, is that her crying?"

Special Importance of the Attachment Bond. At this second interview, other spouses made indirect references to attachment when they commented specifically on the growing bonds between themselves and the baby, or between their spouse and the baby. One husband reported being fascinated by these bonds:

It's just a joy. It's just fascinating, the bond I can see, well, the bond between myself and the baby, but also the bond I can see and feel between W and the baby. To me, that's amazing. It's just hard to describe, because there's nothing you can really compare it to … It's just an amazing experience. The baby's beautiful, you know – but then I'm just a bit biased.

In the next comment, a new mother is similarly pleased by the bond that she sees forming between her husband and baby. This reaction reflects, in part, her earlier concern about whether her husband would show a strong emotional response to the baby:

It's nice seeing how H is doting on her. It really brings out the strongest feelings. I don't think H knew what his feelings would be like, and I couldn't have imagined how his feelings would have shown. I've always been clucky my whole life, so I didn't worry – I sort of knew I'd be okay. But I didn't know what H would be like.

A final point concerning attachment bonds that emerged during the second interview was the sense that for some parents, the bond with the child was the single most important thing in their lives. One new father expressed this feeling as follows:

The best thing for me, in terms of parenting, I guess, is just the fact that I've got a child now. Which is like – oh, I mean, that's really the best thing possible. And then everything else sort of fits in around that.

Another father expressed a similar reaction when he described his thoughts about the importance of family bonds:

I guess between W and B, there's just nothing else that's important in my life, pretty much. And I couldn't imagine – like you hear about these people hitting their kids, and doing all that stuff, and I just think that is the lowest thing in the world, you know. Because I can't think of anything more important than W and B at the moment. Like – if somebody came along and said "All right, you guys, we're taking your house away from you," all right – like that would mean a lot, but we can always go somewhere else.

SUMMARY

In this chapter, we have described two ways of looking at spouses' attachment figures: first, in terms of the questionnaire reports of "most important persons," and second, in terms of interview comments about spouses' emotional and caregiving responses to their infants. The questionnaire reports showed that parenthood brings substantial changes to the attachment network, at least for mothers. These changes are not restricted to the obvious fact that the couple relationship needs to accommodate the new infant. Rather, new parenthood tends to result in increased reliance on parents as attachment figures, and decreased reliance on the spouse and on close friends. Both questionnaire and interview responses also highlighted the wide variability in parents' initial sense of attachment to their babies. Some parents reported an almost immediate sense of very strong attachment, whereas others reported some difficulty in relating to the baby. These difficulties were generally fairly short-lived, however. For wives, lower levels of relationship anxiety were associated with the tendency to name the baby as an attachment figure, suggesting that new mothers' relationships with their partners and with their babies tend to be interwoven. Parents reported a steadily growing attachment to their babies over the course of the study, especially in terms of separation distress. Clearly, as the quote at the beginning of the chapter reminds us, the arrival of the baby changes parents' emotional lives.

ELEVEN

Six Months into Parenting

"Life has certainly changed! Nine pounds of absolute power, that's what a baby is. And so much control over two grown people. If she screams, we run!"

The measures we obtained soon after the birth showed the enormous range of responses to new parenthood (see Chapters 6 and 7). Some parents were finding their infants relatively easy to manage, and reported increased feelings of closeness and partnership with their spouses. Others reported a range of concerns, including difficulty in soothing the baby or "connecting" to it, loss of intimacy with the spouse, and a sense of restriction of general lifestyle. We were interested in whether this wide range of responses would still be evident four to five months later, when the parents had had more time to become attached to their babies and to develop routines for doing the chores and caring for the infant. At the final assessment, both transition and comparison couples again completed measures that evaluated their relationships and their psychological adjustment. In this chapter, we explore changes across the entire course of the study for each group. In addition, for the transition group, we look at the extent to which different couples struggled with new parenthood, and explore factors related to the ease of their transition.

PATTERNS OF CHANGE OVER TIME

As we noted in Chapter 7, our focus in this study was on tracking changes in spouses' psychological adjustment and marital relationships. Again, at this final point, we were especially interested in patterns of change that differed for transition and comparison couples, because such a finding points to a significant impact of new parenthood. To explore these issues, we examined responses to the major questionnaires that couples completed at each assessment: relationship satisfaction, attachment, caregiving, sexuality, and psychological adjustment.

In contrast to the second assessment, when we found few changes that were specific to new parents, the final assessment showed several areas of impact. Transition and comparison couples showed different patterns of change on two aspects of relationship satisfaction (affective communication and time together), two aspects of the behavioral systems that underpin couple relationships (discomfort with closeness and sexual desire), and two aspects of psychological adjustment (general anxiety and stress). On the other hand, the two groups showed only a slight difference in patterns of overall relationship satisfaction, and no difference for relationship anxiety, spousal caregiving, sexual communication, or depression. In the following section, we discuss the areas of differential change and their implications for new parents.

Relationship Satisfaction

As detailed in Chapter 3, we looked at four aspects of relationship satisfaction: global distress, problem-solving communication, affective communication, and time together. Interestingly, the impact of parenthood was restricted to affective communication (the amount of affection and understanding expressed in the marriage), and time together (the quality and quantity of shared interests and leisure time). In other words, parenthood was associated with changes in those scales that reflected partners' feelings about *companionship and intimacy*. (Although new parents showed a decline in "global distress" soon after the birth, this decrease in general unhappiness with the marriage was no longer evident at the end of the study.)

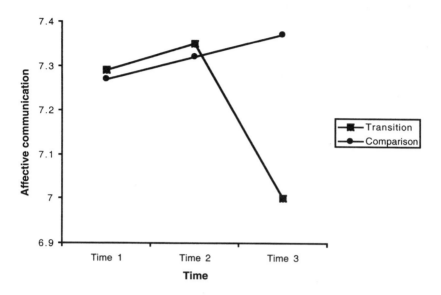

Figure 11.1. **Mean scores on affective communication according to group and time.**

Satisfaction with both affective communication and time together declined for new parents across the 10-month period, but was stable for comparison couples. (Similarly, only new parents showed a slight decline in overall satisfaction.) In the case of affective communication, the drop in satisfaction occurred quite late in the study; there was no evidence of change in the weeks immediately following the birth (see Figure 11.1).

On the other hand, the drop in satisfaction with time together occurred at different points for mothers and fathers. Mothers' satisfaction with shared couple time dropped soon after the birth, but fathers' satisfaction did not drop until the final assessment, when the babies were six months old (see Figure 11.2).

These findings fit with a number of other studies of new parenthood, as we discussed in Chapter 1. In particular, they suggest that the demands of infant care tend to disrupt couples' shared leisure time, intimacy, and expressions of warmth and affection. The idea that women may feel the impact of these demands sooner than men has also been raised by previous studies. Because women are more likely to be involved in full-time parenting and less likely to have regular

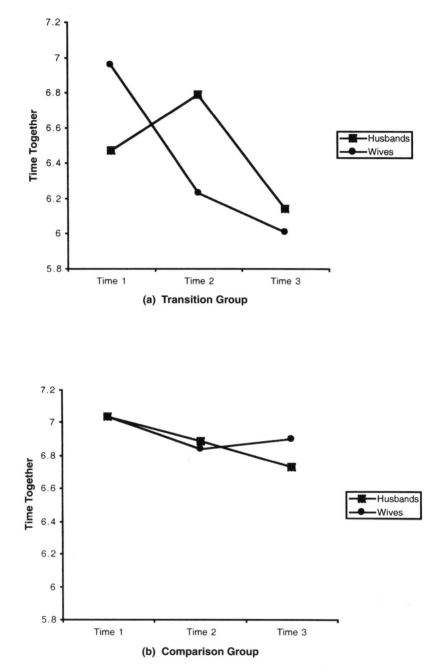

Figure 11.2. Mean scores on time together according to group, gender, and time.

social contacts outside the home, it is not surprising that they are quicker to experience concerns about companionship and intimacy. It seems that, in the early weeks of parenting, men may not necessarily be attuned to these concerns, unless their partners communicate their needs and feelings.

It is important to keep these changes in perspective, however. We have seen that first-time parenthood had relatively little effect on *overall* levels of relationship satisfaction. This finding suggests that most couples can accept the changes in their day-to-day interactions as an understandable (and perhaps anticipated) part of new parenthood. In other words, partners seem to attribute the declines in intimacy to the specific pressures of parenthood, rather than to a general failing on the part of the spouse or the relationship.

Behavioral Systems

New parenthood also had an impact on attachment security and sexuality (although not on patterns of spousal caregiving). In terms of attachment security, the changes were confined to the "discomfort with closeness" dimension. Levels of discomfort with closeness were stable over the 10 months of the study for all groups except *new fathers,* whose scores showed a small but steady decline (see Appendix C for further details of this effect). The idea that parenthood might have an impact on adults' sense of security has seldom been explored; many studies have looked at how parenthood changes couple relationships, but these studies have focused almost exclusively on specific kinds of interactions (such as expressions of affection), or on general evaluations of relationship quality.

The direction of the change in attachment security is interesting: New fathers reported feeling *more* comfortable in situations involving intimacy. Given that researchers have tended to dwell on the problems and difficulties of parenting, it is reassuring to find this evidence of a more "positive" change. Moreover, any decline in fathers' feelings of discomfort and unease with intimacy is likely to benefit the developing bond with the baby, as well as the marital relationship. Of course, it is possible that some of these fathers were feeling more comfortable because their wives were heavily involved

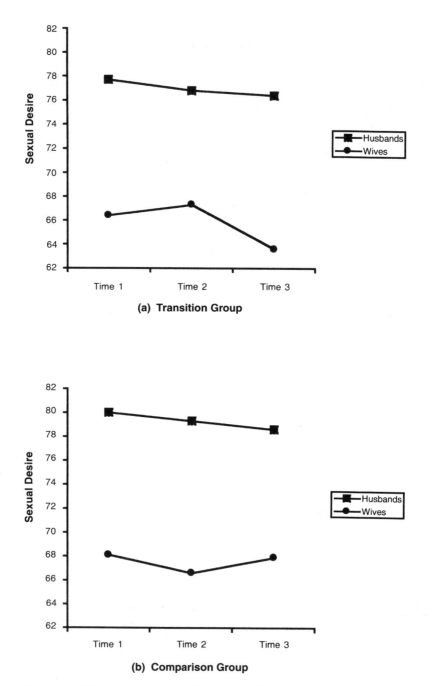

Figure 11.3. Mean scores on sexual desire according to group, gender, and time.

in attending to the infant, and were making fewer demands for couple intimacy.

On a less positive note, new mothers showed the greatest drop in sexual desire, although this change did not emerge until the end of the study (see Figure 11.3). Given the timing of the change, the drop in desire does not seem to be a reaction to the immediate physical and emotional changes of pregnancy or childbirth. Rather, the various demands on mothers' time and energy are likely to have cumulative effects on their levels of sexual interest. Although this drop in sexual interest is understandable, it points to a more general link between new parenthood and reduced opportunities for intimacy. We have already seen that parents were aware of changes in the quality and quantity of couple time, and in expressions of love and understanding. For some couples, difficulties in sexual relating are likely to add to these concerns.

Psychological Adjustment

Parenthood had an impact on spouses' psychological adjustment, as well as on their couple relationships, but the various indicators of adjustment showed different types of change. Unlike comparison couples, new parents showed a *drop* in general feelings of worry and anxiety from the initial assessment to the later times. However, their initial levels of anxiety were somewhat higher than those of comparison couples (although the difference was not significant, in statistical terms; see Appendix C for details). In other words, some of the expectant parents reported quite high levels of worry and anxiety, perhaps reflecting their concerns about the pregnancy and the impending birth. The drop in anxiety after the baby's arrival probably signals a return to couples' more "typical" levels of adjustment.

On the other hand, new mothers reported feeling more stressed after the birth than beforehand. They were the only group in the study to show a significant increase in feelings of impatience, tension, and irritability, with this increase being evident immediately after the birth and maintained over the following months (see Figure 11.4). As with the drop in sexual desire, this change can be understood in terms of the demands and pressures on mothers' time and energy.

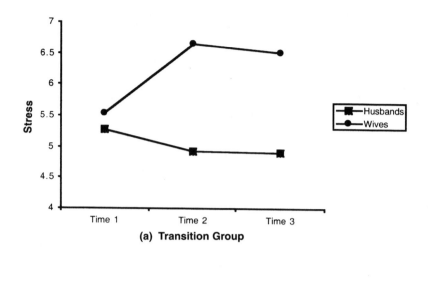

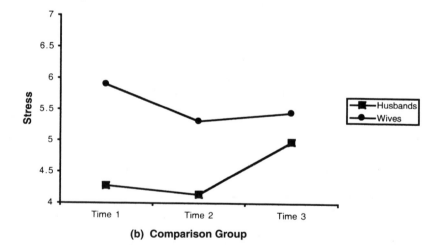

Figure 11.4. Mean scores on stress according to group, gender, and time.

Summary of Changes

In summary, first-time parenthood brought a number of changes for couples in this study. Changes in psychological adjustment tended to appear soon after the birth: New mothers and fathers felt less anxious than they had at the beginning of the study, but new mothers also felt more stressed than before. With the exception of wives' evaluations of time together, measures of the couple relationship were slower to show change. The apparent stability of the relationship from pregnancy to six weeks post-birth is not really surprising: In the weeks immediately after the birth, partners often experience a sense of shared achievement and satisfaction that helps counter the fatigue and tension that might otherwise take its toll. By six months after the birth, however, both mothers and fathers were reporting reduced satisfaction with their relationship, in terms of expressions of affection and shared couple time. At this stage, new mothers were also reporting a dampening of sexual desire. Collectively, these changes suggest that partners had substantially fewer opportunities for intimate interactions. At the same time, new fathers reported feeling somewhat more comfortable with closeness than they did before the birth.

DIFFERENCES BETWEEN GROUPS, GENDERS, AND POINTS IN TIME

Although our main focus in this study was on changes specific to the transition couples, it is useful to take a brief look at overall differences between the two groups, between husbands and wives, and between the different points in time.

Differences Between Groups

The only consistent difference between transition and comparison couples was in the area of sexual communication: Transition couples were less satisfied, on average, with their communication about sexual issues. As we argued earlier (see Chapter 7), this is one aspect of couple relationships that is likely to change during pregnancy, as well as after the arrival of the baby.

For both expectant and new parents, topics related directly to pregnancy and parenthood are likely to become a central focus of couple communication, and there may simply be less talk about sexual issues. In addition, new concerns about sexuality tend to emerge at this time, including physical discomfort during intercourse, fatigue, and concern about one's own sexual attractiveness and about the partner's sexual satisfaction (von Sydow, 1999). Some spouses are probably reluctant to discuss these concerns, given the highly emotional nature of sexual issues.

Gender Differences

At the final assessment, husbands and wives differed in a number of respects. Specifically, wives (regardless of group) reported less discomfort with intimacy in their couple relationships, more responsive care, more compulsive care, less sexual desire, more satisfaction with their sexual communication, and more stress in their lives.

These differences were also present earlier in the study and, as we mentioned in Chapters 4 and 7, generally fit with other data comparing the interaction patterns of men and women. As before, however, it is important to keep in mind that the gender differences were quite small, and that men and women clearly share a common core of relationship experience.

Differences over Time

As we noted in the first chapter, longitudinal studies can be useful in charting development and change in couple relationships. In this study, we have discussed a number of changes that were specific to the group of new parents. The only change that applied to *both* groups was in the area of sexual communication. Over the 10 months of the study, spouses (regardless of gender and group) reported a small drop in satisfaction with their communication about sexual issues.

Given that this change applied to *both* groups, it represents a fairly general development in long-term couple relationships. Perhaps, over time, partners tend to assume that issues concerning their sexual needs and preferences have already been negotiated. The drop in satisfaction with sexual communication suggests that this assumption can be problematic, and that partners might benefit from more open communication on these issues. We need to keep in mind, however, that sexual desire was fairly stable over the course of this study, except for new mothers. In other words, these long-term relationships generally involved quite high and steady levels of sexual interest.

LINKING ATTACHMENT SECURITY WITH RELATIONSHIP QUALITY AND INDIVIDUAL ADJUSTMENT

In Chapter 7, we explored the possibility that attachment security affected the way that couples were faring at the second assessment, especially in the context of first-time parenthood. We found that secure attachment was associated with better individual adjustment and more constructive styles of relating; however, this pattern tended to apply *regardless of* whether couples were childless or dealing with new parenthood. In other words, it seemed that attachment security generally helped to foster a sense of well-being and satisfying patterns of interaction.

We wanted to see whether this pattern also applied at the final assessment. To address this question, we assessed links between the initial scores on the attachment dimensions and the final reports of individual and couple functioning, taken about 10 months later. Again, we found that attachment security was associated with better individual adjustment and more constructive styles of relating, for both new parents and childless couples. For example, discomfort with closeness was associated with lower relationship satisfaction and higher ratings of stress. In addition, as at the earlier follow-up, anxiety over relationships predicted a wide range of difficulties: individual adjustment problems (more depression, anxiety, and stress), less effective style of caring for the spouse (more compulsive caregiving), and less satisfaction with the marriage (less satisfaction overall, and less satisfaction with time together).

At this final assessment, however, one clear difference emerged between new fathers and other husbands: Attachment insecurity (both discomfort with closeness and relationship anxiety) was linked with less sexual desire and less satisfaction with sexual communication, but for the new fathers only. (At the earlier follow-up, attachment insecurity was linked with more negative reports of sexual desire and sexual communication, for *both* groups of men.)

As we have mentioned throughout this book, theory and research suggest that insecure attachment becomes more problematic when people have to deal with stressful events. Similarly, in the present study, we found that relationship anxiety contributed to the onset of depression for new mothers, but not for other wives (see Chapter 8). The fact that men's attachment security was able to predict their sexual desire and sexual communication some 10 months later, but only in the context of parenthood, provides further support for this claim. New fathers certainly face extra demands and responsibilities related to their parenting role; in addition (as we saw earlier in this chapter), their wives experience less sexual desire than they once did. In these potentially difficult conditions, it seems that a secure attachment bond may help husbands to communicate more openly about sexual issues and concerns, and to maintain an active interest in the sexual aspect of their relationships.

THE COURSE OF RELATIONSHIP SATISFACTION

Earlier in this chapter, we compared levels of relationship satisfaction for transition and comparison couples, at each of the three assessment points. We were also interested in considering the transition group separately, and looking more closely at the *course* of relationship satisfaction (because the comparison group did not change on any measure of satisfaction, it was of no further interest in this regard). In other words, we were interested in identifying the pattern, or trajectory, of change, for the transition couples. It is possible, for example, that new parents might actually experience some increase in satisfaction with their relationships around the time of the birth, followed by a decrease as the realities of parenthood become more apparent.

The course of satisfaction was assessed using a method related to growth curve analysis. This method simply involves testing whether any change over time is in a single direction (linear increase or decrease), or up-and-down (curvilinear change). Using this method, we found that the overall satisfaction reported by transition couples showed linear change only: Satisfaction dropped slightly for these couples, although this change occurred mainly in the later part of the study.

It is important to keep in mind that the drop in overall satisfaction was small for new parents, perhaps because the transition involves different forces that largely counteract each other. For instance, the euphoria that often accompanies the arrival of the baby may pass, but at the same time, parents become much more confident in their ability to care for their infant. In fact, when we interviewed parents shortly after the birth, several talked about their initial anxiety and lack of confidence, and about the steep "learning curve" that parenthood entailed (see Chapter 6).

To obtain a more fine-grained picture of the course of relationship satisfaction associated with parenthood, we carried out a similar analysis on each of the four aspects of satisfaction: global distress, affective communication, problem-solving communication, and time together. We found change (of a linear form) in affective communication, and time together, consistent with the findings reported earlier in this chapter. The decline in these areas, then, seems to underlie the small change in overall satisfaction. At the same time, we need to emphasize that the drop in satisfaction represents an *average* pattern; as we discuss in the next section, it certainly did not apply to all of the new parents.

SATISFACTION WITH INTIMACY: STABILITY VERSUS DECLINE

A major goal of this final assessment was to explore the different outcomes experienced by new parents, and the reasons behind them. In particular, we were interested in looking more closely at couples' ratings of their relationships, and seeing whether some couples had managed to maintain (or even enhance) their initial evaluations.

To explore this issue, we focused on those areas of relationship satisfaction that were most vulnerable to the effects of new parenthood: affective communication and time together. (The importance of these areas is supported not only by our own findings, but also by previous studies linking new parenthood with declines in couple intimacy.) We combined these two scales into a single measure of satisfaction with relationship intimacy, so that we could assess the extent of change across the transition period. This composite measure contained 16 items, each rated as true or false; total scores could range from 0 to 16, with higher scores indicating greater satisfaction with intimacy.

Using a technique called cluster analysis, we looked for groups of transition couples who showed particular patterns of change on this measure. On this basis, we identified two groups of new parents. The larger group, consisting of 50 couples, showed almost no change in satisfaction with intimacy throughout the transition; in fact, the average scores of both husbands and wives were between 13 and 14, at each assessment. The second group, consisting of 24 couples, showed a marked drop in satisfaction with intimacy between the post-birth and final assessments; the average scores of husbands and wives were again between 13 and 14 at the first two assessments, but were close to 10 by the end of the study.

To sum up what we have discussed so far, the effects of parenthood on relationship satisfaction were largely confined to the area of couple intimacy (expressions of affection and understanding, and time together). However, not all couples in this study were unhappy with this aspect of their relationships. Roughly two-thirds of couples found their relationships just as satisfying as they had before the arrival of the baby. The remaining one-third were unhappy about their limited opportunities for intimacy (companionship, leisure activities, conversation, and sexual interactions).

Because we go on to explore these two groups in more detail (and to avoid confusion with the transition and comparison groups), we will call these groups the Survivors and the Strugglers, respectively. It is important to emphasize, however, that these terms refer only to their current levels of *satisfaction with intimacy*, and are not intended to imply that the relationships of the Strugglers were necessarily under threat.

It is also important to acknowledge that some couples may actually become *more* satisfied with their relationships when they become parents. Our study provided limited support for this suggestion (new parents showed a drop in feelings of unhappiness and disappointment with their marriage soon after the birth, but this change was short-lived; some also commented during interviews that parenthood had brought them closer together). On the other hand, in an earlier study of the transition to parenthood, Belsky and Rovine (1990) identified increasing relationship satisfaction as one of four possible outcomes.

SURVIVORS AND STRUGGLERS:
EXPLAINING THE DIFFERENT OUTCOMES

To understand *why* some couples emerged unscathed from the transition to parenthood while others found it more of a struggle, we looked for differences between the attitudes and experiences of the two groups. We were interested in several issues that might help to explain the relative ease or difficulty of the transition. The first three issues concerned general characteristics of the spouses and their relationships.

Did the Survivors

- have better general psychological adjustment at the start of the study?
- have better coping resources at the start of the study?
- show more constructive patterns of relating to each other at the start of the study?

In contrast, the remaining four issues focused on experiences related to the transition itself; that is, on various aspects of pregnancy, birth, parenting, and management of infant care and other household tasks.

Did the Survivors

- have a more positive attitude to the pregnancy?
- report easier experiences of birth and early parenting?
- use more effective strategies to cope with parenting?
- devise more equitable ways of allocating domestic tasks?

To explore these issues, we compared the scores of the Survivors and Strugglers on various measures taken throughout the study. These measures were drawn from responses to the questionnaires, the interviews, and the structured diary records. (The statistical technique used to examine these issues was discriminant analysis, and scores from both husband and wife were always included. See Appendix C for further results from these analyses.)

General Characteristics of Spouses and Their Relationships

Psychological Adjustment. In trying to identify the characteristics of Survivors and Strugglers, an obvious question is whether spouses who struggle with the transition are simply more prone to general anxiety, depression, and stress. It could be argued that these kinds of chronic adjustment problems interfere with spouses' ability to maintain their relationships amidst the pressures of parenthood. However, this was certainly not the case in this sample: When we looked at the measures taken at the beginning of the study, there were no differences between Survivors and Strugglers on any aspect of adjustment.

Coping Resources. Another plausible explanation for the difficulties experienced by Strugglers is that they had fewer resources to help them deal with new and challenging situations. Although it was clearly impossible to measure every resource available to couples, we did assess levels of self-esteem and social support at the beginning of the study (see Chapter 3). These measures gave us some indication of both the internal and the external resources on which partners could draw during the transition period. Again, we found that Survivors and Strugglers were very similar on these measures.

Patterns of Relating. Given that Survivors and Strugglers did not differ in individual adjustment or coping resources, it seemed likely that the drop in satisfaction experienced by the latter could be linked to relationship patterns within the marriage. That is, the two groups might differ in their approaches to the key areas of couple relationships: attachment, caregiving, and sexuality. In view of the changes in sexual relating that occurred throughout pregnancy and parenthood, problems in this area might be expected to be particularly central to couples' satisfaction with intimacy.

Despite the logical appeal of this argument, we found that Survivors and Strugglers did not differ in their prenatal levels of sexual desire or sexual communication. On the other hand, husbands in the two groups differed in their levels of attachment security: Husbands who struggled with the transition were more anxious about their relationships than other expectant fathers at the beginning of the study. Similarly (although the effect was weaker), husbands in the "struggling" group reported a less responsive style of caring for their spouse at the first assessment.

These findings highlight the far-reaching effects of the interaction style that partners establish *before* the arrival of their first child. They also point to the key role of *husbands'* relationship behavior throughout the transition period: When husbands are secure and confident in their relationships and respond supportively to their wives' needs, the outcome for both members of the couple is more positive. In other words, although the direct load of infant care may fall primarily on wives, husbands have a major role in terms of providing practical and emotional support. Husbands who are able to perform this role effectively can make parenthood an easier and more enjoyable experience, whereas those who become overwhelmed by their own problems and concerns tend to add to the strain.

Pregnancy, Birth, and Parenting

Despite the importance of the interaction patterns that partners establish before the baby's arrival, it is reasonable to expect that Survivors and Strugglers might also be distinguished by their reactions to the specific experiences of pregnancy and parenthood. As mentioned earlier, we wanted to compare Survivors and Strugglers in terms of their attitudes to the pregnancy, experiences of birth and parenting, coping strategies, and division of domestic labor.

Attitudes to Pregnancy. Common wisdom suggests that the difficulties experienced by Strugglers six months after the birth might reflect partners' basic concerns about pregnancy and parenthood. For example, these couples may not have planned to become parents (or at least, not yet), may have been shocked or ambivalent to learn of the pregnancy, or may have experienced severe physical or emotional difficulties during the course of the pregnancy. However, our findings showed that Survivors and Strugglers did not differ on any of these variables.

Birth and Early Parenting. Just as an unwanted or difficult pregnancy might be expected to impede partners' adjustment to parenthood, problems related to the birth or to basic infant care might create ongoing difficulties. Parenting a fussy baby, for instance, might leave partners with very little time and energy to devote to each other. To address this question, we compared Survivors and Strugglers in terms of the length of labor, extent of pain relief required during the birth, prematurity of the birth, and parents' ratings of the infant's temperament. Again, no differences were found between the two groups.

Coping Strategies. As we discussed in Chapter 7, couples completed a measure of coping strategies when their babies were six weeks old. This measure required them to report on the various strategies they used to deal with the demands of parenthood, and provided scores on three types of coping: problem-focused, emotion-focused, and support-seeking. Problem-focused coping and support-seeking are usually considered to be more effective strategies than emotion-focused coping, in terms of reducing stress. We found, however, that Survivors and Strugglers did not differ in their methods of coping with parenthood.

In interpreting this finding, it is important to remember that Survivors and Strugglers were defined in terms of their satisfaction with couple intimacy. In other words, we have established that spouses who tended to rely on emotion-focused coping were not dissatisfied with their marriages at the end of the study. On the other hand, they were experiencing considerable personal distress: Emotion-focused coping was associated with increases in depression, especially for husbands.

Division of Domestic Labor. Finally, using the diary records described in Chapter 9, we checked whether Survivors and Strugglers could be distinguished in terms of their allocation and performance of domestic work. This question is important, because many studies have suggested that dissatisfaction with the division of household and baby-care tasks is a key factor in predicting a difficult transition (see Chapter 1).

To explore this question, we first compared Survivors and Strugglers in terms of the actual amount of time that husbands and wives reported devoting to child care and other domestic chores. We found no differences between the two groups on this relatively objective measure of contributions to domestic work. Neither did the two groups differ in terms of the *relative* contributions made by each spouse (i.e., the ratio of number of hours spent by husband to number of hours spent by wife).

Next, we considered the other key aspect of domestic work: evaluation of the spouse's effort (in other words, partners' subjective feelings about the division of labor). As in Chapter 9, two measures were used to explore this issue. The first measure focused on the absolute difference between partners' current and desired effort, or "perceptions of unfairness." This measure did not differentiate between Survivors and Strugglers. The second subjective measure, "desired spousal effort," took account of the *direction* of difference between current and desired effort; that is, it focused on whether more or less effort was desired from the spouse. For wives, scores on this measure differentiated between Survivors and Strugglers. On average, wives in the Survivor group scored close to zero, indicating that they were satisfied with their husbands' effort around the home. In contrast, wives who were struggling wanted their husbands to increase their effort quite substantially, both on child-care tasks and on other domestic chores.

Reviewing the Risk Factors

Although we found few differences between the Survivors and Strugglers, two critical areas predicted dissatisfaction with couple intimacy:

- husbands' relationship style
- satisfaction with division of domestic labor

The first difference involved husbands' relationship style (attachment security and spousal caregiving). At the beginning of the study, husbands in the couples later categorized as Strugglers were more anxious about their relationships than were other expectant fathers. In other words, they were more concerned about issues of love and commitment, and less confident that their relationships could withstand stresses and threats. We know from previous studies that these concerns tend to be manifested in jealousy, conflict, dependence, and preoccupation with relationship issues. Behaviors of this kind can put considerable pressure on a marriage, especially during periods of major adjustment. Similarly, at the beginning of the study, husbands later categorized as Strugglers reported being less sensitive and responsive to their wives' needs. Again, this interpersonal style is likely to put pressure on the relationship, particularly when wives are feeling stressed by their new responsibilities.

The second difference between Survivors and Strugglers centered on the performance of household and baby-related tasks. Wives in the couples categorized as Strugglers wanted their husbands to increase their involvement in both types of tasks, whereas other new mothers were relatively satisfied with their husbands' involvement. At the same time, Survivors and Strugglers did not differ in the actual amount of time that husbands or wives spent on domestic tasks. Hence, the crucial issue seems to be that, for wives in the Strugglers group, *expectations* about the division of labor were not matched by the reality of their daily lives. In other words, violated expectations seemed to have created disappointment and dissatisfaction with the spouse's contribution. As we discuss in more detail in the following chapter, couples may need to be very clear about their expectations, and to negotiate ways of allocating tasks that are acceptable to both partners.

SUMMARY

In this chapter, we have reported patterns of change across the entire period of the study, and looked at differences between those who were doing well and those who were struggling in their attempts to deal with this major life transition. In terms of couple relationships, changes specific to the new parents included declines in satisfaction with expressions of affection and time together, in husbands' discomfort with closeness, and in wives' sexual desire. Individual adjustment was also affected: New parents reported a decline in general anxiety over the course of the study, but mothers reported increased levels of stress in their lives. Although these findings point to widespread effects of parenthood on couple relationships and individual well-being, these changes affected some couples more than others. Declines in satisfaction with intimacy were more marked in couples where the husband was anxious about relationship issues, and the wife's expectations about her husband's involvement in domestic tasks were not met. In short, couples' experiences of new parenthood varied greatly, with some couples maintaining their sense of closeness and cohesion, and others experiencing a loss of intimacy in their relationships. This loss of intimacy is likely to be linked to problems in communication, which may make it even more difficult for partners to work together as a couple and develop effective parenting styles.

TWELVE

New Parenthood in Perspective

> "When the baby is not happy about something, this means that my wife is not happy, and this means that I'm not happy – so it's a challenge, but you try to figure out what's wrong and correct the problem."

Throughout this book, we have seen that responses to new parenthood varied enormously from couple to couple. In addition, the patterns of relationship functioning that couples reported at the end of the study were rather different from those evident soon after the birth. Clearly, the transition to parenthood is an ongoing process, and change is not restricted to the weeks immediately following the birth. In this chapter, we sum up the main findings of the study, and discuss the implications for new parents and those wishing to help and support them.

DIVERSITY OF EXPERIENCE

It has been known for many years that overall relationship satisfaction can decline following the birth of the first baby. However, one of the unique features of this study has been the focus on specific aspects of relationship satisfaction that are likely to be affected by the addition of the new family member. Based on couples' reports of their recent feelings about their relationships, it seems that declines in satisfaction occurred mainly in the areas of expressions of affection and understanding, and quality and quantity of time together. In other words, couples tended to be dissatisfied with the lower levels of intimacy they were experiencing. In contrast, there was generally little change in overall levels of satisfaction. This finding suggests that many couples *anticipate* some reduction in intimacy with the arrival of the baby, and are able to accept this change as a normal part of the transition.

Even in the area of marital intimacy, declines in satisfaction were not reported by all couples. Roughly two-thirds of couples (that we called the Survivors) managed to maintain their previous levels of satisfaction with intimacy, despite the impact of the new arrival; during the interviews we conducted, some even reported a renewed sense of closeness and partnership. However, for the other third (the Strugglers), changes in couple intimacy were a real concern.

Another finding that highlighted the diverse reactions of different couples concerned the varying rates at which mothers and fathers became engrossed with their babies. Some parents reported immediate and intensely strong feelings for their infants, to the point where they hated being away from them, even for a very brief period of time. Others reported that they were still grappling with feelings of "disconnection" some weeks after the birth, or that they were looking forward to a greater sense of involvement in the future, as the child developed and became more active.

The diverse reactions to new parenthood were also apparent in relation to patterns of household work. For both mothers and fathers, there was huge variability in the amount of time spent on infant care and other household tasks. Interestingly, the actual amount of time spent on these tasks did not predict spouses' satisfaction with their relationships at the end of the study; nor did it predict declines in satisfaction. From this finding, it seems clear that there are different ways of allocating household tasks that suit different couples. For example, where both husbands and wives share traditional expectations about gender roles, wives may be happy for their husbands to concentrate on providing for the family, and to have less involvement around the home. Other couples prefer to establish a less traditional approach to paid and unpaid work, although the pressures of parenthood can sometimes make this rather difficult to achieve.

ADJUSTMENT AS A PROCESS

As we mentioned at the start of this chapter, adjustment to parenthood involves an ongoing process. In the course of this process, partners gain new experiences, learn new skills, and develop new ways of relating to each other. Changes in general adjustment (e.g., the stress experienced by new mothers) were apparent quite soon after the birth, reflecting the immediate demands of infant care. On the other hand, changes involving the relationship (declines in satisfaction with intimacy, and for new mothers, declines in sexual desire) were generally not apparent until some months later.

Throughout the adjustment to parenthood, changes that may begin with one partner and one aspect of the relationship tend to precipitate further changes that affect both spouses. For example, wives who were insecure about their relationships during pregnancy were more likely to experience high levels of depression in the weeks following the birth (see Chapter 8). By the end of the study, these wives were reporting increases in depression, stress, discomfort with closeness, and relationship anxiety; in addition, their husbands were reporting increases in both relationship anxiety and general anxiety. In other words, both partners were caught up in this negative cycle of insecurity and depression. The link between postnatal depression and wives' insecurity about their couple relationships has not been shown previously, and may be of vital importance in understanding these processes. Given that depressed mothers struggle to maintain their relationship with their partner, their relationship with their baby, and their involvement in daily activities, it is not surprising that their husbands are affected by this difficult situation.

The diary reports discussed in Chapter 9 also point to complex cycles of change. Dissatisfaction with the spouse's task performance was particularly central in this regard. Husbands' dissatisfaction with partners' task performance in the weeks following the birth was greater if the husbands were depressed, insecure, or unhappy with their relationships at the beginning of the study. Further, husbands' dissatisfaction with task performance was associated with increases in their own levels of stress, and with negative changes for their wives (i.e., increases in stress, depression, and anxiety, and declines in relationship satisfaction). Similarly, wives were more dissatisfied with partners' task performance if their husbands were depressed, anxious, or unhappy with their relationships at the beginning of the study, and in turn, wives' dissatisfaction led to increased insecurity for husbands.

In short, it is clear that the experiences of each partner affect, and are affected by, what is happening for the other. This finding can be understood in terms of the high levels of interdependence that characterize relationships between husbands and wives: The thoughts, feelings, and actions of one spouse have a strong impact on the other. In fact, this may be particularly true during periods of transition, when new interaction patterns are being shaped. Because of this interdependence, the transition to parenthood has to be understood from the perspectives of both women and men.

EXPECTATIONS

The diary reports also highlighted the role of partners' expectations about parenthood and about family tasks and responsibilities. The importance of expectations is supported by many other studies of new parenthood. Where partners hold very different expectations of household work patterns or other aspects of couple interaction, problems tend to arise. For example, if a wife spends much more time caring for the infant than her husband expected her to, he may begin to resent the attention the baby is getting. In turn, his resentment and disappointment are likely to have a negative impact on the couple relationship, and perhaps on his wife's overall psychological adjustment. Similarly, if a husband fails to provide the practical and emotional support that his wife expected, the transition to parenthood is almost certain to prove difficult.

Expectations can affect adjustment, even if both partners hold *similar* expectations and standards. If those expectations do not match the reality of parenthood, dissatisfaction tends to result. For instance, partners may underestimate the amount of time and energy involved in caring for a new baby. Similarly, they may not realize the restrictions on their lifestyle that a new baby will bring; in this case, they may resent the fact that they cannot go out at a moment's notice, but have to find a baby-sitter and attend to all the things the baby will need over the next few hours.

A further issue concerns wives' expectations of themselves, especially in the areas of housework and baby care. Some wives hold rather unrealistic standards, expecting to be able to attend to the baby's needs while keeping the house in the condition they used to achieve before the baby arrived. Equally important, they may assume that their husbands hold the same high standards. As we saw in Chapter 9, however, most husbands in this study actually wanted their wives to *reduce* their involvement in domestic chores, and to "slow down."

We noted earlier that expectations also seem relevant to the way that partners handle declines in couple intimacy. Given that overall relationship satisfaction was fairly stable, it seems that most couples are able to cope with this decline, without seeing it as having long-term implications for their marital relationship. Presumably, this ability to accept the restriction of intimacy stems from the fact that the change is anticipated, at least to some extent.

ATTACHMENT SECURITY

One of our main aims in this study was to examine the transition to parenthood from the perspective of attachment security. That is, we were interested in partners' concerns about their couple relationships, and the impact of these concerns on their experiences of the transition. Theory and research into adult attachment suggest that couple interactions are influenced by two main dimensions of attachment security: anxiety over relationships, and discomfort with closeness.

Anxiety over Relationships

The findings of this study point to the particular importance of anxiety over relationships, that is, of individuals' concerns about whether their partners' feelings of love and commitment are deep and lasting, and whether the relationship can survive any threats or challenges. For both husbands and wives, relationship anxiety (measured at the beginning of the study) was associated with more negative reactions to the news of the pregnancy, with less sensitivity and responsiveness to the partner's needs, and with less relationship satisfaction. Spouses high in relationship anxiety also tended to respond to the stresses of parenthood with emotion-focused coping (a form of coping that often fails to reduce levels of stress, because it does not directly confront the source of the difficulties).

On the other hand, some of the implications of relationship anxiety were specific to husbands or wives. According to the diary reports, husbands who were anxious about their relationships at the beginning of the study felt unhappy about their wives' involvement in household tasks; that is, they wanted their wives to spend less time on these tasks. Husbands who were anxious about their relationships were also more likely to be identified as Strugglers, rather than Survivors, at the end of the study. In other words, husbands' insecurity seemed to increase both partners' concerns about declines in affection, attention, and intimacy.

Wives' relationship anxiety also created problems in coming to terms with parenthood: Wives who reported relationship concerns at the beginning of the study were prone to depression following the birth of their babies. As we saw in the previous section, this sense of insecurity on the part of wives, and the associated depression, tend to set in motion a destructive cycle of reactions that has serious implications for both partners and for their relationship.

Part of this destructive cycle involved increases in wives' discomfort with closeness and relationship anxiety, and in husbands' relationship anxiety. These findings are important because they show that attachment insecurity not only *affects* relationship processes, but can be *affected by* them. In other words, difficult relationship experiences can have a profound impact on partners' sense of security. Similarly, wives' dissatisfaction with husbands' involvement in baby-related tasks tended to increase husbands' relationship anxiety. Presumably, some husbands interpret their wives' complaints about their lack of involvement with the baby as threatening the future of the relationship.

In contrast to the widespread effects of *relationship anxiety*, the measure of *general anxiety* showed few links with spouses' adjustment to parenthood. In other words, anxiety about relationship issues is distinct from the more generalized and pervasive sense of anxiety that can have a debilitating effect on some people. The former type of anxiety reflects concerns that are specific to close relationships (concerns about loss and rejection), and is a particularly strong predictor of relationship outcomes.

Although relationship anxiety can clearly have negative effects on couple relationships, it is important to keep this problem in perspective. Everyone experiences some level of anxiety about relationship issues from time to time, particularly when relationships are new or in the midst of change. Relationship anxiety is not necessarily a cause for concern unless it is severe or ongoing, and having a negative impact on the relationship. For example, high levels of relationship anxiety can lead to jealousy, conflict, and a tendency to interpret even benign relationship events in negative ways. These attitudes and behaviors are obviously destructive, and need to be addressed.

Discomfort with Closeness

Although relationship anxiety was particularly important to spouses' adjustment to parenthood, discomfort with closeness also showed some effects. Spouses who felt uncomfortable with intimacy were less satisfied with their sexual communication, and less effective in caring for their partners in times of need. These findings can be understood in terms of the intimacy that is implicit in certain types of couple interactions. For example, sexual issues are highly emotional and intimate in nature, and sexual communication requires that partners be willing and able to handle personal disclosure. Similarly, supporting a distressed or vulnerable spouse usually calls for the provision of physical and emotional intimacy. These behaviors may not come easily to those who prefer to maintain their independence, and to "keep some distance."

The second area concerned stress and coping. Wives who were uncomfortable with closeness were less likely to adopt support-seeking as a response to the stresses of new parenthood. Again, this finding is not surprising, because support-seeking inevitably involves close interactions, and may make people who prefer to be self-reliant feel quite vulnerable. In the context of new parenthood, however, an overemphasis on self-sufficiency tends to put additional pressure on the new mother.

Effects of Partner's Attachment Security

In line with the concept of interdependence (mentioned earlier in this chapter), we found that individuals' reactions to pregnancy and parenthood were affected not only by their *own* attachment security, but also by that of the *partner*. For example, when husbands reported feeling anxious about their relationships, their wives reacted more negatively to the discovery that they were pregnant. Perhaps these wives feared, with some justification, that their relationships were not yet solid enough for them to embark on parenthood. In addition, when wives were uncomfortable with closeness, their husbands tended to engage in more support-seeking. It seems likely that these wives do not respond very sensitively to their husbands' needs for comfort and support, leaving them to seek support in the broader social network.

Advantages of the Attachment Perspective

Although it has been known for some time that the couple relationship is a key factor in the transition to parenthood, the attachment perspective has provided a unique way of looking at these issues. Unlike studies that focus on general reports of relationship satisfaction, the attachment perspective allowed us to explore *why* particular individuals might experience particular kinds of relationship problems. For example, discomfort with closeness and anxiety over relationships are both key aspects of attachment insecurity, but we have been able to show that they are played out quite differently in couple relationships, particularly when the relationship is in transition.

The attachment perspective has also highlighted the importance of looking at the couple as a *unit*, or system. That is, we have seen that the behavior of each partner can be influenced by the attachment characteristics of both. In other words, a couple with one secure partner and one insecure partner is likely to respond quite differently to relationship issues from a couple with two secure partners (or one with two insecure partners).

Another useful feature of attachment theory lies in its ability to link current relationship functioning to earlier experiences, both in the family of origin and in other close relationships. These prior experiences shape behavior through the expectations that partners have of one another and, as a result, different individuals can interpret the same relationship event quite differently. For instance, someone who has consistently experienced warm and affectionate relationships is likely to have positive expectations of others, and to see partners' behavior as generally well-intentioned. On the other hand, someone who has consistently experienced hostility or rejection tends to have more negative expectations of others. Of course, these expectations are quite reasonable, given the context in which they developed, but they can nevertheless interfere with the development of a strong and secure partnership.

Attachment theory is particularly appropriate for studying the transition to parenthood. The key task at this point in the life cycle is for each partner to develop an attachment bond with the infant, while at the same time maintaining a strong and stable couple relationship. As we have seen throughout this book, a sense of insecurity makes this task more difficult, and can serve to undermine the couple relationship.

SOCIAL SUPPORT

Although the couple relationship plays a central role in smoothing the transition to parenthood, new parents also need support from a wider network of family and friends. The importance of this network has emerged as a strong theme throughout this book. Unfortunately, our findings indicate that interactions with others can be a source of conflict and strain to new parents, as well as a source of comfort and support.

During their pregnancy, some couples reported a considerable amount of interference from others, usually involving advice directed at the wives about what they should and should not be doing "in their condition." On the positive side, other expectant couples reported being pleasantly surprised by the support that they were receiving from other people. This support was sometimes practical in nature (e.g., providing baby clothes or other items for the nursery), and sometimes emotional (e.g., responding with great excitement to the news of the impending birth). This sense of shared pleasure seemed to further enrich the whole experience for these couples.

After the birth, some couples again reported problems with social interactions, although these problems took various forms. For some couples, the difficulty stemmed from having no family members close by who could help with the baby or provide emotional support. For others, the difficulty lay in the tendency of friends or family members to intrude in the couple's lives, either by continually demanding hospitality, or by "taking over" tasks that the parents wanted to do themselves. On the positive side, several couples talked about the great enthusiasm with which friends and family members welcomed the new arrival, and the various ways in which they provided help and support.

Both during pregnancy and after the birth, wives were more likely than husbands to mention support from others, whether in positive or negative terms. On the measure assessing overall support from spouse, family, and friends, wives also perceived greater availability of support. Support is likely to be especially important to women at this time, given that they are the ones experiencing firsthand the physical and emotional changes of pregnancy, and generally the ones taking primary responsibility for the infant's daily care.

In the overall social network, some relationships play a special role in meeting needs for comfort and security. In this study, we were interested in tracking changes in this "attachment network" across the transition to parenthood. Over this period, new mothers and fathers reported a slight drop in the extent to which they relied on their spouse for a sense of comfort and security. Mothers also reported less reliance on friends, together with more reliance on parents. The idea that new mothers become more reliant on their parents is fairly widely accepted; parents are an important source of support and advice, and new mothers often develop an increased appreciation of their parents' wisdom and greater life experience. Parents may also be useful in providing practical support and advice. Of course, another change that occurs for new parents involves the gradual inclusion of the baby into their attachment network. Even in the first few months of the baby's life, many parents were keenly aware of the distress they would feel if they were separated from their baby for any length of time.

As well as these general changes in patterns of relating to others, more fine-grained changes also tend to occur. For example, some parents reported that they now felt closer to particular people, but that others seemed to have dropped out of their circle of friends. These changes generally reflected their newfound focus on child-related issues, which brought them closer to friends who had children of their own, but could create distance from those who were still childless. In short, the social network undergoes complex changes at this time of transition.

JOYS OF BECOMING PARENTS

Although parenthood brings many changes and pressures, it is important to keep in mind that couples also reported very positive experiences. For many parents, the sheer fact of having the baby was a source of joy and wonder, particularly if they had been wanting a family for some time. Others were particularly excited when their baby smiled at them, appeared to recognize them, or responded to their attempts at soothing and pacifying. In other words, parents were excited by these early attempts at mutual exchange. Another thrill for parents was watching the baby change and develop day by day, and feeling part of this visible "progress."

The addition of a new family member was also an exciting idea for many couples. Some of these couples were overwhelmed by the knowledge that they had created a new life, and felt that the baby provided a real sense of "continuity." Other couples reported experiencing an increased sense of closeness to the spouse, a new sense of identity as a family, excitement at the idea of doing things together as a family, or a stronger feeling of inclusion within the extended family.

IMPLICATIONS OF THE FINDINGS

The findings of our study have implications for three groups of people: parents themselves (including prospective parents), their friends and family members, and professionals who deal with new parents. We will discuss the implications of the findings for these three groups, and suggest things they can do that may help during this transition period.

Implications for Parents

Two key issues distinguished between the Survivors and the Strugglers in our study (see Chapter 11 for more details). These two issues centred around the division of household tasks (both general and baby-related), and partners' insecurities about their relationships.

Division of Household Tasks. Many couples were concerned about the division of household tasks, with the main issue being the perceived *fairness* of partners' input. According to the diary records completed when the babies were three months old, wives generally tended to see husbands as failing to do their "fair share." When wives were particularly unhappy with their husbands' effort, both partners experienced a drop in satisfaction with the level of intimacy in their relationship. Presumably, wives who are dissatisfied with their husband's effort see themselves as bearing the brunt of the workload, and feel rather angry and resentful. It is not surprising that this situation leads to both partners becoming dissatisfied with their time together, and with the degree of affection and understanding expressed in the marriage.

On the other hand, the diary records showed that husbands tended to want wives to spend *less* time on household and baby tasks. When this perception of wives' over-involvement was quite strong, wives became increasingly stressed and depressed. We can speculate that husbands who wanted their wives to cut back on domestic chores felt somewhat neglected and unwanted; they may have responded to these feelings either by complaining to their wives, or by withdrawing emotionally and leaving them confused and unsupported. These behaviors are likely to make things even more difficult for their wives, who, even if aware of husbands' dissatisfaction, may find it hard to see how they can cut back on basic household chores and infant care.

Although it is obviously important for husbands and wives to share their concerns about each other's involvement in tasks around the home, they need to communicate in ways that promote effective problem-solving, rather than ways that lead to aggressive or defensive responses. Both husbands and wives need to be "up-front" about their expectations for each other's involvement, but also to acknowledge the pressures that the partner is facing. It is critical that couples work on these issues as a team, rather than becoming involved in an unproductive tug-of-war.

Preferably, couples should begin to think and talk about these issues even before the baby is born, because it is much more difficult to resolve problems when both partners are tired and stressed. In negotiating these issues, wives need to be aware that husbands sometimes feel a sense of neglect at this point in the marriage, and that this problem can fuel husbands' complaints about partners' involvement in household tasks. Husbands, on the other hand, may need to be more realistic about the amount of work involved in caring for a new baby; when husbands complain about the amount of attention and affection received from their wives, they only add to the stress these mothers experience. Perhaps if couples were more willing to share in these tasks, the work would get done more quickly, and more time would be left for partners to work at maintaining their relationship. Using some of this time to have fun together would also enrich the relationship. In short, a helpful approach is to try to organize household tasks in a way that minimizes stress for both partners and maximizes time together. This approach may entail considerable adjustment for each spouse, since new priorities need to be discussed and agreed upon.

Although we have said that expectations need to be shared and negotiated, it is also important for partners to be flexible in their allocation of household work. Babies have good days and bad days, and having rigid expectations about who will do what, and about how much should be accomplished on a particular day, can be counterproductive. In fact, these issues may need to be negotiated and reevaluated quite frequently.

Relationship Insecurities. The other key issue distinguishing Survivors from Strugglers was the nature of the couple relationship and, more specifically, issues about security and insecurity. As we have seen throughout this book, attachment insecurity (especially anxiety over relationships) predicted a number of difficulties in the transition to parenthood, including more negative reactions to the pregnancy, dissatisfaction with levels of couple intimacy and with partner's involvement in household tasks, and mothers' postnatal depression.

These findings have several implications for couples facing new parenthood. First, it is important to note that attachment insecurity is best seen as a couple issue, rather than as one person's problem. In fact, the effects of relationship anxiety depend to some extent on the response of the partner: A partner who is sensitive to the spouse's needs and concerns can often reassure the insecure spouse, and help prevent the feelings of insecurity from escalating. For this reason, attachment insecurity should not be regarded as a problem with no solution; consistently sensitive responses from a spouse can help partners to change the negative expectations that are linked with insecurity. In fact, individuals' sense of security can be either enhanced *or* eroded, depending on their relationship experiences, and a stable and satisfying long-term relationship is particularly important in this regard. At the same time, because *both* partners contribute to the relationship, we would not want to place all the responsibility for the relationship on the more secure partner. Especially where husbands are insecure and new mothers are already very stressed, it is unrealistic and inappropriate to expect wives to take full responsibility for the relationship.

Second, where there are serious relationship concerns that are disrupting partners' interactions, counseling and therapy should be considered. It is important for couples to realize that help is available, and that counseling can assist partners to get a new perspective on their difficulties. Particularly when partners are feeling very stressed or insecure, the presence of a third party can provide a more controlled environment in which they are able to listen to each other's concerns and gain a better understanding of each other's positions. Although some people may see counseling as a sign of weakness or inadequacy, or as relevant only to those with extreme adjustment problems, it makes good sense to address relationship problems as they emerge. In fact, intervention is usually much more effective if it takes place before problems have become severe.

Third, it is important for prospective parents to be aware of the changes that may occur in their relationships, and in their own sense of well-being, with the arrival of a baby. Changes in sexual relating, and in couple intimacy more generally, are not uncommon; it may be helpful for partners to discuss their thoughts and feelings about these issues as they plan for parenthood, and throughout the transition period. Similarly, if partners are aware that new mothers may be vulnerable to feelings of stress and depression, they can discuss possible strategies for dealing with these concerns (including seeking professional help).

Finally, couples need to be aware that having a baby will not solve any difficulties in their relationship. In fact, parenthood is much more likely to exacerbate relationship problems, especially if these problems involve deep-seated feelings of insecurity. For example, we have seen that women who are insecure about their relationships are more likely to feel depressed after the birth of the baby, and that this can lead to stress and insecurity for both partners. Similarly, men who are insecure about their relationships are more likely to resent their wives' involvement in household work, again increasing the stress of both partners. In other words, the clear message is that having a baby to save the relationship does *not* work. Rather, partners need to make sure that their relationship is very solid before they embark on parenthood.

Implications for Friends and Family

Friends and family members play a crucial part in the transition to parenthood: New parents tend to need considerable support, and people who are close to them are especially important in this regard. People can help in many ways, providing both practical and emotional support. For example, when a friend buys a toy or an item for the nursery, expectant parents can be pleased about the practical nature of the gift, but also about the fact that their friends share their excitement about the impending birth. Similarly, after the arrival of the baby, friends and family members can help with meal preparation and other basic household chores, leaving the parents more time to devote to their infant.

New parents may also seek advice from others, particularly those in their social network who have already become parents. First-time parents often talk about how much they have to learn, and they may have many questions about others' experiences of pregnancy, birth, and infant care. Friends and family members may be useful sounding boards for these young couples. Just being there to listen and to provide companionship can help a great deal.

Both before and after the birth, couples in this study commented on the problems associated with lack of support, particularly the absence of family members living close by. Given that new parents emphasize the difficulties associated with this lack of support, it may be important for family members to provide whatever support they can from a distance. Even a phone call can let new parents know that family members are thinking of them and are concerned about their welfare. Any expression of interest or concern is likely to buoy parents' spirits, no matter how stressed they are feeling.

Some couples also complained about interactions that they found unhelpful or worrisome. For example, some reported that people told them stories about pregnancy and birth that were frightening, or that ignored any positive aspects of these experiences. Stories about the supposed dangers of being active during pregnancy, and about long and difficult labors, were seen as particularly unhelpful. Couples also complained about receiving unwanted, unfounded, or contradictory advice.

In short, friends and family members need to be sensitive in the way they provide support to new parents. Both tangible and emotional support are appreciated, but it is important that people try not to "take over" from the parents, or erode their sense of being in control of the situation. This latter issue seemed to apply mainly to family members, and particularly to mothers and mothers-in-law. New parents generally appreciated the support they received from friends and family members, but some reported feeling overwhelmed by the demands associated with having other people in the home. In other words, those who visit the new parents need to be careful not to wear out their welcome. For new parents, lack of time alone together tends to be a major source of concern, and can interfere with the development of a sense of family cohesion. Having to provide continual hospitality to friends and family members can exacerbate this problem. Hence, a major way in which support can be demonstrated is to provide the couple with regular opportunities to spend time alone together as a couple; for example, by providing baby-sitting on a regular basis.

Implications for Professionals

In the course of pregnancy and new parenthood, couples are likely to have contact with a variety of professional people, including general practitioners, obstetricians, nursing staff, counselors, pediatricians, and other experts in early childhood development. All of these groups play a vital role in making the transition to parenthood as smooth as possible for each couple.

From the comments made by couples in this study, a number of points emerged that may help professionals in their dealings with couples at this stage. One factor that many couples emphasized was the need for professionals to provide prospective parents with accurate and comprehensive information. Parents tended to report feeling very anxious about the lack of information available to them. For example, several parents commented that although breastfeeding is considered "natural," they needed considerable help in getting it working effectively. Problems of this kind are exacerbated by mothers being pressured to go home from hospital soon after the birth, often before the milk flow is well established.

Whereas couples reported wanting more information, they were also troubled by the inconsistent advice they sometimes received from professionals. In fact, they reported that conflicting advice was a major source of stress in its own right, and tended to make them feel quite anxious and helpless. Given the variety of professionals involved in the transition to parenthood, and the different types of training they receive, some of this inconsistency is probably inevitable. Professionals are generally highly trained and informed in their own area of expertise, and cannot be expected to know a great deal about all other aspects of pregnancy and parenthood. Nevertheless, it would seem important for those professional groups that deal with new parents to try to cooperate in providing information that is as current and consistent as possible. The type of inconsistency reported by some of the couples in this study may be minimized by professionals ensuring that couples have a good sense of where to go for further information, particularly regarding concerns that lie outside their own area of expertise.

Although providing factual information is important, professionals should not neglect the emotional aspects of this transition. With regard to breast-feeding, for example, factual information about milk flow can be helpful, but it may be equally crucial to deal with parents' emotional concerns. For many mothers, in particular, breast-feeding is a highly emotional issue, involving social pressures about the advantages of breast-feeding and their expectations of themselves as "good mothers." In fact, emotional concerns can sometimes affect the physical processes involved in breast-feeding. More generally, parents reported anxieties about their babies' progress, and uncertainties about the best ways to care for them. These issues were especially salient in the first few weeks after the birth; during this time, the development of parenting skills can be made more difficult by the fragile emotional state that accompanies lack of sleep, hormonal changes, and so on. Professionals generally recognize the need to offer both factual information and reassurance, but may not always know how to communicate their support. Discussing these issues with colleagues and members of other professional groups may help in this regard.

For counselors, in particular, the findings of this study highlight the importance of the couple relationship in the transition to parenthood. Partners who have unresolved relationship issues are likely to find the transition much more difficult, because these issues tend to be intensified by the stresses of parenthood. Attachment insecurity is especially relevant, and may underlie various problems that are experienced at this time. Problems as diverse as perceived inequity of household chores and postnatal depression may stem from anxieties about partners' love and commitment, and about the future of the relationship. Professionals may also need to be alert to very early signs of stress and depression, since this study clearly showed that these problems can escalate over the first few months of parenthood.

SUMMARY

Perhaps the most striking finding of this study concerned the diverse experiences reported by new parents. Both the joys and the challenges of parenthood were seen very differently by different couples. In describing their reactions to parenthood, some couples focused on the baby itself, describing both the excitement and wonder of the new arrival, and the stresses and anxieties associated with infant care. Similarly, the changes that couples described in their relationships ranged from a sense of increased closeness and partnership, to concerns about the lack of intimacy and affection. Social networks also showed complex patterns of change: New mothers reported greater reliance on their own parents, and relationships with friends became somewhat less important, particularly if those friends were not parents themselves.

There is no doubt that first-time parenthood is a time of substantial change. Some changes, such as increases in feelings of stress, became apparent soon after the birth, whereas changes in the couple relationship generally became apparent some months later. Throughout this adjustment period, problems experienced by one partner tended to affect the other's adjustment, as well as the couple relationship. Parents' expectations played a major role in their adjustment, with discrepant and unrealistic expectations making the transition more difficult.

A unique aspect of this study has been the potential to explore the implications of attachment security for the couple relationship, and for partners' general psychological well-being. Basic insecurities about love and commitment are likely to have negative effects on individuals and couples, especially when they are facing new and challenging situations. A key challenge that comes with new parenthood involves juggling the various demands on time and energy; in particular, parents need to manage the practical tasks of the household, while tending to the emotional needs of each of its members. In both these areas, a sense of security seems to play a key role in facilitating adjustment.

Core Questionnaires Completed by Couples

MARITAL SATISFACTION

For each of the following, if the statement is TRUE *or* USUALLY TRUE *as applied to you, please circle the letter T. If the statement is* FALSE *or* USUALLY FALSE *as applied to you, please circle the letter F.*

1. My marriage has been very satisfying.
2. There is a great deal of love and affection expressed in our marriage.
3. My spouse often fails to understand my point of view on things.
4. It seems that we used to have more fun than we do now.
5. I am quite happily married.
6. Just when I need it the most, my spouse makes me feel important.
7. Minor disagreements with my spouse often end up in big arguments.
8. My spouse and I spend a good deal of time together in many different kinds of play and recreation.
9. There are some serious difficulties in our marriage.
10. My spouse almost always responds with understanding to my mood at a given moment.
11. A lot of our arguments seem to end in depressing stalemates.
12. My spouse likes to share his/her leisure time with me.
13. Whenever I'm feeling sad, my spouse makes me feel loved and happy again.
14. My marriage is an unhappy one.

15. My spouse seems to enjoy just being with me.

16. My spouse and I seem to be able to go for days sometimes without settling our differences.

17. Even when angry with me, my spouse is able to appreciate my viewpoints.

18. The recreational and leisure life of my spouse and myself appears to be meeting both our needs quite well.

19. My marriage has been disappointing in several ways.

20. Sometimes I wonder just how much my spouse really does love me.

21. My spouse does many different things to show me that s/he loves me.

22. Our arguments frequently end up with one of us feeling hurt or crying.

23. I am fairly satisfied with the way my spouse and I spend our available free time.

24. My marriage is as successful as any I know.

25. When my spouse and I have differences of opinion, we sit down and discuss them.

26. About the only time I'm with my spouse is at meals and bedtime.

27. I get pretty discouraged about my marriage sometimes.

28. Whenever s/he is feeling down, my spouse comes to me for support.

29. Frankly, our marriage has not been successful.

30. When arguing, we manage quite well to restrict our focus to the important issues.

31. My spouse and I enjoy the same types of amusement.

32. My marriage is less happy than the very successful ones.

33. Sometimes I feel as though my spouse doesn't really need me.

34. I believe that our marriage is as pleasant as that of most people I know.

35. My spouse seems committed to settling our differences.

Items used to form the scales are as follows (R indicates reverse scoring):
Global distress: 1 (R), 5 (R), 9, 14, 19, 24 (R), 27, 29, 32, 34 (R)
Affective communication: 2, 6, 10, 13, 20 (R), 21, 28, 33 (R)
Problem-solving communication: 3 (R), 7 (R), 11 (R), 16 (R), 17, 22 (R), 25, 30, 35
Time together: 4 (R), 8, 12, 15, 18, 23, 26 (R), 31

ATTACHMENT STYLE QUESTIONNAIRE

Please answer the following questions using the rating scale:

1 = strongly disagree; 2 = moderately disagree; 3 = slightly disagree; 4 = slightly agree; 5 = moderately agree; 6 = strongly agree

1. Overall, I am a worthwhile person.

2. I am easier to get to know than most people.

3. I feel confident that other people will be there for me when I need them.

4. I prefer to depend on myself rather than other people.

5. I prefer to keep to myself.

6. To ask for help is to admit that you're a failure.

7. People's worth should be judged by what they achieve.

8. Achieving things is more important than building relationships.

9. Doing your best is more important than getting on with others.

10. If you've got a job to do, you should do it no matter who gets hurt.

11. It's important to me that others like me.

12. It's important to me to avoid doing things that others won't like.

13. I find it hard to make a decision unless I know what other people think.

14. My relationships with others are generally superficial.

15. Sometimes I think that I am no good at all.

16. I find it hard to trust other people.

17. I find it difficult to depend on others.

18. I find that others are reluctant to get as close as I would like.

19. I find it relatively easy to get close to other people.

20. I find it easy to trust others.

21. I feel comfortable depending on other people.

22. I worry that others won't care about me as much as I care about them.

23. I worry about people getting too close.

24. I worry that I won't measure up to other people.

25. I have mixed feelings about being close to others.

26. While I want to get close to others, I feel uneasy about it.

27. I wonder why people would want to be involved with me.

28. It's very important to me to have a close relationship.

29. I worry a lot about my relationships.

30. I wonder how I would cope without someone to love me.

31. I feel confident about relating to others.

32. I often feel left out or alone.

33. I often worry that I do not really fit in with other people.

34. Other people have their own problems, so I don't bother them with mine.

35. When I talk over my problems with others, I generally feel ashamed or foolish.

36. I am too busy with other activities to put much time into relationships.

37. If something is bothering me, others are generally aware and concerned.

38. I am confident that other people will like and respect me.

39. I get frustrated when others are not available when I need them.

40. Other people often disappoint me.

Items used to form the scales are as follows (R indicates reverse scoring):
Discomfort with closeness: 3 (R), 4, 5, 8, 9, 10, 14, 16, 17, 19 (R), 20 (R), 21 (R), 23, 25, 34, 37 (R)
Anxiety over relationships: 11, 13, 15, 18, 22, 24, 27, 29, 30, 31 (R), 32, 33, 38 (R)

CAREGIVING

How well does each of the following statements describe your feelings and behavior towards your spouse? Not like me (1) to Completely like me (6)

1. When my partner seems to want or need a hug, I am glad to provide it.

2. I feel comfortable holding my partner when s/he needs physical signs of support or reassurance.

3. I don't like it when my partner is needy and clings to me.

4. Too often, I don't realize when my partner is upset or worried about something.

5. I sometimes "miss" or "misread" my partner's signals for help and understanding.

6. I can help my partner work out his/her problems without taking control.

7. I often end up telling my partner what to do when s/he is trying to make a decision.

8. I create problems by taking on my partner's troubles as if they were my own.

9. When it is important, I take care of my own needs before I try to take care of my partner's.

10. When my partner is troubled or upset, I move close to provide support or comfort.

11. I'm very good at recognizing my partner's needs and feelings, even when they are different from my own.

12. I tend to be too domineering when trying to help my partner.

13. I tend to get over-involved in my partner's problems and difficulties.

14. I sometimes draw away from my partner's attempts to get a reassuring hug from me.

15. I am very attentive to my partner's nonverbal signals for help and support.

16. When helping my partner solve a problem, I am much more "cooperative" than "controlling."

17. I frequently get too "wrapped up" in my partner's problems and needs.

18. I sometimes push my partner away when s/he reaches out for a needed hug or kiss.

19. I can always tell when my partner needs comforting, even when s/he doesn't ask for it.

20. When I help my partner with something, I tend to want to do things "my way."

21. I tend to take on my partner's problems – and then feel burdened by them.

22. When my partner cries or is distressed, my first impulse is to hold or touch him/her.

23. I sometimes miss the subtle signs that show how my partner is feeling.

24. I am always supportive of my partner's *own efforts* to solve his/her problems.

25. I help my partner without becoming over-involved in his/her problems.

26. When my partner is crying or emotionally upset, I feel like withdrawing.

27. I'm good at knowing when my partner needs my help or support and when s/he would rather handle things alone.

28. When my partner tells me about a problem, I sometimes go too far in criticizing his/her own attempts to deal with it.

29. When necessary, I can say "no" to my partner's requests for help without feeling guilty.

30. I'm not very good at "tuning in" to my partner's needs and feelings.

31. I always respect my partner's ability to make his/her own decisions and solve his/her own problems.

32. I can easily keep myself from becoming overly concerned about or overly protective of my partner.

Items used to form the scales are as follows (R indicates reverse scoring):
Responsive caregiving: 1, 2, 3 (R), 4 (R), 5 (R), 6, 7 (R), 10, 11, 12 (R), 14 (R), 15, 16, 18 (R), 19, 20 (R), 22, 23 (R), 24, 26 (R), 27, 28 (R), 30 (R), 31
Compulsive caregiving: 8, 9 (R), 13, 17, 21, 25 (R), 29 (R), 32 (R)

SEXUALITY

Please answer the following questions using the rating scale:

1 = Strongly disagree; 2 = Moderately disagree; 3 = Slightly disagree; 4 = Slightly agree; 5 = Moderately agree; 6 = Strongly agree

1. I tell my partner when I am especially sexually satisfied.

2. I am satisfied with my partner's ability to communicate her/his sexual desires to me.

3. I do not let my partner know things that I find pleasing during sex.

4. I am very satisfied with the quality of our sexual interactions.

5. I do not hesitate to let my partner know when I want to have sex with him/her.

6. I do not tell my partner whether or not I am sexually satisfied.

7. I am dissatisfied over the degree to which my partner and I discuss our sexual relationship.

8. I am not afraid to show my partner what kind of sexual behavior I find satisfying.

9. I would not hesitate to show my partner what is a sexual turn-on for me.

10. My partner does not show me when s/he is sexually satisfied.

11. I show my partner what pleases me during sex.

12. I am displeased with the manner in which my partner and I communicate with each other during sex.

13. My partner does not show me things s/he finds pleasing during sex.

14. I show my partner when I am sexually satisfied.

15. My partner does not let me know whether sex has been satisfying or not.

16. I do not show my partner when I am sexually satisfied.

17. I am satisfied concerning my ability to communicate about sexual matters with my partner.

18. My partner shows me by the way s/he touches me if s/he is satisfied.

19. I am dissatisfied with my partner's ability to communicate her/his sexual desires to me.

20. I have no way of knowing when my partner is sexually satisfied.

21. I am not satisfied in the majority of our sexual interactions.

22. I am pleased with the manner in which my partner and I communicate with each other after sex.

23. Just thinking about having sex with my partner excites me.

24. I try to avoid situations that will encourage my partner to want sex.

25. I desire more sex than my partner does.

26. I look forward to having sex with my partner.

27. I enjoy using sexual fantasy during sex with my partner.

28. It is easy for me to go weeks without having sex with my partner.

29. My motivation to engage in sex with my partner is low.

30. I enjoy thinking about having sex with my partner.

31. My desire for sex with my partner is strong.

32. I feel that sex is not an important aspect of the relationship I share with my partner.

33. I think my energy level for sex with my partner is too low.

34. It is hard for me to get in the mood for sex with my partner.

35. I lack the desire necessary to pursue sex with my partner.

36. I try to avoid having sex with my partner.

37. I feel that my partner enjoys our sex life.

38. My sex life is very exciting.

39. Sex is fun for my partner and me.

40. I feel that my partner sees little in me except for the sex I can give.

41. I feel that sex is dirty and disgusting.

42. My sex life is monotonous.

43. When we have sex it is too rushed and hurriedly completed.

44. I feel that my sex life is lacking in quality.

45. My partner is sexually very exciting.

46. I enjoy the sex techniques that my partner likes or uses.

47. I feel that my partner wants too much sex from me.

48. I think that sex is wonderful.

49. My partner dwells on sex too much.

50. I feel that sex is something that has to be endured in our relationship.

51. My partner is too rough or brutal when we have sex.

52. My partner observes good personal hygiene.

53. I feel that sex is a normal function of our relationship.

54. My partner does not want sex when I do.

55. I feel that our sex life really adds a lot to our relationship.

56. I would like to have sexual contact with someone other than my partner.

57. It is easy for me to get sexually excited by my partner.

58. I feel that my partner is sexually pleased with me.

59. My partner is very sensitive to my sexual needs and desires.

60. I feel that I should have sex more often.

61. I feel that my sex life is boring.

Items used to form the scales are as follows (R indicates reverse scoring):
Sexual communication: 1, 2, 4, 7 (R), 8, 10 (R), 11, 12 (R), 13 (R), 14, 15 (R), 16 (R), 17, 18, 19 (R), 20 (R), 21 (R), 22, 37, 39, 43 (R), 44 (R), 46, 54 (R), 58, 59, 61 (R)
Sexual desire: 23, 24 (R), 26, 28 (R), 29 (R), 30, 31, 33 (R), 34 (R), 35 (R), 36 (R), 47 (R), 48, 49 (R), 57

DEPRESSION ANXIETY STRESS SCALES (DASS)

Please read each statement and circle the number which best indicates how much this applied to you over the past week. There are no right or wrong answers. Do not spend too much time on any one statement. The rating scale is as follows:

0 = Did not apply to me at all; 1 = Applied to me to some degree, or some of the time; 2 = Applied to me to a considerable degree, or a good part of the time; 3 = Applied to me very much, or most of the time.

1. I felt that I was using a lot of nervous energy.
2. I experienced breathing difficulty (e.g., excessively rapid breathing, breathlessness in the absence of physical exertion).
3. I felt that life was meaningless.
4. I found it difficult to work up the initiative to do things.
5. I found myself getting upset rather easily.
6. I felt that I had lost interest in just about everything.
7. I was worried about situations in which I might panic and make a fool of myself.
8. I had a feeling of shakiness.
9. I could see nothing in the future to be hopeful about.
10. I felt that I was rather touchy.
11. I found it hard to wind down.
12. I was aware of the action of my heart in the absence of physical exertion (e.g., sense of heart rate increase, heart missing a beat).
13. I felt I was close to panic.
14. I couldn't seem to get any enjoyment out of the things I did.
15. I felt sad and depressed.
16. I felt scared without any good reason.
17. I found it difficult to tolerate interruptions to what I was doing.
18. I found myself getting agitated.
19. I felt I was pretty worthless.
20. I found it difficult to relax.
21. I experienced trembling (e.g., in the hands).

Items used to form the scales as follows:
Depression: 3, 4, 6, 9, 14, 15, 19

Anxiety: 2, 7, 8, 12, 13, 16, 21

Stress: 1, 5, 10, 11, 17, 18, 20

Summary of Sample Characteristics

TABLE B1. Sources of Recruitment		
Source	**Transition Couples**	**Comparison Couples**
Newspaper/newsletter	17 (15.9%)	53 (53.0%)
Public hospitals	35 (32.7%)	0 (0.0%)
Snowballing	15 (14.0%)	16 (16.0%)
Student pool	1 (0.9%)	17 (17.0%)
Flyers in offices/stores	11 (10.3%)	4 (4.0%)
Radio advertisements	9 (8.4%)	5 (5.0%)
Parenting Expo	14 (13.1%)	0 (0.0%)
Not known	5 (4.7%)	5 (5.0%)
TOTAL	107 (100.0%)	100 (100%)

TABLE B2. Highest Educational Level Attained				
	Transition Group		**Comparison Group**	
Education Level	**Husbands**	**Wives**	**Husbands**	**Wives**
Year 8–10	10 (9.3%)	6 (5.6%)	6 (6.0%)	3 (3.0%)
Year 11–12	29 (27.1%)	21 (19.6%)	20 (20.0%)	19 (19.0%)
Technical college	25 (23.4%)	23 (21.5%)	14 (14.0%)	10 (10.0%)
Undergraduate degree	28 (26.2%)	36 (33.6%)	37 (37.0%)	41 (41.0%)
Postgraduate degree	15 (14.0%)	20 (18.7%)	23 (23.0%)	27 (27.0%)

Note: Percentages shown are column percentages; one transition wife did not report her educational level, thus reducing the effective sample size to 106.

	TABLE B3. Current Occupation			
	Transition Group		Comparison Group	
Current Occupation	Husbands	Wives	Husbands	Wives
Professional	39 (36.4%)	38 (35.5%)	49 (49.0%)	42 (42.0%)
Administrative/managerial	13 (12.1%)	23 (21.5%)	15 (15.0%)	19 (19.0%)
Clerical and sales	7 (6.5%)	17 (15.9%)	3 (3.0%)	9 (9.0%)
Skilled or semiskilled	39 (36.4%)	7 (6.5%)	19 (19.0%)	7 (7.0%)
Student	4 (3.7%)	10 (9.3%)	11 (11.0%)	18 (18.0%)
Homemaker	1 (0.9%)	11 (10.3%)	0 (0.0%)	1 (1.0%)
Unemployed	4 (3.7%)	1 (0.9%)	3 (3.0%)	4 (4.0%)

Note: Percentages shown are column percentages.

Summary of Major Statistical Analyses

	Transition Group		Comparison Group	
TABLE C1. Correlations between Initial Anxiety over Relationships and Post-Birth Measures of Relationship Quality and Individual Adjustment (Chapter 7)				
Measures	**Husbands**	**Wives**	**Husbands**	**Wives**
Relationship satisfaction				
Overall	−.26*	−.29*	−.26*	−.34**
Global distress	.34**	.01	.19	.18
Affective	−.28*	−.15	−.09	−.30**
Problem-solving	−.16	−.20*	−.21*	−.33**
Time together	−.14	−.34**	−.28**	−.26*
Caregiving				
Responsive	−.25*	−.36**	−.38**	−.08
Compulsive	.21*	.09	.21*	.24*
Sexuality				
Communication	−.39**	−.10	−.39**	−.14
Desire	−.21*	−.14	−.24*	−.14
Psychological adjustment				
Depression	.35**	.31**	.41**	.45**
Anxiety	.32**	.28**	.44**	.46**
Stress	.32**	.24*	.42**	.22*

Note. * $p < .05$, ** $p < .01$.

TABLE C2. Correlations between Initial Discomfort with Closeness and Post-birth Measures of Relationship Quality and Individual Adjustment (Chapter 7)

	Transition Group		Comparison Group	
Measures	Husbands	Wives	Husbands	Wives
Relationship satisfaction				
Overall	−.21*	−.15	−.33**	−.09
Global distress	.11	.03	.31**	−.07
Affective	−.28**	−.12	−.32**	−.12
Problem-solving	−.17	−.13	−.16	−.05
Time together	−.13	−.11	−.27*	−.17
Caregiving				
Responsive	−.30**	−.29**	−.21*	−.17
Compulsive	.08	.04	.17	.13
Sexuality				
Communication	−.29**	−.12	−.24*	−.28**
Desire	−.18	−.02	−.08	−.15
Psychological adjustment				
Depression	.21*	.10	.31**	.15
Anxiety	.08	.07	.23*	.30**
Stress	.20	.02	.19	.18

Note. * $p < .05$, ** $p < .01$.

TABLE C3. Goodness of Fit Indices for the Final Structural Equations Models (Chapter 7)

Coping Strategy	Akaike's Information Criterion	Model Chi Square Statistic	Comparative Fit Index
Support-seeking	−23.35	$\chi 2\,(37) = 50.65$	.947
Emotion-focused	−33.53	$\chi 2\,(44) = 54.47$	.971

TABLE C4. Path Coefficients for the Prediction of Support-Seeking (Chapter 7)

Wives' discomfort with closeness to wives' support-seeking	−.25
Husbands' parenting stress to wives' support-seeking	.26
Wives' discomfort with closeness to husbands' support-seeking	.23
Wives' anxiety over relationships to husbands' support-seeking	−.22
Husbands' parenting strain to husbands' support-seeking	.45

TABLE C5. Path Coefficients for the Prediction of Emotion-Focused Coping (Chapter 7)	
Wives' discomfort with closeness to wives' social support	−.25
Wives' anxiety over relationships to wives' social support	−.27
Wives' social support to wives' emotion-focused coping	.24
Wives' parenting strain to wives' emotion-focused coping	.56
Wives' anxiety over relationships to wives' emotion-focused coping	.41
Husbands' discomfort with closeness to husbands' self-esteem	−.25
Husbands' anxiety over relationships to husbands' self-esteem	−.59
Husbands' self-esteem to husbands' emotion-focused coping	−.42
Husbands' anxiety over relationships to husbands' parenting strain	.22
Husbands' parenting strain to husbands' emotion-focused coping	.42
Wives' discomfort with closeness to wives' social support	−.25
Wives' anxiety over relationships to wives' social support	−.27
Wives' social support to husbands' emotion-focused coping	.18

TABLE C6. Correlations Between Husbands' Prenatal Characteristics and Spouses' Perceptions of Division of Labor (Chapter 9)				
	Unfairness in Household Tasks		Unfairness in Baby-Related Tasks	
Measures	Husbands' Perception	Wives' Perception	Husbands' Perception	Wives' Perception
Relationship measures				
Relationship satisfaction	−.28*	−.26*	−.25*	−.07
Discomfort with closeness	.04	.03	.06	.12
Anxiety over relationships	.23*	.17	.16	−.01
Psychological adjustment				
Depression	.43**	.20	.30**	.24*
Anxiety	.15	.32**	.16	.25*
Stress	.18	.09	.14	.12

Note. * $p < .05$, ** $p < .01$.

TABLE C7. Partial Correlations Between Perceived Unfairness of Division of Labor and Relationship and Individual Outcomes at Final Follow-Up (Chapter 9)

	Unfairness in Household Tasks		Unfairness in Baby-Related Tasks	
Measures	Husbands' Perception	Wives' Perception	Husbands' Perception	Wives' Perception
Relationship measures				
Relationship satisfaction	−.02	.02	.07	.01
Husbands	−.12	−.22+	−.27*	−.18
Wives				
Discomfort				
Husbands	.23*	−.11	.12	.06
Wives	.14	−.12	.18	−.01
Relationship anxiety				
Husbands	−.09	−.02	−.20	.30*
Wives	.14	−.11	.19	.19
Psychological adjustment				
Depression				
Husbands	.19	−.15	.21+	−.08
Wives	.26*	−.08	.31**	.18
Anxiety				
Husbands	−.07	−.27*	−.03	−.03
Wives	.21+	−.16	.33**	.17
Stress				
Husbands	.23*	.14	.25*	.04
Wives	.37***	−.17	.39***	−.02

Note: These correlations control for initial (Time 1) scores on the outcome variable.
+ $p<.10$, * $p<.05$, ** $p<.01$, *** $p<.001$.

TABLE C8. Mean Scores on Discomfort with Closeness According to Group, Gender, and Time (Chapter 11)

	Transition Group		Comparison Group	
Assessment	Husbands	Wives	Husbands	Wives
Time 1	50.67	45.31	49.30	43.71
Time 2	49.19	44.27	48.12	43.38
Time 3	48.44	45.76	49.50	43.26

TABLE C9. Mean Scores on DASS Anxiety According to Group, Gender, and Time (Chapter 11)		
Assessment	Transition Group	Comparison Group
Time 1	1.80	1.30
Time 2	1.39	1.06
Time 3	1.27	1.63

TABLE C10. Mean Scores of Survivors and Strugglers on Prenatal Questionnaire Measures (Chapter 11)				
	Husbands		Wives	
Measure	Survivors	Strugglers	Survivors	Strugglers
Psychological adjustment				
Depression	1.82	2.71	2.27	2.37
Anxiety	1.10	1.54	2.16	2.21
Stress	4.75	6.17	5.10	5.92
Attachment security				
Discomfort with closeness	49.82	50.92	44.36	47.17
Anxiety over relationships	35.36a	41.00b	36.96	37.92
Caregiving				
Responsive caregiving	111.22a	103.70b	113.49	113.70
Compulsive caregiving	24.37	25.83	25.84	25.17
Sexuality				
Sexual communication	124.19	120.96	129.27	129.57
Sexual desire	78.21	75.78	66.37	67.30

Note. Within each row, the letters a and b indicate that these two mean scores differ significantly from each other.

TABLE C11. Mean Scores of Survivors and Strugglers on Post-Birth Measures of Domestic Work (Chapter 11)				
	Husbands		Wives	
Measure	Survivors	Strugglers	Survivors	Strugglers
Total hours spent on tasks				
Household tasks	6.87	5.64	11.55	10.75
Baby-related tasks	12.87	14.05	35.80	41.93
Perceived unfairness of division				
of labor				
Household tasks	.27	.31	.31	.45
Baby-related tasks	.12	.19	.19	.36
Effort desired from spouse				
Household tasks	−.11	−.20	.21a	.45b
Baby-related tasks	−.13	−.19	.10a	.36b

Note. Within each row, the letters a and b indicate that these two mean scores differ significantly from each other.

References

Ainsworth, M. D. S. (1989). Attachments beyond infancy. *American Psychologist, 44,* 709–716.

Ainsworth, M. D. S., Blehar, M. C., Waters, E., & Wall, S. (1978). *Patterns of attachment: A study of the strange situation.* Hillsdale, NJ: Erlbaum.

Apt, C. V., & Hurlbert, D. F. (1992). Motherhood and female sexuality beyond one year postpartum: A study of military wives. *Journal of Sex Education and Therapy, 18,* 104–114.

Argyle, M., & Henderson, M. (1985). *The anatomy of relationships.* London: Heinemann.

Barich, R. R., & Bielby, D. D. (1996). Rethinking marriage: Change and stability in expectations, 1967–1994. *Journal of Family Issues, 17,* 139–169.

Bartholomew, K. (1990). Avoidance of intimacy: An attachment perspective. *Journal of Social and Personal Relationships, 7,* 147–178.

Bartholomew, K., & Horowitz, L. M. (1991). Attachment styles among young adults: A test of a four-category model. *Journal of Personality and Social Psychology, 61,* 226–244.

Bates, J. E., Freeland, C. A. B., & Lounsbury, M. L. (1979). Measurement of infant difficultness. *Child Development, 50,* 794–803.

Bell, D. C., & Richard, A. J. (2000). Caregiving: The forgotten element in attachment. *Psychological Inquiry, 11,* 69–83.

Belsky, J. (1984). The determinants of parenting: A process model. *Child Development, 55,* 83–96.

Belsky, J., & Kelly, J. (1994). The transition to parenthood: How a first child changes a marriage. New York: Delacorte Press.

Belsky, J., & Pensky, E. (1988). Marital change across the transition to parenthood. *Marriage and Family Review, 12,* 133–156.

Belsky, J., & Rovine, M. (1990). Patterns of marital change across the transition to parenthood: Pregnancy to three years postpartum. *Journal of Marriage and the Family, 52,* 5–19.

Benedek, T. (1959). Parenthood as a developmental phase: A contribution to the libido theory. *Journal of American Psychoanalytic Association, 7,* 389–417.

Bibring, G. L., Dwyer, T. F., Huntington, D., & Valentine, A. F. (1961). A study of the psychological processes in pregnancy and the earliest mother-child relationship. *The Psychoanalytic Study of the Child, 16,* 9–72.

Bittman, M. (1991). *Juggling time: How Australian families use time.* Canberra, Australia: Office of the Status of Women, Department of the Prime Minister and Cabinet.

Bowlby, J. (1969). *Attachment and loss: Vol. 1. Attachment.* New York: Basic Books.

Bowlby, J. (1973). *Attachment and loss: Vol. 2. Separation: Anxiety and anger.* New York: Basic Books.

Bowlby, J. (1979). *The making and breaking of affectional bonds.* London: Tavistock.

Bowlby, J. (1980). *Attachment and loss: Vol. 3. Loss.* New York: Basic Books.

Brennan, K. A., Clark, C. L., & Shaver, P. R. (1998). Self-report measurement of adult attachment: An integrative overview. In J. A. Simpson & W. S. Rholes (Eds.), *Attachment theory and close relationships* (pp. 46–76). New York: Guilford.

Brown, M. A. (1986). Social support during pregnancy: A unidimensional or multidimensional construct? *Nursing Research, 35,* 4–9.

Buss, D. M. (1994). *The evolution of desire: Strategies of human mating.* New York: Basic Books.

Caplan, G. (1957). Psychological aspects of maternity care. *American Journal of Public Health, 47,* 25–31.

Clements, M., & Markman, H. J. (1996). The transition to parenthood: Is having children hazardous to marriage? In N. Vanzetti & S. Duck (Eds.), *A lifetime of relationships* (pp. 290–310). Pacific Grove, CA: Brooks/Cole.

Condon, J. T. (1993). The assessment of antenatal emotional attachment: Development of a questionnaire instrument. *British Journal of Medical Psychology, 66,* 167–183.

Cook, T., & Campbell, D. T. (1979). *Quasi-experimentation: Design and analysis issues for field settings.* Chicago: Rand McNally.

Cooper, P. J. & Murray, L. (1997). The impact of psychological treatments of postpartum depression on maternal mood and infant development. In L. Murray & P. J. Cooper (Eds.), *Postpartum depression and child development* (pp. 201–220). New York: Guilford.

Coopersmith, S. (1981). *Self-esteem Inventories.* Palo Alto, CA: Consulting Psychologists Press.

Corijn, M., Liefbroer, A. C., & de Jong Gierveld, J. (1996). It takes two to tango, doesn't it? The influence of couple characteristics on the timing of the birth of the first child. *Journal of Marriage and the Family, 58,* 117–126.

Cowan, C. P., & Cowan, P. A. (1988). Who does what when partners become parents: Implications for men, women, and marriage. *Marriage and Family Review, 12,* 105–131.

Cowan, C. P., Cowan, P. A., Heming, G., & Miller, N. B. (1991). Becoming a family: Marriage, parenting, and child development. In P. A. Cowan & M. Hetherington (Eds.), *Family transitions* (pp. 79–109). Hillsdale, NJ: Erlbaum.

Crohan, S. E. (1996). Marital quality and conflict across the transition to parenthood in African American and White couples. *Journal of Marriage and the Family, 58,* 933–944.

Deutsch, F. M., Lussier, J. B., & Servis, L. J. (1993). Husbands at home: Predictors of paternal participation in childcare and housework. *Journal of Personality and Social Psychology, 65,* 1154–1166.

Dyer, E. (1963). Parenthood as crisis: A re-study. *Marriage and Family Living, 25,* 196–201.

Emmons, C., Biernat, M., Tiedje, L. B., Lang, E. L., & Wortman, C. B. (1990). Stress, support, and coping among women professionals with preschool children. In J. Eckenrode & S. Gore (Eds.), *Stress between work and family* (pp. 61–94). New York: Plenum Press.

Feeney, J. A. (1998). Adult attachment and relationship-centered anxiety: Responses to physical and emotional distancing. In J. A. Simpson & W. S. Rholes (Eds.), *Attachment theory and close relationships* (pp. 189–218). New York: Guilford.

Feeney, J. A. (1999). Adult romantic attachment and couple relationships. In J. Cassidy & P. R. Shaver (Eds.). *The handbook of attachment: Theory, research, and clinical applications* (pp. 355–377). New York: Guilford.

Feeney, J. A., Noller, P., & Hanrahan, M. (1994). Assessing adult attachment: Developments in the conceptualization of security and insecurity. In M. B. Sperling & W. H. Berman (Eds.), *Attachment in adults: Theory, assessment, and treatment* (pp. 128–152). New York: Guilford.

Field, T. (1997). The treatment of depressed mothers and their infants. In L. Murray & P. J. Cooper (Eds.), *Postpartum depression and child development* (pp. 221–236). New York: Guilford.

Goodnow, J. J., & Bowes, J. M. (1994). *Men, women and household work.* Melbourne, Australia: Oxford University Press.

Grossman, F. K. (1988). Strain in the transition to parenthood. *Marriage and Family Review, 12,* 85–104.

Grossmann, K. E., Grossmann, K., & Zimmermann, P. (1999). A wider view of attachment and exploration: Stability and change during the years of immaturity. In J. Cassidy & P. R. Shaver (Eds.). *The handbook of attachment: Theory, research, and clinical applications* (pp. 760–786). New York: Guilford.

Harris, K., & Campbell, E. (1999). The plans in unplanned pregnancy: Secondary gain and the partnership. *British Journal of Medical Psychology, 72,* 105–120.

Hazan, C., & Shaver, P. R. (1987). Romantic love conceptualized as an attachment process. *Journal of Personality and Social Psychology, 52,* 511–524.

Hazan, C., & Shaver, P. R. (1994). Attachment as an organizational framework for research on close relationships. *Psychological Inquiry, 5,* 1–22.

Hazan, C., & Zeifman, D. (1994). Sex and the psychological tether. In K. Bartholomew & D. Perlman (Eds.), *Advances in personal relationships Vol. 5: Attachment processes in adulthood* (pp. 151–178). London: Jessica Kingsley.

Hazan, C., Zeifman, D., & Middleton, K. (1994). *Adult romantic attachment, affection, and sex.* Paper presented at the 7th International Conference on Personal Relationships, Groningen, The Netherlands, July.

Hill, R. (1949). *Families under stress.* New York: Harper & Row.

Hobbs, D. (1965). Parenthood as crisis: A third study. *Journal of Marriage and the Family, 27,* 367–372.

Hobbs, D. (1968). Transition to parenthood: A replication and an extension. *Journal of Marriage and the Family, 30,* 413–417.

Hudson, W. W., Harrison, D. F., & Crosscup, P. C. (1981). A short-form scale to measure sexual discord in dyadic relationships. *Journal of Sex Research, 17,* 157–174.

Huston, T. L., McHale, S. M., & Crouter, A. C. (1986). When the honeymoon's over: Changes in the marriage relationship over the first year. In R. Gilmour & S. Duck (Eds.), *The emerging field of personal relationships* (pp. 263–286). Hillsdale, NJ: Erlbaum.

Huston, T. L., & Vangelisti, A. L. (1995). How parenthood affects marriage. In M. A. Fitzpatrick & A. L. Vangelisti (Eds.), *Explaining family interactions* (pp. 147–176). Thousand Oaks, CA: Sage.

Johnson, E. M., & Huston, T. L. (1998). The perils of love, or why wives adapt to husbands during the transition to parenthood. *Journal of Marriage and the Family, 60,* 195–204.

Kerns, K. A., & Barth, J. M. (1995). Attachment and play: Convergence across components of parent-child relationships and their relations to peer competence. *Journal of Social and Personal Relationships, 12,* 243–260.

Kilmartin, C. (2000). Young adult moves: Leaving home, returning home, relationships. *Family Matters, 55,* 34–40.

Kobak, R. R., & Sceery, A. (1988). Attachment in late adolescence: Working models, affect regulation, and representations of self and others. *Child Development, 59,* 135–146.

Kunce, L. J., & Shaver, P. R. (1994). An attachment-theoretical approach to caregiving in romantic relationships. In K. Bartholomew & D. Perlman (Eds.), *Advances in personal relationships Vol. 5: Attachment process in adulthood* (pp. 205–237). London: Jessica Kingsley.

LeMasters, E. E. (1957). Parenthood as crisis. *Marriage and Family Living, 19,* 352–355.

Levy-Shiff, R. (1994). Individual and contextual correlates of marital change across the transition to parenthood. *Development Psychology, 30,* 591–601.

Lovibond, S. H., & Lovibond, P. F. (1995). *Manual for the Depression Anxiety Stress Scales (DASS)* (2nd ed.). Sydney, Australia: Psychology Foundation of Australia.

Miller, B. C., & Sollie, D. L. (1980). Normal stresses during the transition to parenthood. *Family Relations, 29,* 459–465.

Miller, R. S. (1997). We always hurt the ones we love: Aversive interactions in close relationships. In R. M. Kowalski (Ed.), *Aversive interpersonal behaviors* (pp. 11–29). New York: Plenum.

Murray, L., & Cooper, P. J. (1997). The role of infant and maternal factors in postpartum depression, mother-infant interactions, and infant outcomes. In L. Murray & P. J. Cooper (Eds.), *Postpartum depression and child development* (pp. 111–135). New York: Guilford.

Newman, P., & Smith, A. (1997). *Social focus on families.* London: The Stationery Office.

Noller, P., & Feeney, J. A. (in press). Communication, relationship concerns, and satisfaction in early marriage. In H. T. Reis, M. A. Fitzpatrick, & A. L. Vangelisti (Eds.), *Stability and change in relationships.* New York: Cambridge University Press.

Noller, P., Feeney, J. A., Peterson, C. C., & Sheehan, G. (1995). Learning conflict patterns in the family: Links between marital, parental, and sibling relationships. In T. J. Socha & G. H. Stamp (Eds.), *Parents, children and communication: Frontiers of theory and research* (pp. 273–298). Mahwah, NJ: Erlbaum.

O'Hara, M. W. (1997). The nature of postpartum depressive disorders. In L. Murray & P. J. Cooper (Eds.), *Postpartum depression and child development* (pp. 3–31). New York: Guilford.

Osofsky, J. D., & Culp, R. (1993). A relationship perspective on the transition to parenthood. In G. H. Pollock & S. I. Greenspan (Eds.), *The course of life, Vol. 5: Early adulthood* (pp. 75–98). Madison, CT: International Universities Press.

Parke, R. D., & Beitel, A. (1988). Disappointment: When things go wrong in the transition to parenthood. *Marriage and Family Review, 12,* 221–265.

Presland, P., & Antill, J. K. (1987). Household division of labour: The impact of hours worked in paid employment. *Australian Journal of Psychology, 39,* 273–291.

Rholes, W. S., Simpson, J. A., Blakely, B. S., Lanigan, L., & Allen, E. A. (1997). Adult attachment styles, the desire to have children, and working models of parenthood. *Journal of Personality, 65,* 357–385.

Rholes, W. S., Simpson, J. A., & Stevens, J. G. (1998). Attachment orientations, social support, and conflict resolution in close relationships. In J. A. Simpson & W. S Rholes (Eds.), *Attachment theory and close relationships* (pp. 166–188). New York: Guilford.

Sanchez, L., & Thomson, E. (1997). Becoming mothers and fathers: Parenthood, gender, and the division of labor. *Gender and Society, 11,* 747–772.

Schwartz, P. (1994). *Love between equals: How peer marriage really works*. New York: Free Press.

Shaver, P. R., & Hazan, C. (1988). A biased overview of the study of love. *Journal of Social and Personal Relationships, 5*, 473–501.

Snyder, D. K. (1979). Multidimensional assessment of marital satisfaction. *Journal of Marriage and the Family, 41*, 813–823.

Sroufe, L. A., & Waters, E. (1977). Attachment as an organizational construct. *Child Development, 48*, 1184–1199.

Tennov, D. (1979). *Love and limerence: The experience of being in love*. New York: Stein & Day.

Terry, D. J. (1988). *Stress, coping and adaptation in married couples*. Unpublished doctoral dissertation, The Australian National University, Canberra, Australia.

Terry, D. J., McHugh, T. A., & Noller, P. (1991). Role dissatisfaction and the decline in marital quality across the transition to parenthood. *Australian Journal of Psychology, 43*, 129–132.

van IJzendoorn, M. H., & De Wolff, M. S. (1997). In search of the absent father – meta-analysis of infant-father attachment: A rejoinder to our discussants. *Child Development, 68*, 604–609.

Vitaliano, P. P., Russo, J., Carr, J. E., Maiuro, R. D., & Becker, J. (1985). The Ways of Coping Checklist: Revision and psychometric properties. *Multivariate Behavioral Research, 20*, 3–26.

von Sydow, K. (1999). Sexuality during pregnancy and after childbirth: A metacontent analysis of 59 studies. *Journal of Psychosomatic Research, 47*, 27–49.

Weiss, R. S. (1982). Attachment in adult life. In C. M. Parkes & J. Stevenson-Hinde (Eds.), *The place of attachment in human behavior* (pp. 171–184). New York: Basic Books.

Weiss, R. S. (1986). Continuities and transformations in social relationships from childhood to adulthood. In W. W. Hartup & Z. Rubin (Eds.), *Relationships and development* (pp. 95–110). Hillsdale, NJ: Erlbaum.

Weiss, R. S. (1991). The attachment bond in childhood and adulthood. In C. M. Parkes, J. Stevenson-Hinde, & P. Marris (Eds.), *Attachment across the life cycle* (pp. 66–76). London: Tavistock/Routledge.

Wheeless, L. R., Wheeless, V. E., & Baus, R. (1984). Sexual communication, communication satisfaction, and solidarity in the development stages of intimate relationships. *The Western Journal of Speech Communication, 48*, 217–230.

Wolcott, I., & Glezer, H. (1995). *Work and family life: Achieving integration*. Melbourne, Australia, Australian Institute of Family Studies.

Author Index

Subject Index